Media Literacies

Media Literacies

A Critical Introduction

Michael Hoechsmann
and
Stuart R. Poyntz

WILEY-BLACKWELL

A John Wiley & Sons, Ltd., Publication

This edition first published 2012
© 2012 Blackwell Publishing

Blackwell Publishing was acquired by John Wiley & Sons in February 2007.
Blackwell's publishing program has been merged with Wiley's global Scientific,
Technical, and Medical business to form Wiley-Blackwell.

Registered Office
John Wiley & Sons Ltd, The Atrium, Southern Gate, Chichester, West Sussex,
PO19 8SQ, UK

Editorial Offices
350 Main Street, Malden, MA 02148-5020, USA

9600 Garsington Road, Oxford, OX4 2DQ, UK

The Atrium, Southern Gate, Chichester, West Sussex, PO19 8SQ, UK

For details of our global editorial offices, for customer services, and for information
about how to apply for permission to reuse the copyright material in this book
please see our website at www.wiley.com/wiley-blackwell.

The right of Michael Hoechsmann and Stuart R. Poyntz to be identified as the
authors of this work has been asserted in accordance with the UK Copyright,
Designs and Patents Act 1988.

Library of Congress Cataloging-in-Publication Data

Hardback ISBN 9781405186117
Paperback ISBN 9781405186100

A catalogue record for this book is available from the British Library.

This book is published in the following electronic formats: ePDFs 9781444344127;
Wiley Online Library 9781444344158; ePub 9781444344134; mobi 9781444344141

Set in 10.5/13 Minion by Thomson Digital, India

1 2012

Contents

Contents

Preface

We live in remarkable times.

Who would have thought it possible even 10 years ago to write a book on a machine that unites all of the functionalities of a typewriter, a fax machine, a library archive, a book store, a telephone, a stereo, a television, a deck of cards, a photo album, a recording studio, and a video editing suite into a sleek and portable package? Sitting studiously with others in a public library, a café, or an airport departure lounge, we wonder what diversity of projects and practices are simultaneously taking place around us. As Michael Wesch so eloquently portrays in the YouTube video 'The Machine is Us/ing Us,' we have adopted cyberskins. If there was any doubt that we are cyborgs – part human/part machine – this doubt is allayed by the very intimacy of technology across our everyday lives. Our communications technologies have become smaller, more convergent, and more comprehensive. We use them to receive, gather, develop, and transmit information. They are proximate with so much of what we do and who we are, and yet, as Richard Lanham points out in *The Economics of Attention* (2006), the consequence is that we are swimming in a sea of data, the only constraint upon which is our limited capacity to take it all in.

If this is so, as much as we are changing, we are also beholden to age-old ways of doing things. The book that you hold in your hands, for instance, is an anachronistic technology that has shown remarkable resilience. Culturally speaking, the book is intimately connected to our identities as learners and participants in the story-telling circle that is central to the human condition. The book speaks to our interior lives. It is silent, yet evocative. It gives us access to the cultural legacies that bind us to the past and teases us with the promise of things to come. Compared with television, the book is often elegant and sophisticated, a repository of stories and information that has, until now, been associated with what the nineteenth-century essayist and poet Matthew Arnold (1993 [1869]) described as 'the best that has been thought and said in the world.' Television, on the other hand, has only occasionally shaken its reputation as the black sheep in the communications media family.

Unlike the book, television is loud and brash; yet, it too can sometimes be smart and provocative. It changes culture, and like earlier forms of mass entertainment – magazines, film, recorded music, and radio – it mobilizes the eyes and the ears, weaving together a visual and audio tapestry that continues to bind together our lives. Among these earlier technologies, it was only film that combined both visual and audio elements (and even that took time to happen), so perhaps we shouldn't be surprised that it was film that first attracted the attention of media educators. Where film helped kick off a movement, television soon became that movement's bread and butter. The combination of audiovisual narrative, commercialism, and the subtext of cultural arbiter made television a rich and important site for teaching and learning. Alongside film, teen magazines, popular music, and, to a lesser extent, radio, television was viewed as a significant site of socialization, acculturation, and learning that deserved to be treated as an educational resource in classrooms and other sites of learning.

This book takes for granted that television and other media forms have become part of the cultural fabric of our lives, and that these media deserve the full attention of educators and should be part of the curriculum in schools. In this regard, we do not stand alone. Media education is a movement that has been largely led at the grassroots by school-based educators and community activists, supported by a small cadre of scholars and media professionals. In this book, we acknowledge and trace the history of media education, and grapple with the fresh challenges posed by the convergent media of the twenty-first century. We develop two parallel models of media literacy that are described as Media Literacy 1.0 and Media Literacy 2.0. These models map out pedagogical responses to distinct media eras, but, because these eras continue to overlap and collide, these models are held together in a dynamic tension. Without the new communication technologies, there could not be a Media Literacy 2.0. But without the accumulated knowledge of critical educational practice drawn from several decades of Media Literacy 1.0, a Media Literacy 2.0 agenda is at risk of becoming shallow and instrumentalist, focused on teaching soon-to-be-redundant software packages to young people who have access to a wide range of media tools and capacities in their out-of-school lives.

In this book, we weave together issues and examples from both Media Literacy 1.0 and Media Literacy 2.0. In Chapter 1, for example, we discuss the history and emergence of media education. Chapter 2 focuses on who young people are today, with particular concern for the nature of their digitally mediated lives. Chapter 3 describes another side of the history of media literacy, the role of the media itself as a site of instruction and learning. Chapter 4 and Chapter 5 have been written as primers for Media Literacy 1.0, one focused on the interpretation of the media and the other on its production. In Chapter 4, we present a holistic model for media interpretation that unites the analysis of media institutions, media texts, the active involvement of audiences, and the give and take between the media and culture, including how one impacts upon and (sometimes) changes the other. In Chapter 5, we articulate four key areas of concern that speak to the way media production aligns with and helps to nurture young people's agency and engagement with the world. Chapter 6 addresses the areas of new and digital literacies, and in Chapter 7 we articulate our understanding of Media Literacy 2.0 by addressing seven key conceptual problematics – consciousness, communication, consumption and surveillance, convergence, creativity, copy-paste, and community – that are at the core of this project. In Chapter 8, we carry the discussion of media literacy forward by addressing a vexed concern – critical citizenship – that continues to be at the center of the field.

Throughout this book, the reader will find a number of sidebars written primarily by emerging researchers and media literacy educators. These sidebars function like hypertext. They draw the reader away from the narrative for an in-depth discussion of an issue or a media phenomenon. In many cases, the sidebars also offer ideas and resources for teaching media literacy in various settings.

As two academics with long histories of working in the field of media education, we view this book as a culmination of two decades of involvement in media literacy, and as a reflection of ideas drawn from a wide range of educators. Writing this text has been a collaborative effort and an equal co-authorship, but a final decision on author sequence ultimately had to be made, and we decided on alphabetical order. These are remarkable times to be working in media education, and we are indebted to the many youth and colleagues who have challenged us and pushed our thinking forward. We cannot thank them all here, but their presence in our lives is reflected throughout this book.

1

What is Media Literacy?

Media literacy is a set of competencies that enable us to interpret media texts and institutions, to make media of our own, and to recognize and engage with the social and political influence of media in everyday life. That is the shortest definition we can provide. The rest of this book is about expanding this definition and situating media literacy within evolving discussions of literacy, media, and technology education.

Media literacy suggests a capacity or competence to do something with media, whether to make sense of it, to produce it, or to understand its role in our societies. Just as more traditional literacy practices enable one to engage with print-based texts, media literacy enables one to engage with a variety of multimodal texts ('texts' that may include visual, audio, and print text elements) that range from a magazine advertisement to a televised rock video, a radio talk show to a video game, a cell phone photograph to a website. In reality, the range of possible multimodal texts that can be studied or produced through the critical lens of media literacy is vast. That said, it is important to note at the outset that media includes both media texts (i.e., a newspaper, a song, a film, or a website) produced by broadcasters, film-makers, and Web designers, and media technologies (i.e., television, film, and digital technologies such as cell phones, iPods, and digital cameras) used to produce these texts.

We recognize that framing the meaning of media in this manner runs the risk of escalating the subject to the point where the center does not hold. But media literacy has long faced the problem of developing a mode of analysis or a way of thinking that speaks across the various technologies, texts, and institutions that make up contemporary media cultures. We are equally

Media Literacies: A Critical Introduction, First Edition. Michael Hoechsmann and Stuart R. Poyntz.
© 2012 Blackwell Publishing Ltd. Published 2012 by Blackwell Publishing Ltd.

aware that we are writing from a privileged vantage point in the history of media, and of media education. Cresting the wave of some powerful new transformations in communication, we are in a position to see patterns that were not as clear even a decade ago, and to view a world powerfully transformed from the one of 20 years ago. In 1990, the personal computer was still a somewhat clunky machine owned mainly by technology buffs and educators. E-mail was primarily an inter-university messaging system and the World Wide Web was a modest, text-driven system. Meanwhile, television was at its apogee, enjoying its last moments as the culturally central communications medium it had become. Neil Postman's *Amusing Ourselves to Death: Public Discourse in the Age of Show Business* (1985) and Allan Bloom's *The Closing of the American Mind* (1987) were influential texts that suggested an era of immanent intellectual decline. Said Bloom (1987): 'Our students have lost the practice of and taste for reading' (p. 62). 'As long as they have the Walkman on,' he continued, 'they cannot hear what the great tradition has to say. And, after its prolonged use, when they take it off, they find they are deaf' (p. 81).

As if art should imitate life imitating art, *The Simpsons* had aired its first episode in December of 1989, and the dumbing down of America seemed in full flower in a revolution symbolized by Homer and Bart Simpson. (In a sidebar in Chapter 4 we demonstrate that *The Simpsons* is not dumb at all where media education is concerned.) The Walkman referenced by Bloom had been in circulation for just over ten years, and MTV, a station where commercials are content and all content is commercial, had been broadcasting for almost a decade. The world of media in 1990 was thus one of consumption by mass audiences, and the trends appeared to be moving towards greater individualization (Walkman), more base content (*The Simpsons*), and greater commercialization (MTV).

If this was true in America, the forces of globalization and the increasing movement of media texts and technologies around the world during this period meant that similar debates and circumstances were underway across the world's regions (Tufte and Enghel, 2009). Throughout this book, we mark some of these developments. Here we note, however, that the late 1980s and 1990s corresponded with a time of dramatic growth of media literacy organizations worldwide, the apogee of an era we will call 'Media Literacy 1.0.'

We use this designation because this period of history was a stage of growth in media education that focused primarily on the power and influence of broadcast media (i.e., the production of film and television studios, record labels, and corporate advertising). Given the circumstances of the era, media education was mainly predicated on reacting to the monolith of the mass media, and the primary method used in media literacy was a critique of *representation* focused on what was being communicated (the 'texts'), by whom (the media 'industry'), and for whom (the 'audience'). We argue in Chapter 4 that there is still much that remains helpful about Media Literacy 1.0 – after all, most web trolling, music listening, television watching, and film going among children and youth is still intertwined with the world of corporate media. If this is true today, however, by 1990 there was already a robust media education sector emerging in many nations in response to the role of the mass media in kids' lives. The UNESCO Grunwald Declaration on Media Education of 1982 had to a great extent set the tone for these developments. Indeed, the UNESCO statement represented an important consensus among the 19 nations assembled at Grunwald, Germany.

> Rather than condemn or endorse the undoubted power of the media, we need to accept their significant impact and penetration throughout the world as an established fact, and also appreciate their importance as an element of culture in today's world [...] The school and the family share the responsibility of preparing the young person for living in a world of powerful images, words and sounds. Children and adults need to be literate in all three of these symbolic systems, and this will require some reassessment of educational priorities. Such a reassessment might well result in an integrated approach to the teaching of language and communication. [Nonetheless,] media education will be most effective when parents, teachers, media personnel and decision-makers all acknowledge they have a role to play in developing greater critical awareness among listeners, viewers and readers.

Shortly after the Grunwald Declaration a new model for articulating a media literacy curriculum emerged from the influential work of Len Masterman. Masterman's seminal text, *Teaching the Media* (1985), would in fact form the basis of much Media Literacy 1.0 work. At root, Masterman argued that students need to engage with issues of media production, language, representation, and audiences to address how meaning operates in the broadcast media. The formula drawn from Masterman and elaborated by media educators across a variety of contexts enabled a rich, critical, and savvy analysis of media institutions, texts, and media reception contexts. This method, still a key component of media education today, responded to the cultural and social conditions of the day, an era of massified and one-way media flow.

Media Literacy 2.000

By 2000, however, the world of communications media was in a period of rapid evolution. The previous decade had seen the entry of a variety of new technologies and applications into the marketplace and a thoroughgoing transformation of others that had still been in primitive forms a decade before. The synthetic World Wide Web of Tim Berners-Lee had made its debut in the early 1990s and had been the biggest transformation in communications media of that decade, enabling the mass adaptation of other Internet applications such as e-mail, instant messaging, and chat, as well as providing an electronic portal to a virtual Library of Alexandria of knowledge, data, information, and nonsense. The staggering growth of the role of the Internet in everyday life and commerce was such that world governments had spent months of preparation for the turning of the clock in 2000, fearing a Millennium bug that was supposed to cause mass chaos. While this turned out to be one of the greatest unauthored hoaxes in communications history, another perfect storm brewing in media education circles in 2000 came from a different technology that had made great advances in the previous decade.

Video games were not new in 2000, but their complexity and popularity seemed to reach new heights. Complicating this, in the previous year, two students at Columbine High School in Littleton, Colorado had come to school with guns and bombs and proceeded to kill as many students as they could. When the rampage was over, 15 people were dead, including a teacher and the two shooters. In seeking answers to this senseless tragedy, pundits and theorists had identified the shooters' interest in violent video games as a potential cause of the incident. We track the debates on media violence and the specific place of video games in these debates in Chapter 3; suffice it to say, however, this interactive media technology came in to media education debates under a hail of suspicion. In truth, for the most part, media literacy did not have a place for video gaming, predicated as it was on the much more active participation of game users. Media education had been, and still was, a discourse well situated to respond to broadcast screen media. Here, the important questions seemed to be: what's on the screen, who makes it, and how does the viewer respond to it? Similar orientations were taken to the pages of magazines and newspapers, and, to a much lesser extent, the audio messaging of radio. But, as discussed at various points throughout this book, different and, in some instances, more complex questions need to be asked of video games. In the early 2000s, however, media education was still predicated primarily on a viewer whose hands were not engaged in making or playing media. It was a discourse that responded primarily to the practices of the eye and the ear.

In the subsequent decade, hands-on interaction and participation in media consumption and production has increasingly become the norm rather than the exception. Henry Jenkins (2006a) describes these practices as part of a culture of convergence. Such a culture is one where there are more opportunities for young people (and others) to express themselves through digital media, 'to transform personal reaction[s]' to the images, sounds, and narratives of consumer media culture into forms of 'social interaction' (Jenkins, 2006, p. 41). In a sense, the contemporary period has involved the most ruptural and transformative shifts in media and communications since the late nineteenth century. This is a period of profound change in how we organize and produce knowledge, and in how we communicate. The most significant element of this change is *participation,* along with two-way media flow. The era of one-way information flow from publishers and broadcasters that Tom Pettit (2007) calls the 'Gutenberg Parenthesis' is over. Of course, we are still in a nascent period, but there have been unmistakable shifts in social and cultural life. The dynamic relationship between Media Literacy 1.0 and Media Literacy 2.0 we argue for in this book is meant to address these shifts. At root, we suggest that the core of media literacy today is the work of empowering young people through meaningful and critical participation in contemporary media environments. We note, as do Jenkins et al. (2006), however, that interactive technologies – including computers, the Internet, and digital cameras – do not guarantee such participation. Rather, the latter must be nurtured, and this is where media educators must play a profound role.

The notion that young people can be empowered through and about media as a means for reshaping public spheres emerged as part of certain media education initiatives as early as the 1960s (see Chapter 5 for a more detailed discussion on this, especially in relation to the development of community-based youth media production initiatives). Nonetheless, until the 2000s, the idea of media education as empowerment had largely been a marginal position, argued most forcefully by educators and scholars such as David Buckingham (1996, 2003a) and Jesus Martin-Barbero (1987). Until the new communication technology r/evolution of the late 1990s and early 2000s, empowerment models of media education offered students a perspective on media use and appropriation that focused on how viewers and consumers of media were not simply brainwashed, but rather participated in far more complex interpretations and mediations with the media in their lives. Unfortunately, this was always a relatively advanced perspective in media education circles, the more subtle perspective of educators who had read and understood some cultural studies and who were skeptical of approaches that only saw the potential negative impacts of media on young people. Most media education in practice continued to be a form of simple response to the idea that the mainstream media largely perpetuates dominant power relationships and ideas (i.e., hegemony), however, and so David Buckingham was still forcefully making the case in 2003 for an empowerment model in his influential *Media Education: Literacy, Learning and Contemporary Culture.* For our purposes, the lessons to be learned from this transitional period are that while a critical media education should always include the analysis of the highly ideological and commercial transmissions of the mainstream media, this perspective is never sufficient to explain the complex mediations made by the people involved in production, reception, and meaning-making with media.

To catalogue the changes in communication technology and media use in the first decade of the twenty-first century is not really the purpose of this chapter. Nonetheless, especially in the domains of Web 2.0, where users are simultaneously producers and consumers of media content, the active involvement of young people in media-making today has dramatically shifted. Extraordinary advances in video gaming and simulative worlds such as *Second Life* have pushed us much further towards a new model of immersive media (see Chapter 2 for more on this) where the user is both at the controls and on the screen. While there continue to be significant digital divides that shape how media environments operate, it is worth noting that, for those with even limited access to the Internet, low-cost, user-friendly software (i.e., audio, video, and music production applications, as well as Web 2.0 distribution platforms) has enabled some forms of cultural expression that were unimaginable only a few years ago.

As a result of these and like developments, media consumption and use have shifted dramatically over the past decade. While television and radio still play dominant roles in media consumption, many people, including children and youth, are now consuming media across platforms, often simultaneously. We document young people's changing media lives extensively in Chapter 2. Here we note, however, that television has taken cues from the Internet, and viewers today are more likely to actively participate in television content, as the wildly popular world of reality television – and its associated web forums – aptly demonstrates. Moreover, with the convergence of the camera, music player, and telephone in pocket-sized cell phones, technologies for media consumption and production have shrunk to the point that many wired young people are now walking broadcasters, able to post images and video to the World Wide Web in real time, all the while listening to their favorite pop music and answering phone calls or texts from friends. In other words, while the technologies of media use change, so too do the perspectives and practices of the users, so much so that debates have emerged that question whether young people's most basic orientation to learning can fit with traditional schooling models.

Natives and Aliens

At the center of discussions about adolescents' learning in relation to contemporary media cultures are ideas about digital natives who are like 'aliens in the classroom.' In an article with that very same title, Bill Green and Chris Bigum (1993) raised the question as to whether educators need to adapt to new types of students whose coming of age has corresponded with the birth of a digital culture. In response, Green and Bigum proposed that teachers should adapt to young people, who are in some ways fundamentally different from previous generations. The questions raised by Green and Bigum are intended as interventions to challenge the traditional skill-and-drill and sage-on-the-stage models of education at a time when students' out-of-school experiences in and with new technologies are setting up a profoundly different engagement with learning. What Green and Bigum tentatively raised as questions, however, hardened in Mark Prensky's (2001) formulation about the differences between Digital Natives and Digital Immigrants. In fact, in Prensky's casting it often seems like students can learn nothing in contemporary classrooms:

> *Today's students are no longer the people our educational system was designed to teach* [...] A really big *discontinuity* has taken place. One might even call it a 'singularity' – an event which changes things so fundamentally that there is absolutely no going back. This so-called 'singularity' is the arrival and rapid dissemination of digital technology in the last decades of the 20th century

[...] Today's average college grads have spent less than 5,000 hours of their lives reading, but over 10,000 hours playing video games (not to mention 20,000 hours watching TV) [...] [As a result,] *Digital Immigrant instructors, who speak an outdated language (that of the pre-digital age), are struggling to teach a population that speaks an entirely new language.* (Prensky, 2001, pp. 1–2, emphasis by Prensky)

Prensky goes on to argue that those raised with the new tools have more than simply a new engagement with learning; he argues they also have entirely new brain structures and wiring.

Whatever one makes of this claim – and the validity of Prensky's brain research has been called into question (McKenzie, 2007) – the more important point is the uncritical manner in which this distinction between educators and learners is posed. The problem with the discourse on newly wired digital natives (i.e., students) versus digital immigrants (i.e., teachers), stuck forever with an accent, is that it upsets the educational apple cart. If the immigrants can never catch up with the natives, how can they be presumptuous enough to teach them new literacies and practices associated with digital technologies?

Fortunately, media educators have long ago crossed this threshold. In fact, the recognition that the media educator can never know everything about evolving media discourses and practices is a central truism in the field. To teach media is to adopt the necessary humility of a Freirean educator who is willing to teach in order to learn. The media educator thus needs to bring strategies, concepts, and frames to the teaching context, but with an open mind towards media content that is often better known by young learners. Ironically, Prensky's formulation seems to ignore this possibility and the history of practices that allow educators to operate at the junction point between new media developments and change in older educational contexts.

Media educators have long harkened to Neil Postman's warning that we are *Amusing Ourselves to Death*, and that the average school-age child spends 900 hours per year in the classroom and watches 1500 hours of television over the same period. To a great extent, this has been a *raison d'être* for media educators, who have insisted that we not ignore a powerful form of communication that challenges, and in many cases overwhelms, traditional print literacy. Finding ourselves in a new era, where electronic participation is multimodal and participatory, it is clear to most educators – not just those dedicated to media education – that new forms of communication require an educational response. This is certainly the case for those who strive to integrate ICT (information communication technology) into the classroom, but also for educators across subject disciplines. Media education too must adjust and adapt to this situation, as we suggest throughout this book. But this is not the first time media educators have had to adjust their practices to new times. Indeed, the type of openness and engagement with evolving modes of communication we see today in education circles has long been the very culture of practice championed within media education.

Media Education has a History to Draw On

If we look back to the 1960s, for instance, we see one of the great periods of growth in media education, much of which was fuelled by the idea that educators could adapt curricula and teaching practices to the increasing role of commercial television and movies in kids' lives. In the UK, this sentiment led educators to develop a screen education movement based around the critical use of movies in classrooms. Drawing from the influential work of writers such as Richard Hoggart (*Uses of Literacy*, 1957) and Raymond Williams (*Culture and Society*, 1958), the purpose of screen education was to study the popular culture texts young people were watching, so that youth would be in a better position to understand their own situation in the world, including the causes of their alienation and marginalization. A similar desire to help young people see connections between school and their everyday lives motivated early initiatives in media education in Australia and Canada. Pedagogically, this led to the development of film analysis and film production courses, which drew inspiration from cultural shifts in the way movies were understood. No longer seen simply as forms of entertainment, film education focused on the way popular Hollywood movies (e.g., *Easy Rider*, 1969 and *Medium Cool*, 1969) reflected social and cultural values, and thus were thought to deserve critical attention. This meant teaching students to understand the language of cinema, as well as the way movies engage with and shape prospects for social and political change.

In the US, school-based media education initiatives were slower to get off the ground. Experiments with television in US classrooms began as early as the 1950s, and throughout the 1960s and 1970s the US Department of State helped to set up instructional television programs in American Somoa, Brazil, El Salvador, India, the Ivory Coast, and Niger in a complicated program that aimed to both extend American influence and shape emerging education systems (Goldfarb, 2002). It was not until 1978, however, in response to kids' increasing television consumption, that the National Parent–Teacher Association in the US convinced the Office of Education to launch a research and development initiative on the effects of commercial television on children. In short order, this initiative led the Office of Education to recommend

> a national curriculum to enhance students' understanding of commercials, their ability to distinguish fact from fiction, the recognition of competing points of view in programmes, an understanding of the style and formats in public affairs programming, and the ability to understand the relationship between television and printed materials. (Kline, Stewart, and Murphy, 2006, p. 135)

Ultimately, attempts to implement this curriculum were hampered in the early 1980s as President Ronald Reagan's move to deregulate the communications industry challenged efforts to develop media education in US schools. Nonetheless, these early developments would prove crucial in establishing the ground from which more recent media education initiatives have grown.

Globally, key curricular documents had been produced by the 1980s and 1990s, and media education entered school curricula in many countries around the world in a formal way for the first time. The Canadian province of Ontario led the way, mandating the teaching of media literacy in the high-school English curriculum in 1987. Primary and secondary students across Canada would be receiving some form of media education by the end of the 1990s. Meanwhile, in the UK, the late 1980s witnessed the integration of media education into the curriculum as an examinable subject for students pursuing university entrance. This helped to fuel the popularity of courses in media studies, film studies, and communication studies in schools, and by the 1990s and 2000s additional intermediate courses in media studies were added to the curriculum. In Australia, the late 1980s and 1990s marked a period of expansion in school-based production and media education training, in part because such training was seen to be an ideal way to equip young people with the technical skills and competencies needed to compete in a globally competitive, highly mediated world (McMahon and Quin, 1999; Quin, 2003). Similarly, in various non-English-speaking countries, including Finland, Norway, and Sweden, the 1990s represented a period in which media literacy developed and expanded (Tufte, 2000). The seeds of change were not, however, confined to countries that had implemented formal media education curricula. Where not included in the formal curriculum, media education also became a pedagogical practice of teachers aware of the impact of the media in the lives of their students. In other words, it is not accurate to assume media education was solely a practice of educators in a select group of countries. In particular, in those countries in the global South, where the broader educational needs of society were still focused on getting children to school and teaching basic literacy and numeracy, media education may not have emerged in the mandated curriculum, but teachers were drawing on media education strategies.

In the US, the development of school-based media education initiatives has been challenging for various reasons. The history of media education in other national contexts indicates that a community of grassroots educators is vital if media literacy is to become part of the school curriculum. Given this fact, the size of the US and the physical distance separating teaching communities has been a problem, as has a lack of state-centered teaching organizations, which can build momentum to support new initiatives (Kubey, 2003). As in many other countries, there is also a shortage of teacher training programs in media education, so interested educators have a difficult time accessing materials and maintaining the momentum needed to sustain media literacy as part of school life. Nonetheless, Kubey (2003) notes that, as of 2000, all 50 states included some education about the media in core curricular areas such as English, social studies, history, civics, and health and consumer education. This does not necessarily mean that media education is taken up in the classroom, however, as issues related to teacher preparation and a return to intensive testing in primary and secondary curricula, as mandated by President George W. Bush's 2001 No Child Left Behind policy, have undercut opportunities to develop school-based media literacy programs.

Because of these difficulties, where media literacy has developed in the US, parents and parent groups have taken a leading role and have generally focused on addressing what are perceived to be the negative effects of media on youth aggression and crime, materialism, sexuality, and alcohol and drug use. Alongside these efforts, a number of key non-governmental organizations have developed over the past two decades and have promoted a more dynamic and, in our judgment, more effective form of media education. The Alliance for a Media Literate America, a national membership organization chartered in 2001 to organize and host the National Media

Education Conference every two years and to promote professional development, is of particular note. So too are the Media Education Foundation, which produces some of the most important media education resources in North America, and the Center for Media Literacy, which offers a helpful MediaLit Kit to promote teaching and learning for a media age.

Media Education in the Twenty-First Century

If media educators have often shown a remarkable ability to adopt and engage with evolving modes of communication, we note that, regardless of national contexts, educators' creative and critical engagement with media is changing, given the emergence and rapid proliferation of new information technologies. In the current period of flux and innovation, the bigger question is thus not whether media education will develop but what type of media education will dominate in schools and other learning environments.

Questions like this have set the stage for a remarkable outpouring of policy discussions and government and inter-governmental policy papers of late in Canada, Europe, and the US, among others (Frau-Meigs and Torrent, 2009; Livingstone, 2009; O'Neill, 2009; Sourbati, 2009; Tornero, 2009). Various organizations (UNESCO; the MacArthur Foundation and the Joan Ganz Cooney Center in the US; the European Commission; the Council of Europe; the Alliance of Civilizations; the Arab League; Nordicom's International Clearinghouse on Children, Youth and Media; and the Media Awareness Network in Canada) are involved in these discussions. In turn, this work is coincident with a series of legislative and policy initiatives – including the 2004 Children's Act in the UK and the United Nations Convention on the Rights of the Child, which is recognized internationally but not always implemented in practice – meant to improve the conditions of childhood. The effects of these developments are nicely captured by Divina Frau-Meigs and Jordi Torrent (2009), who note in the introduction to an important collection of essays (*Mapping Media Education Policies in the World*) that:

> The importance of media education is being gradually recognized worldwide. After the time of the lonesome innovators isolated in their classrooms, after the time of extended communities of practice around researchers and field practitioners working at the grassroots level, the moment of policy-makers has arrived. A threshold has been reached, where the body of knowledge

concerning media literacy has matured, where the different stakeholders implicated in education, in media and in civil society are aware of the new challenges developed by the so-called 'Information Society,' and the new learning cultures it requires for the well-being of its citizens, the peaceful development of civic societies, the preservation of native cultures, the growth of sustainable economies and the enrichment of contemporary social diversity. (p. 15)

This sentiment is, of course, important. We note, however, that with the advent of personal computing and the integration of educational technology approaches in schools and teacher education, a training curriculum that focuses on learning software and mastering camera use and design skills can now be undertaken in a way that ignores a critical analysis of consumer broadcast media altogether. We argue, however, that media literacy must always involve an analysis of media texts and dominant and powerful institutions, in conjunction with opportunities for creative media production that speaks to and builds from the challenges, dreams, and visions that are part of young people's lives. What we reject, in other words, are those approaches to the use of new communication technologies in schools where technological mastery is seen as an end in and of itself. We recognize that newly accessible video editing suites and broadcasting (or narrowcasting) opportunities made available through Web 2.0 platforms (e.g., Facebook, YouTube, wiki spaces, and so on) can enable forms of production by young people that were until recently only possible in the well-resourced and highly specialized workplaces of the media industries. We further recognize that technical skills training (in camera use, sound design, and new forms of media distribution, etc.) helps young people to learn key competencies that can open up important and meaningful job opportunities, so it must be part of media education. But to conceive of media literacy as only a form of technical training oriented towards job markets is to woefully understate the critical and civic concerns that have long informed the field. And these concerns matter today not only because they speak to the history of media literacy but because consumer media culture, including new digital technologies, have a direct bearing on key normative ideals in our lives, including our ideas about democracy, community, and our own social futures. Understanding contemporary media, including newly available digital tools, can thus never just be about technical training, because the meaning and effects of this media extend well beyond questions of skills. Indeed, to understand contemporary media environments, we need to ask more fundamental questions, including about how the social and political influence of the media is changing and remaking our everyday lives.

To write a book about media literacy today, we not only have to consider what role media education has played up to the present but also recognize what role it could or should play in the future. We argue for an approach that unites the robust tradition of media analysis and production that has been the hallmark of media education for the past forty years with the emerging domain of new communication technologies in education – an approach that focuses on those elements of these technologies that are participatory, collaborative, and creative. Following Roger Silverstone (2004), we also contend that media literacy must always have a moral agenda. It is not enough that media literacy be understood in relation to the development of the individual and his or her skills, nor to think of media literacy as a tool that primarily serves economic interests and fosters 'skills for [...] employability' (O'Neill, 2009, p. 8). Rather, media literacy must serve the common good by enabling young people to become active citizens, contributors to the public life of our shared worlds.

> Media literacy should be a moral agenda, always debated, never fixed, but permanently inscribed in public discourse and private practice, a moral discourse which recognizes our responsibility for the other person in a world of great conflict, tragedy, intolerance and indifference, and which critically engages with our media's incapacity (as well as its occasional capacity) to engage with the reality of that difference, responsibly and humanely. For it is in our understanding of the world, and our willingness and capability to act in it, that our humanity or inhumanity is defined. (Silverstone, 2004, pp. 440–441)

To advance this media literacy project, we note that there are widely differing discourses in scholarly circles on what constitutes 'literacy' today, each of which has quite distinct effects on how media, technology, and literacy are considered and taught. Literacy, whether new or multiple, whether digital or traditional, continues to hold a place of importance in public and educational debates worldwide (Lankshear and Knobel, 2006). It is a competence that is indispensable in the 'semiotic economies' (Luke, 2003) of the twenty-first century; yet, its very qualities are the subject of intense contestation in educational and governmental circles. As we are well aware, the meaning of literacy is unstable and in flux, a vehicle for empowerment now lying in pieces on the garage floor while we work diligently with new tools to repair it.

Given this backdrop, throughout this book we are somewhat reluctant to transpose the term literacy from its associations with alphabet-driven textual reading and writing to multimodal (text, image, sound) encoding and decoding. A new term such as 'mediacy' might be more useful going forward, because some of the new codes and conventions of encoding and decoding with contemporary media technologies are radically different from traditional ideas about reading and writing. We accept, however, that there is an established and sophisticated discourse on media literacy to which we wish to contribute. Like literacy, media literacy can be a schooled capacity and competency, an ability to interpret and produce media texts that results from a formal media education. But, like speech, media literacy is also a domain of learning outside of schools, one children begin to develop years before they come to school. The difference between that which is formally presented as media education and that which is learned in streets and rec rooms often rests on criticality. As consumers and sometimes producers of media, young people learn a great deal about the workings of media and about the world around them. Formal media education takes what may appear natural in a media-saturated environment, however, and challenges learners to see through facets of media that may have been uncritically absorbed. To a great extent, this is the common understanding among educators and scholars of the process of media education and its outcome, media literacy.

This said, three key points should be raised in relation to this definition of media literacy and media education. First, media literacy is not something only learned from teachers. Inhabiting a media-saturated world by necessity involves immersion in the codes and conventions of media, and a learning process, though later in childhood, equivalent to that of learning a first language. Examples of this are the critical capacities of eight-year-olds to see through the false promises of advertising and the gradual accumulation by children of procedural knowledge of media cues (e.g., this is a flashback sequence; there was a cut in the dramatic sequence from one location to another; a close-up of an object – a knife, for example – suggests a future development in the plot). To see how television teaches its viewers these cues over time, starting simply and gradually and becoming more complex, one only has to look at a typical demographic progression, say from *Barney* through *Scooby Doo* to *90210* or *The O.C.* Thus, if media literacy is not something learned only in structured learning environments, there are two wild cards embedded in media education from the start. On the one hand, there is the hand of the powerful in the mix – media corporations and those corporations whose products are pitched in the media. On the other, there is an insider knowledge already possessed by the learner, one that in many instances outstrips that of the teacher.

The second point to be made is that media literacy is more than just something we should teach – a necessary component of citizenship education that is essential in increasingly semiotic societies. Rather, media education offers an alternative to school curricula that were developed in the nineteenth century and have only slowly evolved. Media education provides an opportunity par excellence to get 'in the paint' with our students (to borrow an expression from the world of professional basketball) and to use contemporary media artifacts and themes to make schooling more engaging and exciting for the average student. Ultimately, the vast majority of our students are consumers and fans of at least some media texts. These texts are produced for the most part by media organizations that relentlessly research their audiences, and who produce a great bulk of material for those demographics that are seen to mobilize spending power in the marketplace. Taking media texts seriously is not only about critically engaging such texts, however; it is also a way to open windows into the lifeworlds our students are inhabiting, valuing, and thinking about in relation to their own futures.

Finally, the third point is to recognize how the ground has shifted in recent years to include media production as an integral component of media literacy and education. If there is a central thread running through contemporary definitions of media literacy, it is in fact that this literacy *should* involve interpreting *and* creating media texts. The notion that media production is an integral component of media literacy is a significant development in the short history of the field. Returning to foundational texts such as Len Masterman's *Teaching the Media* (1985), one sees that it is the interpretation of texts and the interests of the (usually corporate) producers that was the central question of the day. Contemporary models of media education, conversely, tie together the consumption and production of media, recognizing both as equally significant elements of media literacy. This book draws on both sides of this coin to develop a model of media education that is responsive to both the powerful influence of the commercial media and the tremendous potentials associated with independent media creation and distribution in an era marked by technological miniaturization and new media expressions. In Chapter 2, we set the stage for this model of media literacy by looking closely at young people's mediated lives, including changes in the way children and youth are growing up today.

2

Children's Media Lives

Perhaps, as they say, life imitates art, but, in an immersive media environment of the sort that many of the world's young people inhabit today, this begs a question: Is there any experience that is as yet unmediated by media influences? Growing up living a partially simulated life of screens, earbuds, and joysticks is now a normal experience, so much so in fact that there is an increasingly fuzzy line that divides what one knows from where one has learned it, or what one has experienced from where it actually happened. The average North American child's impression of history is conditioned by Disney, just as the average Latin American child's impression of family life has developed through the storylines of popular soap operas (or *telenovelas*). When it comes to matters of the heart, many children will learn of love, sexuality, death, and violence in relation to screen-borne narratives. The media plays a central role in our lives, at times distracting us from pressing issues and at others directing our attentions to these very questions. The social media site Facebook, for instance, is an extraordinary parallel universe, offering people an alternative way in which to project their identities and to socialize with a community of 'friends.' At the same time, Facebook is a tremendous networking tool for mobilizing activists, groups, individuals, and sometimes governments to take action on pressing issues of the day. (See, as examples of this work, the President Barack Obama group; the group for the Media Education Foundation; or the group for Open Media (openmedia.ca), which lobbies for informed participation in and activism toward Canadian media.) That Facebook can be the point of departure for activating people's civic engagement demonstrates the power

Media Literacies: A Critical Introduction, First Edition. Michael Hoechsmann and Stuart R. Poyntz.
© 2012 Blackwell Publishing Ltd. Published 2012 by Blackwell Publishing Ltd.

and pedagogical potential of the media, but it also presents the irony of lives lived through a screen filter.

The media is, and always has been, larger than life. We live in its constant presence, even when we are not plugged in and turned on. Today's young people are in many ways no different from previous generations, but it is fair to say that, if the media is a bath, the water levels are constantly rising. Media-filled childhoods have been common since the early days of television in the late 1940s, and to some extent since radio was popularized in the 1920s to add an in-home complement to early cinema. But the early days of television, movies, comic books, and AM radio look quaint compared to the immersive media life we now live. During these earlier periods in fact, media technologies and texts were in general part of discrete public spaces (i.e., the movie theatre or the Major League ball park) and private spheres (i.e., the living room). As older analogue media has given way to digital media, however, it is increasingly true that everything in our lives has become mediated.

It is now virtually impossible, for instance, for youth to imagine what it would be like to grow up without the Internet, television, video games, and pop music. Such media welcome young people into the culture, values, and mores of contemporary life in most of the world's cultures. Among other things, this means that the division between formal places of learning – such as schools – and the rest of our lives no longer holds, because we are learning all the time. The stories, experiences, and practices we encounter in the electronic and digital media are in fact the fodder and teachers through which our lives and identities become sensible. It is in this sense that we mean our lives are mediated today; who we are, what we know, and how we act in the world are all experiences now lived out as electronic and digitally mediated life.

To be sure, this does not mean that any of us – including children and youth – are mere dupes of the mass media, always willing to believe what we see, hear, or read. It does mean, however, that our lives are inescapably intertwined with the images, sounds, and words of a consumer-mediated culture. From *Teletubbies* to *Sponge Bob Square Pants*, the kinder-narratives of television and the Internet provide children with the fodder from which their dreams and nightmares take shape. Such programs and their associated web spaces also train young viewers in the codes and conventions of media viewing and media use, scaffolding learning so that young people's literacy with media develops as each program becomes more sophisticated.

At a young age, the mysteries of the ocean's floor are taught by Sponge Bob, while Barney shows kids how to get along. *Teletubbies*, we believe, eschews content for form, teaching kids how to sit and watch television, while Scooby Doo demonstrates struggle and teamwork, and reveals that the world is not a safe place. As kids get older, Disney's grand narratives introduce young people to history and geography. From *The Lion King's* Africa to *Beauty and the Beast's* France and *Pocahontas'* North America, the world is revealed to children through Disney's distorting lens. And what is learned on the screen is reinforced in the public spheres of kid culture, as the following popular playground refrain illustrates: 'Scooby Dooby Doo took a poo, Shaggy thought it was candy. He took a bite, turned all white, and that's the end of the story.' Here irony, humor, and linear narrative interweave with the formation of a touchstone of kid culture. To belong, you've got to master the common tropes and themes of contemporary kid culture, many of which are media-derived.

In this chapter, we illustrate the degree to which young people inhabit media-saturated environments. We begin by looking at the changing context of young people's lives, and the way children and youth are linked to a complex and changing web of media participation. We focus particular attention on the Internet, digital media, and video games, and examine what we know about how young people are interacting with these media and how this participation differs between genders, classes, and ethnicities. We examine how media concentration and branding practices have changed the way children are growing up, and suggest what this means for media education practice. In subsequent chapters, we turn our attention to what educators, parents, and young people might do in response to children's contemporary mediated worlds.

Researching Young People in Mediated Environments

It is ironic, although certainly not new, that in the wall-to-wall, immersive media environment we live in today the people paying most attention to how young people adopt and adapt to media participation come from the media industries themselves (Montgomery, 2009). While there is a substantial amount of research, both formal and informal, produced by the educational sector, it is those with a vested interest in media effects on children's habits of media participation, and the consumption of both media products and other consumer goods, that study young people most closely.

Early in the 2000s, the PBS (Public Broadcasting System) documentary *Merchants of Cool* (2001) documented this process, revealing the relentless quest on the part of those involved in the advertising industry to unearth youth trends as they emerge. The point, as the documentary tells us, is to integrate these trends into the appeals and strategies advertisers use to sell any number of products and services to kids. Marketers act as culture spies so that they are better able to stay close to the lives and experiences of young people. *Merchants of Cool* goes on to explain that what this creates is a 'feedback loop' between advertisers and youth: youth perform cultural practices – dressing in a particular way, listening to certain music, using new forms of slang, or developing new linguistic practices specific to online environments – that are then studied and adapted into advertising texts (and media programming more generally). These, in turn, are then retransmitted back to youth, who adopt these practices. Keeping ahead of the game means marketers are constantly cool-hunting 'trendsetters,' whose practices are marketed back to a broader 'mainstream' of youth. The process puts a premium on research: the better research and analysis marketing companies have about young people, the better able they are to move the aforementioned feedback loop along. The end result is a constant game of trying to understand kids in order to connect their lives and how they use popular media resources to the products and services various corporations have to sell.

The upshot of this is that the contemporary generation of young people is the most studied demographic in the history of marketing. Whether through detailed focus groups, conferences, industry seminars, new trade publications, or the use of cultural anthropologists hired to study what kids do online, in the mall, or with their friends, a relentless eye is cast toward understanding who young people are and how they might be integrated into consumer life. Importantly, these developments are part of a series of changes that have marked the experience of adolescence over the past three decades.

Getting Older Faster, Staying Younger Longer

What is so confusing about adolescents' experiences today is that they often seem to add up to a paradox. On the one hand, children seem to be staying younger longer, living in a time of 'extended youth.' Sonia Livingstone (2009) observes, for instance, that Western industrial societies 'have seen the extension of formal education from early to late teens and a commensurate rise in the average age of leaving home, thus pushing back the start of employment and delaying the traditional markers of adulthood' (p. 5). If this creates longer-term financial dependence on families, such dependence is exacerbated because youth labor markets have largely remained stagnant in countries across the global North over the past two decades. The result is that youth is extended as young people's entrance into an adult world is delayed.

On the other hand, we are also seeing evidence that children are getting older faster. The age of sexual knowledge and consent for young people has declined over the past two decades, for instance, as has the age at which kids learn about drugs and alcohol, not to mention the range of lifestyle choices available to them. Moreover, there is the sense that children face unprecedented risks today. For example, in 2007 the UK Risk Commission testified that each year, for every million children, six are abducted by a stranger, 2400 are involved in accidents on the road, 40,000 are sexually abused by someone they know, approximately 50,000 (young adolescents) have extreme gambling difficulties, 140,000 are obese, and 270,000 (10–25-year-olds) report that they have been victims of crime in the last year (Livingstone, 2009, p. 9; see also Madge and Barker, 2007). Suicide rates for boys have risen by more than 50 percent since the late 1980s and so there is a palpable sense today of living in uncertain and changing times that force kids to grow up faster.

Market research can be understood as an effort to track these paradoxical changes in order to better introduce and integrate young people into consumer life. To be sure, youth market research is not new. Looking back at the history of young people's experiences in the US, the UK, and other highly developed consumer societies, in fact, it is clear that something like this kind of research has been ongoing since the 1940s (Osgerby, 2004). The urgency and sophistication of contemporary research is of a different order than in the past, however, and it is a response to the fact that the spending power of children and youth has itself risen dramatically over the past decades. In the US, for instance, young people's spending power tripled between 1960 and 1990. By the second half of the 2000s, US teens were spending 155 billion dollars of their own money annually, and children aged between four and 12 were influencing or controlling the spending of 500 billion dollars each year (Montgomery, 2009). Similar trends are apparent in other Western countries – indeed, global estimates suggest that children aged six to 12 influence more than a trillion US dollars' worth of spending (Wasko, 2008) – and, in many ways, such trends are the result of various demographic, social, and economic changes that have occurred since the end of the 1980s (Livingstone, 2009).

With the arrival of the 'Echo boom' – i.e., the children of baby boomers – for instance, the number of young people in Western societies and the marketplace has grown dramatically as compared to the late 1970s and 1980s. Changes in family structures, and in particular the advent of dual-income families where women work both inside and outside the home, has meant that children are taking on more family responsibilities and 'becoming the household experts on the latest products, especially new technologies' (Wasko, 2008, p. 462). Some suggest the added pressures families feel from overburdened work schedules have encouraged parents (and grandparents) to buy more for their kids as a way to ameliorate 'absence' guilt. If this creates new opportunities to target children as consumers, there is also evidence from the US that children are taking on more part-time jobs than in the past to make more money to spend on consumer goods (Montgomery, 2009). Conversely, though, reports from other Western countries (in particular those of the European Union) suggest that 'the new youth market is largely funded by parents rather than by any growth in youth employment' (Livingstone, 2009, p. 6). Regardless, in both situations the point is that young people have access to more spending power and often increased latitude in their choice of what to spend money on today.

Where consumer market research has influenced how this money is spent, we cannot ignore the fact that young people's spending habits are also shaped by the pleasure and satisfaction many experience through media. Roger Silverstone (1999) noted this some time ago, but as educators and researchers we sometimes ignore this fact. As we discuss at various points throughout this book, however, the joys and thrills young people associate with using and consuming media cannot be ignored if media education is to have a meaningful and critically effective place in kids' lives. Moreover, as childhood itself changes, young people seem to be turning to media as a space for freedom and exploration, a relatively safe and secure environment that offers them resources and opportunities to explore their identities and sense of freedom beyond the gaze of adult mentors. This cannot help but create tensions between adults, teachers, and young people, but, as traditional adolescent spaces (e.g., playgrounds, malls, the street) increasingly become sites of fear and surveillance for youth, it should not be a surprise that electronic and digitally mediated experience has come to fulfill roles that have traditionally been associated with other kinds of places and relationships. All this is to say, it matters more than ever today that we develop a clear picture of how young people are involved with mediated culture, and where and how critical media education can be effective in this context.

Life Inside a Media Wonderland

While many statistics have been collected over the years on the time adolescents spend immersed in media, the general impression these numbers convey is that most children and youth are more involved than ever with media technologies and content. At the center of this engagement is a new terrain of children's and youth media, a world in which the Internet, mobile phones, and 'television' consumed through web spaces and iPods compete for attention with and often surpass the influence of older media (i.e., radio, appointment television, and movies). The prominent studies conducted in recent years have sought to understand these developments and in particular the role of the Internet and video games in young people's lives. Regular television and radio continue to hold a place among kids' media choices, particularly in developing world contexts where the digital divide holds back young people's rapid adoption of some new technologies (others, including mobile phones, have spread dramatically in such contexts). Still, the more salient point is young people's time with media in general has tended to increase significantly over the decades (Livingstone and Haddon, 2009; Tufte and Enghel, 2009).

Between the 1960s and 1980s, for example, young people's media use mostly amounted to more time spent in front of the television. Today, however, across classes, genders, and ethnicities in the global North, traditional forms of television viewing are on the decline (Media Awareness Network, 2005; Livingstone and Haddon, 2009; Rideout, Foehr, and Roberts, 2010). In the 1970s, for instance, young people in Canada, the UK, and the US typically watched 25–28 hours of television each week. Today, however, US teens spend approximately 50 hours each week with various media, of which only about 17 hours is spent watching regularly scheduled television in front of the set (Rideout, Foehr, and Roberts, 2010, p. 3). Similar figures and trends were found in studies of young people's media use in the European Union and Canada (Media Awareness Network, 2005; Livingstone, 2009). These figures do show some differences in relation to class, with less-well-off young people typically spending more time watching television and playing console-based video games then their more affluent peers. The point to be made, however, is that changes in the amount of time young people spend with media are taking place as part of longer-term trends in how media is knit into adolescents' lives.

At the center of these trends is the fact that young people simply have more media options today – both in terms of the media technology used and the content available – and these options are tightly intertwined with the daily lives of children and youth. For instance, nearly three quarters of 8–18-year-olds in the US have a television in their bedroom, half have a video game console and/or cable/satellite television, and a third have their own computer and Internet access (Rideout, Foehr, and Roberts, 2010). As Livingstone (2009) notes, these figures reveal a shift to a screen rich 'bedroom culture,' which is increasingly becoming the norm for kids in countries across the global North (p. 21). Adding to and fostering media use in this screen-rich bedroom culture is the fact that cell phones are now media content delivery platforms. In other words, whereas cell phones have historically been used to hold a conversation, this use now only accounts for only 30 minutes of the nearly three hours per day that 8–18-year-olds spend using cell phones. The rest of the time, teens are using their phones for texting (90 minutes per day) or listening to, playing, or watching other media (Rideout, Foehr, and Roberts, 2010).

With all these media options available, it won't be a surprise that young people are also now much more likely than in the past to be media multitaskers, capable of packing more media into any given hour of consumption than was true of previous generations. While young people in the US spend more than seven hours a day consuming media, for example, they actually manage to pack nearly 11 hours of media content into those seven or so hours. This is the case because almost 75 percent of teens say they multitask some or all of the time they are using media (Rideout, Foehr, and Roberts, 2010, p. 33). Consequently, the typical image of the teenage user today is someone doing homework while listening to music and responding to the occasional text or instant message (IM). Other teens of course manage to do much more as media multitaskers. For instance, one of our sons composes and mixes music between bouts of homework while still in IM contact with his friends. Another son produces videos and elaborate photo galleries in the same manner. In this way, the new digital media environments kids in the global North are growing up in are becoming the kind of active media domains in which the contemporary couch potato is also sometimes a DJ, an occasional movie producer, and always a switchboard operator, taking several calls or texts at once.

With more computers and Internet access in homes in the global North, few will be surprised that across the Western world Internet use is on the rise. In Europe, for instance, children are using the Internet at a younger age, and on average 75 percent of 6–17-year-olds across the European Union are regularly online. The World Internet Project (2009) found similarly that 95 percent or more of young people in Canada, Israel, and the UK regularly use the Internet. In the US, 99 percent of youth use the Internet and most teens spend an hour and a half on the computer daily, outside of school work. This represents an increase of almost half an hour since 2004, and is a reflection of the fact that home Internet access in the US has increased from 74 to 84 percent and the quality of Internet access has improved significantly, with high-speed Internet now available to 59 percent of US teens, as compared to 31 percent in 2004 (Rideout, Foehr, and Roberts, 2010, p. 3). Perhaps more importantly, kids' increased time online is a reflection of the popularity of social media sites. While such sites were not available five years ago, the social networking site Facebook and the video sharing site YouTube now represent two of the three most favored Internet destinations for young people.

Inequities and Parents' Worries about Media Use

Of course, around the world these kinds of developments are unevenly realized due to the prevalence of a digital divide between haves and have-nots. In Mexico, for example, 50 percent of the population do not participate in the new media at all, while another 20 percent have only sporadic contact with the Internet. As a relatively wealthy global South country, Mexico has a well-developed fiber optic system and an enviable digital participation rate in global terms. Nonetheless, the notion that participatory, collaborative media – such as music mixing software, digital cameras, and editing software – is available to all is misleading in a world that is stratified by economic inequalities that do not make for an even playing field.

Closer to home, other research results suggest that the time youth in the global North spend with media is not always educationally productive or socially equitable. We know, for instance, that kids who are heavy media users – more than eight hours per day – report getting low or poor grades in school. In the US, we also know that there are important disparities in media use in relation to age and race. In particular, there is a noticeable jump (more than three hours per day) in media use between the ages of 11 and 14 for both boys and girls, with the biggest increases coming in television and video game use. Perhaps more revealing, African-American and Hispanic youth in the US consume about 13 hours of media daily, of which, 5.5–6 hours is spent watching television.

For many parents, these and like statistics have been cause for alarm and worry. The fear is that 'sitting in front of a computer or television for extended periods of time can lead to weight gain, or that endless instant messaging can interfere with children's ability to form face-to-face relationships' (Montgomery, 2009, p. 6). Fears about how young people consume contemporary media are also layered with longstanding fears about how old and new media bring violent images and stories into adolescents' lives. Violent video games such as *America's Army* and *Grand Theft Auto* epitomize these concerns because they only seem to add to the array of violent images kids watch on television and in movies. The result is a sense of deep uncertainty and wariness among parents, many of whom 'feel behind the curve, only learning about their children's favourite media pastimes from the front page of the newspaper or evening newscasts' (Montgomery, 2009, p. 7). Many parents feel ill-equipped to respond to this situation, and yet they simultaneously feel a tremendous pressure to address the changing media culture that is so much a part of their kids' lives.

We take up the question of violence in the media and its impact on young people in Chapter 3, but the question of video gaming is the nexus of new concerns that are important to situate in relation to what we know about what and how kids are playing and the way gaming is fitting into their lives. On this, it is absolutely clear that just about all kids play video games. In fact, the recent study *Teens, Video Games and Civics* notes:

> Video gaming is pervasive in the lives of American teens – young teens and older teens, girls and boys, and teens from across the socioeconomic spectrum. Opportunities for gaming are everywhere, and teens are playing video games frequently. When asked, half of all teens reported playing a video game 'yesterday.' Those who play daily typically play for an hour or more. (Lenhart et al., 2008, p. i)

Video game playing among teenagers is somewhat less popular in European countries; nonetheless, it is still pervasive (Livingstone and

Haddon, 2009). Not surprisingly, younger boys and girls play games most often, while teenage girls tend to play less, although more than 50 percent of teen girls still play. Interestingly, kids play all sorts of games, rarely sticking with one genre (i.e., first-person shooter games such as *America's Army*). Moreover, of the six most popular kinds of games among US teens, only one (*Grand Theft Auto*, an action game) is associated with violence. The rest cover the gamut from racing games (*Burnout, Mario Kart*) to puzzle games (*Solitaire, Tetris*), sports (*Madden, Tony Hawk*), and rhythm (*Dance Dance Revolution, Guitar Hero*). Kids do, of course, play a mixture of violent and non-violent games, but, contrary to another concern among parents, gaming is in general a highly social activity. Less than one quarter of teens only play games on their own, for instance, and most play with others most of the time. It is also of note that, as games have become increasingly common, parents either play with their kids or more often keep track of the kinds of games their children are playing (Lenhart et al., 2008; Livingstone and Haddon, 2009). In the *Teens, Video Games and Civics* study, it was also shown that the quantity of game play did not relate to young people's interest in civic engagement. Indeed, kids who play games together tend to be more interested in politics and more willing to commit to civic participation (Lenhart et al., 2008, p. vi). This does not mean that we should have no concerns about video games and young people. In fact, we take up some of these concerns and the educational possibilities video games present in Chapter 7. The point to be made here, however, is that gaming is a complex activity in kids' lives, one that often attracts concern but one that we need to approach with a degree of wariness toward easy criticisms that suggest gaming is undermining kids' social, ethical, and political lives.

What is true today is that young people are growing up in an increasingly complex communication environment. The Internet allows for both one-to-one communication (like the telephone and face-to-face interaction) and one-to-many communication (which is true too of older broadcast or mass media, such as the television and movies). It also allows for many-to-many forms of communication (as in massive multiplayer online games), something that is a unique characteristic of digital networks (Castells, 2001). This allows today's media to expand in new directions and places, finding new routes into young people's lives. This in turn contributes to 'the reconfiguration of opportunities and risks in children's lives in relation to social, cultural, educational, civic, health, and still important leisure activities' (Livingstone, 2009, p. 21).

Media Concentration and the Big Four

Where media environments pose new challenges and opportunities for young people, it is crucial that we think about these developments in relation to recent changes in the political economy of children's media. Calling attention to the political economy of media and communications is not meant to deny the ways young people are finding pleasure and important forms of social engagement through contemporary media. However, it does draw our attention to the way systems of media production – including the dominant companies that produce and advertise new media products and technologies – constitute power relationships that shape how media (e.g., magazines, music, television shows, web spaces) is created, distributed, and consumed by children and youth.

Thinking in these terms, four major transnational media companies (Disney, News Corp., Time Warner, and Viacom) dominate children's media and entertainment markets. A group of other 'large multinationals dominate the business of toys, video games, candy, soft drinks, and food,' but the big four in children's media have 'spread their influence globally, drawing on their financial muscle and extensive program libraries' to shape the media worlds children now inhabit (Wasko, 2008 p. 465). The history of each of these companies is significant, but what distinguishes all of them is two key factors. First is their ability to develop and introduce a vast range of new media products and services that can be distributed to young consumers globally across an array of media platforms, including movies, television channels, Internet sites, theme parks, magazines, and music distribution networks. Second are the new branding and marketing strategies that have developed in conjunction with the growth of media conglomerates, which are changing the way children are growing up.

Many educators and students have some sense that companies such as Disney, News Corp., and Viacom have an incredible reach into young people's lives, but pointing out just how wide and deep that reach actually is always has an eye-opening effect. On this, Janet Wasko (2008) offers a revealing portrait of the various media properties owned by Disney, which continues to be a global leader, if not the only dominant player, in the development and promotion of media products for children and youth. She (2008) notes that Disney now includes:

- Various live-action and animated film companies, including Hollywood, Merchant-Ivory, Miramax, Pixar, Touchstone, and Walt Disney Studios;
- Various television businesses, including ABC, Buena Vista, Touchstone, and the Walt Disney label;
- Cable channels, including Toon Disney and the ESPN franchise (which is actually a global group of cable channels, radio, Internet, retail, print, and food operations designed for a youth market);
- Extensive product merchandising companies including Disney Consumer Products, one of the largest licensors of branded characters and logos in the world;
- A chain of retail outlets and online catalogue sites, including the Disney Catalogue;
- Children's book and magazine publishers including Disney Publishing, which is thought to be the largest publisher of children's literature in the world;
- Various online services, interactive television, and Internet websites, produced by Disney Online, including one of the most popular sites on the web, www.disney.com;
- Six major theme parks, including Disneyland, Disneyland Paris, Hong Kong Disneyland, Tokyo Disneyland, and Walt Disney World, all of which are designed to reinforce and extend the monetary value of Disney films, characters, television shows, and other associated products;
- Various radio stations, including Radio Disney, which develops programming specifically for kids; and
- Branded characters central to children's culture including Mickey and Minnie Mouse, Winnie the Pooh, and so on.

Through this library of media products and services, Disney is the dominant global player in baby and toddler merchandising, and is also deeply associated with 'young people and families, having built a strong and enduring reputation that is almost "naturally" associated with children' (Wasko, 2008, p. 467). For some educators, researchers, and students, it is this overly naturalized (ideological) association between Disney and childhood that is problematic today. For others, it is not just the intimate relationship between Disney and childhood that matters but the way branding practices have developed alongside and in conjunction with the growing influence of Disney (and other media companies) that is of greatest concern.

Creating Cradle-to-Grave Consumers

Branding matters in children's media lives because brands themselves are not just about 30-second television advertisements anymore. Rather, brands (such as Apple, Disney, Lego, Mattel, or Nike) are complicated meaning systems that have an impact on kids' identities and operate across different media forms, using different techniques, resources, and appeals to address audiences. Brand marketing to children really began in the 1930s with the early merchandising of Disney characters (Kline, 1993). In the 1960s, the popularity of young people's cross-over products led to the use of animated characters as branding devices in children's advertising. This began with cereal but the practice expanded as television and its characters came to have a more central role among adolescents. Over the next 20 years, these practices would develop, but it was really in the 1980s that the full evolution of branding emerged.

What enabled this evolution was the onset of a neoliberal policy environment that changed how media industries and companies are regulated (by governments) and the way marketing to young people works. At the core of neoliberalism is the contention that markets are best able to provide for the wellbeing, development, and happiness of all. For the past 30 years this idea has been tremendously influential among policy-makers, economists, and some educationalists across the global North and, as a consequence, the marketplace has been empowered as the best arbiter of the ideas, experiences, and products that should be part of kids' lives. The work of empowering markets – and the companies that dominate them – has come about through government deregulation of those media industries that play a central role in children's and youths' lives. In the US, in particular, the 1980s and 1990s were a time of massive government withdrawal from the regulation of how media companies operate and target all audiences, including young people (Kline, 1993; Buckingham, 2000). In part, this helped create the conditions for global media conglomerates – such as Disney, Time Warner, and Viacom – to emerge as major players across young people's culture. Just as importantly, however, these developments created the conditions wherein new branding and marketing strategies could develop to reach in and target children and youth across their everyday lives. The end result has been that brands have become more prevalent, influential, and common features across kids' experiences. Indeed, one commonly cited statistic suggests that the average

10-year-old can recall between 300 and 400 brands (del Vecchio, 1997; Wasko, 2008).

For many, this matters because brands reference and articulate complicated psychological needs (i.e., childhood, family, love, friendship, self-esteem, a sense of freedom) as a way of ensuring that various products are bought, regardless of their real value. Brands in fact speak to us about our basic emotions, desires, and social needs and then translate these on to products as though these material objects can be the conveyors of the more basic emotional needs and desires we all share (Danesi, 2006). Many are suspicious of this, but perhaps the more significant issue is that, as media deregulation has advanced, we have seen the emergence of a new set of branding strategies that have in many ways changed the experience of childhood.

One example of this kind of strategy is exemplified by the product spin-offs and successes of the *Star Wars* brand. The first *Star Wars* films were popular enough but the franchise showed real innovation in using the films as a platform to cross-market clothes, toys, television specials, cereals, animated cartoons, and eventually video games to kids. By doing this, the *Star Wars* brand generated tremendous sales (two billion dollars by 1989 alone), but, in leveraging the new opportunities a deregulated environment afforded to media producers, the franchise also helped to change the context of young people's play (Kline, 1993). After *Star Wars*, in fact, what we began to see is that characters crafted for film or television became 'the predominant social identities' at the very heart of children's leisure time (Kline, 1993, p. 138). A major shift in Federal Communications Commission policy in the US in the mid 1980s accelerated these developments by allowing television networks to create programs – such as *Strawberry Shortcake, Teenage Mutant Ninja Turtles,* and *Transformers* – specifically designed to market new toys, comics, cups, candies, and a vast range of other products to children. As a consequence, by the 1990s and 2000s, the full effects of the 'Strawberry Shortcake' strategy – so called in recognition of the first toy to benefit from this policy change – were evident. The effect of this today is that it is rare that a new television show or film is produced without a whole range of product spin-offs. Japanese phenomena such as Pokémon and Yu-Gi-Oh! moreover have emerged as holistic and intact cultural systems, with highly integrated and complex cultural practices that knit together movies, video games, trading cards, and websites under the auspices of a single brand that becomes entwined in kids' lives.

The larger impact of these developments has been to expand the role of brands across kids' social spaces. Today, in fact, there is little in children's and youths' culture that has not been branded. Sports (the UEFA Champions League, the NBA, etc.), fashion, search engines, computers, games, personalities (Tiger Woods, Miley Cyrus) – all are now pitched to kids through intricately developed branding programs. As a consequence, 'there is [...] a constant dynamic interplay' between kids' lives and 'the promotion of brand products' (Danesi, 2006, p. 19). This happens through celebrity endorsements, the creation of 'events' that promote branded goods, and the placement of products in television shows, movies, and video games. Branding also operates through and has encouraged the development of a highly segmented marketplace in which young people are targeted as 'tweens,' 'kidults,' 'middle youth,' 'adultescents,' and so on (Cook, 2004; Willett, 2005; Buckingham, 2006a). The end result is that branding and the language of marketing have become a kind of *lingua franca* for kids, a set of practices that locates the meaning and impact of any number of experiences and ideas for young people.

Now, we want to emphasize again that this does not mean young people are naïve about the way brands target them as consumers. In a 24/7 culture of branding, in fact, it is difficult for kids not to evolve some sensitivities to ads and marketing-speak, if only because this is the water they now swim in. What we are learning, however, is that, while young people begin to recognize and distinguish between advertisements on the basis of their persuasive intent beginning around age eight (Buckingham, 2006a), they are also typically unaware of how new marketing strategies are weaving brands into their lives. But this is a significant problem, especially where young people's online experiences and practices are concerned, because it is here where growth in the amount and sophistication of children and youth-oriented branding practices is most apparent.

The big four media conglomerates are major players in these developments, which perhaps accounts for the fact that online advertising is 'a booming market' (Willett, 2008, p. 53). At the center of this market are several new strategies used for online marketing (Montgomery, 2009) including:

- The integration of advertising and online content, which is often described as 'immersive advertising' because the user cannot easily distinguish between what is an advertisement and what is content (see, for instance, the Neopets website, www.neopets.com);

- The use of other immersive advertising in 'the form of e-cards, ring tones, wallpaper, contests, clubs, games, and quizzes ... in everything from computer games to children's edutainment websites [e.g., Club Penguin]' (Willett, 2008, p. 53);
- The use of viral marketing that leverages instant messaging and peer-to-peer digital and social networks to integrate branded messages into ongoing communication between children and teens – one of the most interesting examples of this practice is the Girls Intelligence Agency (www.girlsintelligenceagency.com); and
- The development of environments – such as www.lego.com – where children spend long periods interacting with branded products.

The appeal of this form of branding is not only that young people have a difficult time recognizing it as advertising. More important is the fact that '[t]he interactive nature of [...] online advertising assures marketers that children are engaging with a promotion or at least more so than TV audiences who may not even be in the room when the ad is shown' (Willett, 2008, p. 53).

Conclusion

The upshot of this is that children's media lives are tremendously complex and challenging today. Heightened levels of media concentration and increasingly sophisticated and ethically challenging forms of branding continue to pose risks to young people. Conversely, though, new digital media technologies that allow young people to mix their own music, mount their own stories, and edit their own images and videos offer tremendous opportunities for children and youth to take a stand and make a mark in their lives and communities. Taken together, then, young people are not just the recipients of images, ideas, and stories broadcast through a mass media system today. Rather, in a convergent media culture (Jenkins, 2006a), one in which multiple media speak to and are used by young people, the characteristic experiences are different.

Young people's media consumption is now characterized by *personalization* (kids create specific identities through their Facebook pages or through the igloos they design and decorate on Club Penguin), *hypersociality* (a constant ability and even expectation to be 'available'), *networking* (young people can reach out to and be reached by media across various platforms, times, and places), and *ubiquity* (there is just much more electronic and digital media than ever before). Moreover, research is telling us that many young people, particularly those who come from middle class homes, are likely to use the Internet daily for a range of purposes, including searching out information, doing school work, sending e-mail, downloading music, and making media content. Children and young people from working class and/or low-income homes are likely to use the Internet less, watch television more, and produce less of their own media content. On the other hand, many youth from across socio-economic categories do not go online as much as is often thought, and, when they do, their use of online resources can be less creative or complex than we might hope (Livingstone, 2009).

We take this to mean that, while contemporary media cultures may engage young people's 'collective imagination and [afford] new "genres of participation,"' many of the old and familiar inequalities – related to questions of race, class, and gender – continue to shape how young people use media and what forms of media consumption they engage with (Ito, 2008; Livingstone, 2009, p. 25). More, a culture of choice and personalized goods that dominates kids' online and offline environments tends to encourage children and youth to 'behave in an individualized way' when it comes to acts and practices of identity formation and personal development (Livingstone, 2009, p. 11). This in turn makes the work of nurturing young people as civic actors more challenging because, in an important way, young people's media lives privilege personalized acts of decision making rather than collective acts of political commitment and community engagement.

Thus, while kids' media lives are indeed rich and complex, we contend that the work of media education is more important than ever. In a sense, media education fills the 'activation gap' (Rheingold, 2008) between the opportunities young people now have to participate in and through media and their involvement in social and political life. Towards these ends, in Chapter 3 we offer a method for understanding the learning possibilities that arise within kids' mediated lives and highlight substantive examples of learning programming (educational media), including initiatives that have engaged media as a form of public pedagogy in the service of progressive educational ends.

3

Media as Public Pedagogy

*Television – once exclusively used to enhance leisure and entertainment –
has evolved to be an essential tool for the classroom.*
(Channel One help site, help.channelone.com)

One of the most controversial television networks in North America is
Channel One News. This network began broadcasting in schools in 1990
and has evolved to become the largest provider of news programming for
teens. With a daily audience of almost six million young people, who view a
12-minute broadcast during school hours, Channel One develops award-
winning news programming made by and for youth. Offered free of charge
to schools, Channel One not only provides the programming but also the
equipment with which it is viewed. The catch in this arrangement is that the
daily 12-minute program includes two minutes of advertising for government and a variety of corporations, who pitch products and services such as
clothing, health and beauty products, sugar-free beverages, anti-drug
messages, and military recruitment to the captive audience of secondary
students. Participating schools are required to show the broadcast during
class hours at least 90 percent of school days and are not allowed to present
content from competing broadcasters. Channel One presents itself as bias-
free, but it makes a number of restrictions on what may be advertised,
banning, for example, messages that advocate contraception, feminine
products, or abortion clinics.

Critics of Channel One such as Henry Giroux (1994) blast the network
for its commercialization of classroom space and its manipulation of
cash-strapped school boards desperate for Channel One's offer of free

Media Literacies: A Critical Introduction, First Edition. Michael Hoechsmann and Stuart R. Poyntz.
© 2012 Blackwell Publishing Ltd. Published 2012 by Blackwell Publishing Ltd.

educational technology. Giroux points out that the list of corporations signed up for ads by Channel One include corporate heavyweights such as Burger King, Gillette, Nike, PepsiCo, Proctor and Gamble, and Quaker Oats and that the network was already reaching a gross annual revenue of more that 100 million dollars in its early days. Clearly, the arguments against Channel One's intrusion into the educational sphere have strong merits as schools are one of the last remaining bastions against the creep of consumerism into everyday life, and the notion that students – who are bound by law to attend school – should be required to view television advertisements is certainly troubling. Despite the profound significance of this critique, however, arguments in favor of a project such as this, which exposes high school students to news produced by and for youth, have some value as well. Among other distinctions, Channel One has twice won the George Foster Peabody Award, in 2003 for a feature entitled 'A Decade of AIDS' and in 2005 for news coverage of the armed conflict in Sudan. While youth today are immersed in media and saturated with information, they are reading less news than previous generations (Bennett, 2008), and thus their exposure to stories such as these cannot be taken for granted. Ultimately, while the noteworthiness of its editorial content does not trump the arguments of Channel One's critics against the corporate intrusion into schools, this case does serve as an interesting anecdote in relation to the dramatically differing views people have regarding the way commercial media operates as a form of public pedagogy, a set of practices that alter and shape the meaning and experience of learning for young people.

This tension between diametrically opposed viewpoints towards Channel One is nothing new. The popular media have long been thought to have powerful ideational, ideological, and pedagogical effects on children and youth. In this chapter, we examine how educators, researchers, and adolescents might usefully understand the role of media – both commercial and educational – as sites of learning for children and youth. In particular, we examine how the media has been framed as threat, exalted as a powerful pedagogical tool, and used as a tableaux for critiques by progressive media educators and culture jammers. Ultimately, we argue that, while public debates on the media's potential for harm to children have exhibited strong strains of moral panic, some progressive broadcasters and media educators long ago discovered the powerful pedagogical capacities of the media. We show how educators and others have exploited these capacities, and in subsequent chapters we focus on the way media education can augment critical learning *through* the media with a focused pedagogy on education *about* the media.

Media as Threat

While we often think of the period we are living in as unique, a time of profound change as compared with the past, it is worth recalling that an awareness of the development of communication technologies, consumerism, and mass media has long been thought important for children's learning. Several critical traditions form the legacy upon which media education was built. For example, the first provisional forms of media education were developed in the 1930s in the UK, largely in response to the growing power of visual culture, including comic books, the cinema, and advertisements. The literary scholars F. R. Leavis and Denys Thompson (1933) led this work with the goal of *inoculating* children and youth against the dangerous effects mass communications and mass culture were thought to pose. In response, media education was promoted as a form of cultural discrimination, a way to ensure young people learned the right kinds of books, pictures, and music – those thought essential for a rich cultural life.

Many shared the notion that a vibrant and meaningful cultural life was under threat during the 1930s. In particular, the German critics Theodor Adorno and Max Horkheimer (1972) saw firsthand the powerful role the media played in the rise of fascism in Germany. Drawing from this experience, as well as their disappointment with the quality of early popular music and Hollywood movies, Adorno and Horkheimer argued that the artifacts and emissions produced by 'culture industries' (that is, the corporations who sold or transmitted film, popular music, magazines, and radio) threatened to undermine rich and autonomous forms of cultural life. By this, they meant that movies, advertisements, and eventually television were signs of the commoditization of culture, an indication that culture itself – epitomized by the rich European traditions of classical music, painting, and literature – was being reduced to a sellable thing, a commodity just like any other in capitalist societies. As a consequence, culture is turned into a series of artifacts and expressions that do not promote critical and autonomous thought; rather, the culture industries promote a kind of sameness, a uniformity of experience and a standardization of life that at best serves to distract people from the truly significant issues of the day. The culture industries thereby produce 'false consciousness' through childish illusion and fantasy, and, for Adorno, Horkheimer, and their Frankfurt School colleague Herbert Marcuse, false consciousness represents a form of thinking that misinterprets the real issues that matter in our lives while leaving children and adults blissfully unaware that key issues demand their attention and action.

In the 1960s and 1970s, the sheer magnitude of US-produced media and its circulation around the world led to related accusations of cultural imperialism. In this era, concern arose over the manner in which ideologies, values, and worldviews from the globe's capitalist centers (i.e., America) permeated the nations on the periphery, in particular those nations that were considered to be a part of the 'developing' 'third world' (see Boyd-Barrett, 1982; O'Sullivan et al., 1994). This new wave of cultural imperialism, or 'coca-colonization' as it was sometimes referred to, was thought to be leading to the homogenization of global cultures as people around the world seemed quick to accept, and gladly embrace, the imposition of a made-in-America cultural ethos in their own cultural contexts. This theory was easily transposed on to children the world over, who were seen to be acutely vulnerable to the power and influence of a centralized and corporate world of mass media.

These perspectives have attracted many advocates over the years, particularly among educators wary of the relationship between consumer media and young people. We should not ignore the fact that childhood itself holds a near mythic place in Western societies and the Western imagination. Consequently, educators' wariness toward media culture is often underpinned by deeper commitments to a sense that childhood itself is a time of innocence, vulnerability, and hope (Buckingham, 2000, 2003a; but also see Prout, 2008). The authority of this ideal can be traced back to *Émile* (1963), Jean-Jacques Rousseau's treatise on the nature of childhood and education. In *Émile*, Rousseau argues that childhood is naturally pure and virtuous and that it is the world that is corrupt. This notion continues to resonate across debates about children's and youths' relationships with the media, but the problem is that it can often underpin unhelpful and overly fearful conceptions about kid's lives.

Contemporary culture industries are assumed to dominate and determine who and what kids are, a proposition that can devolve into claims that childhood itself is vanishing. Overwhelmed by a powerful media system controlled by a small group of corporate conglomerates – for example, Disney, News Corp., Time Warner, and Viacom – the assumption is that childhood is no longer recognizable as what it once was. Rather than being a free and natural space, childhood is thought to be contaminated by a consumer media culture that is filled with images of violence, sexuality, drugs, alcohol, junk food, and stereotypical beliefs (Willett, 2008). Further, while much has been made of the participatory potentials of the new communication technologies and the platforms of Web 2.0 (Benkler, 2006; Jenkins et al., 2006), what many educators are most aware of are those panic-laden stories about youth transgressions and victimization through these same technologies and platforms (Hoechsmann and Low, 2008). Youth are cyberbullying one another (with cell cams), risking their reputations online and making themselves vulnerable to 'stranger danger' (on social networking sites), developing violent behaviors (in video games), becoming intellectually handicapped (by multitasking), and once again buying in to consumer culture (on websites such as Club Penguin and Facebook). We do not, of course, ignore these concerns, but we also note that this way of framing kids' mediated lives is too narrow and one-sided. More to the point, overly pessimistic conceptions – such as the culture industries and cultural imperialism theses noted above – misrepresent the complex relationships and possibilities that underlie the connections between young people, media, and learning experiences.

Media as a Form of Public Pedagogy

We suggest, in fact, that the problem with arguing that the media either produces a whole series of negative effects that endanger young people's health and vitality, or carries tremendous potential for young people's learning and growth, is that both of these positions misrepresent how media culture actually operates in our lives. Another way to say this is that both positions misunderstand the sociological problem of structure and agency (Buckingham, 2003a). Structure and agency questions have occupied scholars in the sociology of culture and communication studies for decades. At the center of this work are concerns about how to understand the influence of social, economic, and technological *structures*, including the media, on our lives. More precisely, the question is: what is the relationship between these structures and our own *agency* – our ability to influence, shape, and take action in the world?

In response, we acknowledge that it is difficult not to see the consumer media as having a determining presence in kids' lives. After viewing several thousand cereal ads, for example, one might be tempted to buy a particular crunchy brand. The tying together of images of the good life with clothing advertisements is a powerful endorsement of the garment industry. And, if you want to make certain running shoes look cool, mobilizing

African-American culture and the personae of basketball stars Kobe Bryant or LeBron James can be persuasive. As we have seen in Chapter 2, media power is concentrated among a select few corporations and owners with vested political and commercial interests. These companies in turn are intent on mobilizing the sale of products in order to generate the greatest profits. Bias and manipulation are thus part of how commercial media so often function in our current system.

Conversely, though, there is plenty of evidence that young people do not simply act out the plans concocted over boardroom tables on Madison Avenue (New York's famous hub of advertising firms) or in Hollywood (the global ground zero of television and film). As we saw in Chapter 2, media executives seek out the best research they can find in order to align their products and texts with the beating heart of the cultural life of young people. As the market researchers know, however, those cultures and subcultures inhabited and performed by teens are complex and constantly in flux. Thus, it is a misconception to suggest that the popular culture of children and youth is simply produced or manufactured. Though the media industry produces content that is incorporated into cultural life, young people's popular culture is more than the sum of the parts of the media industry. Ultimately, the term 'popular culture' is too often misused to refer solely to the artifacts and emissions of the media industries, the *products* of the media rather than the *practices* of youth that give meaning and value to these products.

Analyses such as these lead us to argue that to understand the way the media interacts with our lives and to see the learning potentials therein it is neither helpful to emphasize the determining power of consumer-media structures nor, more optimistically, simply to highlight the role of human agency and choice in consumerism. Where neither of these responses is wholly adequate, we suggest an alternative direction.

For some time now, various theorists, including, most importantly, Anthony Giddens (1976, 1984, 1990), have argued that questions about social, economic, and technical structures, including the media, should not be approached separately from questions about human agency. In other words, media structures should not be thought of as something like an objective set of institutions, technologies, and practices that determine human experience. Instead, such structures need to be understood in terms of their interdependence with human agency (see Parker, 2000). Social structures such as media institutions and technologies are never just objective forces that bear down on our lives. Rather, where such structures shape our experiences, they also open up new possibilities for acting in the world and are shaped by our ability to take concerted action that channels the impact and meaning of media experiences in particular ways. To understand how changes in our media culture impact the lives of children and youth, then, it is necessary to see how human agency and media structures act through one another (Willett, 2008).

How, then, to make sense of the relation of media culture to the lives of children and youth? We suggest it is helpful to think of this relationship in terms of the notion of public pedagogy (Buckingham and Sefton-Green, 2003; Sefton-Green, 2006). The notion that the media is pedagogical may fly in the face of much educational discourse. The etymology of pedagogy in fact reveals that the term 'refers to the science of teaching children,' and in common parlance it 'is used interchangeably with "teaching" and "instruction" referring, with various degrees of specificity, to the act or process of teaching' (Gore, 1993, p. 3). But examining media culture as a site of pedagogy focuses attention on two crucial and interconnected themes. First, it draws attention to how this culture operates through a set of formative institutions, technologies, texts, and practices that shape and open up new possibilities in relation to how and what young people learn. Second, *given the characteristics or affordances (the technical features and aesthetic qualities) of different media*, thinking of media culture as a site of pedagogy focuses attention on how various media technologies, texts, and practices can be repurposed by educators and students as potential resources for learning and democratic empowerment. Pedagogy thus acts as a bridging concept between structure and agency. In what follows, we document the ways consumer media culture has been taken up as a force that, while shaping young people's lives, can be seen to offer new possibilities for children.

New Learning Horizons

Education of young people through and about mass media has been going on for well over a century, both inside and outside of schools. Concerns about the place of violence, vulgarity, and sexual desire in early popular culture (e.g., penny novels and mass sporting events, including professional baseball) drove these developments. With the rise of mass media such as film, however, these concerns took on a new urgency, largely because movies have an impact on all age groups, most importantly children.

The emergence of the cinema at the turn of the twentieth century forever changed the nature of the intergenerational transmission of knowledge, fixing the attention of the new cinema-going publics on the silver screen. Early cinematographers were able to stage dramas of a scale unheard of in theatre, to command an audience much greater than could literature, and hence to infiltrate the popular imaginary like never before. But, because movies work through the language of images, they were considered both highly emotional and intellectually deceitful. Images were thought to leave audiences in something like a trance, a state of passivity that left them open to forms of manipulation that were morally suspect and politically dangerous.

If these were the fears, for some the very fact that movies could reach larger and more diverse audiences – including women and the working class – meant that the medium contained a kind of promise and potential for learning that could not be ignored. Such responses were not only common among film's boosters; they also reflected a rather more nuanced sense of how life – including the experience of learning – was changing in the twentieth century. In a remarkable series of essays written in the 1930s (Demetz, 1986), Walter Benjamin was unique in arguing that movies could widen audiences' horizons through the technology of the shot and the power of editing, which afforded novel opportunities for people to experience distant lands, other times, and new and fantastical experiences. In this way, Charlie Chaplin's *The Gold Rush* (1925), MGM's *The Great Ziegfeld* (1936), and Victor Fleming's *The Wizard of Oz* (1939) seemed capable of helping people to dream about a different life, to escape vicariously from the confines of everyday experience and imagine a different and perhaps better world.

If these examples suggest the promise of movies as resources for imaginative and even creative learning, we are not suggesting movies should be thought of as simple learning resources. Indeed, the challenge with movies is that they may be a little too easy to understand. They allow for a mode of participation – on the surface at least – that does not require tuition. The fact that movies are easy on, and even seductive to, the eye, however, sometimes causes children to misunderstand what they see. More precisely, children can under-read or misinterpret the visual and story conventions (the 'modality cues') in more sophisticated media texts (Hodge and Tripp, 1986).

Any parent who has watched their younger children try to keep up with the viewing habits and interests of older siblings is likely to recognize this problem. What research tells us is that, while from an early age children distinguish between reality and fiction when they watch movies and television, they often lack the precision and experience necessary to read complex forms of representation. Because of this, children – as compared to their older siblings, for instance – sometimes respond to movies and television shows with a kind of misplaced intensity, or even a sense of confusion and uncertainty that indicates they may not know what they are seeing. Younger audiences can misunderstand film and other forms of mass media, in other words, because a lack of experience can lead to straight-forward interpretations of otherwise complex forms of representation. This issue has been especially important where debates about violent images and stories in the media are concerned.

Debating Dangerous Screens

Debates about the effects of violent media on young people's behavior have been ongoing for decades. What is interesting about these disputes is that they are often haunted by the same oversimplifications that have long characterized thinking about consumer media and young audiences. Where violent media is concerned, this oversimplification is most evident in the so-called 'effects' debates. At the center of these debates are efforts to show a direct or causal learning relationship between 'depictions of visible, manifest, physical violence, and the threat of violence' (von Feilitzen, 2009, p. 9) in all kinds of media (movies, comic books, and video games) and young people's behavior in the real world. Attempts to show this kind of connection have been ongoing since before the 1940s. There are now in fact between 3000 and 4000 studies on the influences of violent content in film and television on children and youth in the US alone (von Feilitzen, 2009).

Given this wealth of research, it is significant that the results continue to be ambiguous and complex. Moral activists have suggested otherwise and point to direct connections between violent media representations and youth aggression (Drotner, 1999; Oswell, 2008). Such charges were leveled during the prominent US Senate Commerce Committee hearing on the regulation of video games following the 1999 Columbine school shootings in Littleton, Colorado (Jenkins, 2006b). The intensity of these debates aside, what is important about the available research is that none of it demonstrates anything like a copycat relationship between media violence and young people's actions in the real world (Anderson et al., 2001; Jenkins,

2006b; von Feilitzen, 2009). No studies show that the media resembles a hypodermic needle inserting violent messages that young audiences learn and act out. At best, studies show a correlation between media violence and youth behavior, not a causal link. This conclusion is important but its meaning is ambiguous. Does a correlation between media violence and aggressive youth behavior indicate a direct connection or does it simply tell us that aggressive people like violent media?

The entertainment industries, whose interests are well served by having few if any restrictions on young people's media, have typically argued that these results mean violent media poses no danger to young audiences (Minow and LaMay, 1995; Kline and Woo, 2008). Others, more skeptical of the self-serving nature of this position, have offered different conclusions.

In a review of research on the influences of mediated violence, for instance, von Feilitzen (2009) notes that one real problem is that media violence encourages and teaches people to exaggerate the amount and types of violence in society, creating what George Gerbner called a 'mean world syndrome,' a sense that society is more dangerous than it actually is. This in turn is a problem, given the feelings and reactions a mean world syndrome creates among those who are most often the victims of media violence. For women and children, for instance, we know that the impact of media violence is at least in part ideological (Schlesinger et al., 1992; von Feilitzen, 2009). That is, when women and/or children regularly see their like victimized on screen, it shapes their own sense of safety in the real world. What results is a sense of vulnerability, a sense that one is less safe and under greater threat than one actually is. The danger this poses is that it challenges and likely undermines the sense of agency women and children and others feel. This in turn disempowers these groups, leaving them with a sense of fear about their ability to control their own futures.

In response to the entertainment industry's position, Kline (2005) has also offered another argument we need to consider. Rather than thinking about the relationship between media violence and young people in terms of effects, Kline suggests that a more helpful approach is to explore this question through an analysis of risk. In other words, while media violence may not lead to direct effects, it is helpful to chart and respond to the *degree of effect* posed by media violence, particularly in relation to specific audiences.

What Kline is getting at is that, while it is true that aggression in young people is caused by myriad factors – including disposition, social background, neighborhood, and family dysfunction – this does not mean media violence plays no part in influencing young people's behavior. Rather, a 'risk factors model' points out that we know from experience and studies (Hodge and Tripp, 1986) that children can misread the modality cues of sophisticated media texts. Longitudinal studies that have followed the same individuals for many years indicate, further, 'that viewing media violence seems to statistically explain 5–10 percent of [...] young people's increased aggression over time' (von Feilitzen, 2009, p. 12). We also know that close to 90 percent of adolescent boys play video games, including violent games such as *America's Army* and the *Grand Theft Auto* series (Jenkins, 2006b); and evidence indicates that playing such games can increase children's violent thoughts and feelings or lead to aggressive forms of play (Robinson et al., 2001). Given this, Kline and others conclude that, while media does not make children violent, this does not mean children's media use is risk-free. Rather, violent media poses a hazard to children and youth, a hazard that is legally recognized in most national contexts – including Australia, Canada, and the UK, but not the US, which designate children as 'developmentally incomplete subjects' (Kline and Woo, 2008, p. 101).

In response, rather than calling for draconian forms of censorship or more moralizing talk, Kline (2005) demonstrates that the risks posed by violent media, including childhood aggression, can be ameliorated through media education interventions. What is important, in other words, is that positively influencing young people's relationship with violent media is not simply a matter of regulation. The more important issue is how to foster and build on young people's meaningful engagement and negotiation with media texts. Approaching the whole issue of media violence in this manner is important because we know that children and youth are far from passive users of media. David Buckingham's (1996) research into the role of television in shaping how children become citizens in their society has, in fact, made clear that

> Children respond to and make sense of television in the light of what they know about its formal codes and conventions, about genre and narrative and about the production process. In these respects, they are much more active [...] users of the medium than they are often assumed to be (p. 7).

The more children and youth learn about how media works, in other words, the more active and engaged they become with it.

If the relationship between young people and violent media is more complicated than is often thought, then, this draws our attention to the value of media education, but also to the potential offered by electronic media as a learning resource. After all, at least one lesson to be drawn from the media violence debates is that young people do not need to be inoculated against the media as much as their meaningful and critical engagement with it needs to be nurtured. Fostering of such forms of engagement has been ongoing for some time, but really developed into its own with the coming of television and the rise of children's learning programs in various nations.

The Merits of Television for Education

First introduced to the general public at the 1939 New York World's Fair, television made a meteoric entrance into modern social life in the late 1940s. In North America, the arrival of television was initially greeted with enthusiasm in education circles. This was less evident in the UK, where it was greeted with familiar charges that it over-stimulated young audiences, leading to 'passivity, eye damage, anxiety, and nightmares' (Starker, 1989, p. 132). In the US, on the other hand, much like digital media today, television was initially seen as a tool for supporting democratic ways of life. For educators, television seemed to offer a way to break down local barriers and class hierarchies by providing an 'electronic window on the world.' Interest in the role of television in education in the US was also fueled by Cold War concerns (Goldfarb, 2002). The successful launch of Sputnik in 1957 accentuated a crisis evident in the US public school system. In response, largely under the leadership of the Ford Foundation and the National Association of Educational Broadcasters, television was taken up as an ideal tool for teaching inner-city kids, whose schools were plagued by under-funding, teacher shortages, and supply gaps. In-class television could reach more children while simultaneously extending the influence of exemplary teachers contracted to deliver lessons. It thus seemed to promise new opportunities and possibilities.

Not surprisingly, if the rhetoric about television instruction held up for a time, the results of these early efforts were mixed. Test scores seemed to rise, but evaluation studies demonstrated that television in the classroom 'was most effective in limited doses, and that it should not take up a major portion of any pupil's day' (Goldfarb, 2002, p. 49). Perhaps more importantly, beyond the schoolhouse walls it was becoming apparent by the late 1950s that 'most children's programming was produced with the size of the audience rather than children's education in mind. [Consequently,] television [became] the source of anxious discourses about mesmerized children entranced by mindless cartoons, punctuated by messages from paying sponsors' (Kline, Stewart, and Murphy, 2006, p. 132; see also Kline, 1993). And why wouldn't this be the case? After all, in many countries – including the US – television was a commercial medium from the outset. Early television stars were both entertainers and hucksters, hawking the products of their commercial sponsors directly in their programs or in commercial spots contiguous with the flow of programs. As a consequence, by the early 1960s, television was becoming synonymous with the selling and marketing of goods to children and youth. Whether this meant early spin-off products drawn from the first children's program, *Howdy Doody*, or later products developed by Disney and Hanna-Barbera (the creators of *The Flintstones*, *The Jetsons*, and Yogi Bear, among others), a 'profusion of dolls, toys, games, comics, lunch pails, and TV books' were in circulation and serving to freeze 'the memories of childhood into consumable objects' (Royal Ontario Museum, 1995, p. 23).

While television clearly raised worries about the role of consumerism in young people's lives, television's reach and increasingly central role within families continued to draw the attention of some educators, who argued that television could be repurposed to have a broader educational impact. This sentiment crept into educational discourses throughout the 1960s. In Chapter 1, for instance, we saw that it was during this decade that the first concentrated efforts to develop film education programs in schools in Australia, Canada, and the UK began. The contention at the center of these efforts was that movies could be treated like novels and used to develop young people's critical thinking through a medium closely connected to kids' lives. In a related but distinct development, other educators argued that television's reach and potential as a learning medium could be exploited through the development of sophisticated educational programming. This seemed especially important because in the 1960s schools themselves often relied on questionable pedagogical strategies, including 'control of the student by others, public humiliation, and the continuous threat of failure' (Spring, 2009, p. 78). Television learning, on the other hand, seemed to offer a different learning experience, a non-punitive form of learning that provided children with 'shelter from the emotional stresses of society' (p. 78).

Children's Learning Television

The challenge taken up with the move toward educational programming was and still is that the boundaries between entertaining and teaching kids are porous. This is not a new idea so much as it extends and contributes to that older tradition of using stories and folktales to teach moral lessons to children (Singhal and Rogers, 1999). Of course, what is different today is that this work is not being undertaken around the local hearth; it is developing through the conventions, institutions, and practices of a highly complex media system.

Using this media system to create successful learning resources has been a delicate business. The idea of using other media – including radio and documentary movies – as informational (and often didactic) educational tools to teach kids social studies, geography, or history has a long tradition in many national schooling systems. But the development of more dynamic forms of educational programming began in the late 1960s, and certainly the most successful example has been *Sesame Street*.

Created by the Children's Television Workshop in 1969 as part of the so-called 'American war on poverty' (Spring, 2009), *Sesame Street* helped launch PBS in the US as a counterweight to the influence of commercial programming in the American mediasphere. Originated by Joan Ganz Cooney and Lloyd Morrisett, *Sesame Street* set out to promote peaceful multicultural societies and to provide inner-city kids with a head start in developing literacy and numeracy skills. To do this, the now well-known strategy was to adapt the conventions of commercial media – muppets, music, animation, live-action films, special effects, and visits from celebrities – to deliver mass literacy in the home.

By the late 1990s, approximately 40 percent of all American children aged 2–5 watched *Sesame Street* weekly. With this success, *Sesame Street* expanded its programming and also developed programs to serve children of war as well as poor kids (Spring, 2009). As a consequence, the reach of *Sesame Street* is now global, extending to 120 countries and including many foreign-language adaptations developed with local educators in Bangladesh, China, Egypt, Germany, Israel, Palestine, Russia, and South Africa, among other countries (Spring, 2009). As *Sesame Street*'s reach has become global, the issues raised in the program have changed. No longer only concerned with the way commercial media conventions can be repurposed to help kids to learn key literacy skills, *Sesame Street* is now engaged in raising awareness and understanding of key issues that demand our attention. For instance, in the South African coproduction, a muppet named Kami who is characterized as HIV-positive was introduced in response to the large numbers of South African children who are HIV-positive. Through Kami and related stories, the goal of the program is 'to create tolerance of HIV-positive children and disseminate information about the disease' across South Africa (Spring, 2009, p. 80). Meanwhile, in Bangladesh, the local version of *Sesame Street* has been used to promote 'equality between social classes, genders, castes and religions' (p. 80).

This kind of success has led to the development of other Children's Television Workshop educational programs, including *The Electric Company*, *3–2–1 Contact*, and *Square One TV*, which have also demonstrated educational promise. The more important point here, however, is that *Sesame Street* has demonstrated the unique pedagogical potential of learning media. Scholarly research and Children's Television Workshop's own formative evaluation have in fact demonstrated that learning television such as *Sesame Street* can help develop young people's literacies and their ethical sentiments toward the world. Further, research by Anderson et al. (1998) has shown that preschool children from across demographic groups experienced marked improvement in literacy and numeracy skills from viewing *Sesame Street*. Moreover, this influence does not appear to fade quickly; rather, the advantages associated with viewing seemed to last as long as three years, well into students' elementary schooling. This is not to say that learning television is a panacea for children and youth. But it does indicate that, used wisely, the conventions, institutions, and practices of an electronic media system can support positive educational outcomes. (In the sidebar AN INCONVENIENT TRUTH AS PUBLIC PEDAGOGY, Jamie Sportun shows how Al Gore's documentary in fact represents a signature example of media as public pedagogy.)

A conviction that electronic and digital media can support progressive educational goals has helped fuel the development of learning media over the past two decades. In the UK, for instance, there is a long tradition of using the radio, television, and now digital media to promote learning and citizenship (see Oswell, 2002). Picking up on this feature of learning media, what is interesting and sometimes problematic about these developments is the way educational media has become its own powerful genre and industry today.

We mean by this that it seems we are witnessing a veritable explosion of educational media. Certainly some of the most potent examples of such

An Inconvenient Truth as public pedagogy

Jaime Sportun, McGill University

With the exception of Dan Quayle, who was famous for all of the wrong reasons, the position of vice president of the US is not one known for pop culture *caché*.

Following his time in office, however, Al Gore went on to star in the 2006 Oscar-award-winning documentary *An Inconvenient Truth*, a film that details the role human activity plays in global warming and urges action on the part of all. In the documentary, Gore discusses widely held scientific views on global warming and uses visual data and computer-simulated images to demonstrate what will happen should this current trend continue.

Setting aside the message of this film for a moment, it is clear to see how Gore's approach makes a smooth transition from theatre to classroom. His method of instruction is not at all unlike a typical teacher or professor, using PowerPoint to transmit information to a live audience in lecture format. If it were not for periodic breaks from this approach to give viewers glimpses into Gore's personal life, the film would likely put many students to sleep. Further, the use of the cartoon *Futurama* to visually represent the causes and effects of global warming, paired with a shot of Gore working on his MacBook, are evident attempts to capture the attention of youth.

Henry Giroux (1995) refers to mainstream films as 'teaching machines' and argues that these works play a major role in shaping public consciousness. The notion of *An Inconvenient Truth* as a 'teaching machine' was taken to an arguably unprecedented level as teachers, school boards, and federal governments began purchasing it for use within their schools. The governments of England, Scotland, and Wales, for example, each distributed the film to all high schools under their jurisdiction (*BBC News*, 2007). Such was the saturation of *An Inconvenient Truth* in schools in fact that one eleventh-grade student in Ontario, Canada reported that he was shown the film in four different classes over the course of one year (*National Post*, 2007).

Gore is the consummate 'edutainer' in this film, using punchy rhetoric, compelling imagery, and a populist style that draws the viewer in as though present for a live, public lecture. In the opening segment of the film, he introduces himself as the man who 'used to be the next president of the United States of America,' to laughter and cheers from the audience assembled for the taping. Humor, however, is not the only way Gore connects with his viewers. He appeals to both Americans and global citizens alike to 'act together to solve this global crisis' and hence to protect the Earth for generations to come.

An Inconvenient Truth is a 'teaching machine' that propelled some students into action. For example, a student in New York was motivated after watching the film to start SAFE (Student Action for the Environment), an initiative aimed at reducing waste by staging small-scale political protests such as boycotting the disposable lunch trays in school cafeterias (Do Something, 2006). College students in Maryland held a 'teach-in' where professors from multiple disciplines were invited to relate their subject-specific content to the issues raised in the film (Footnotes, 2007). Many more have sought the coveted opportunity to be trained by Gore himself, so that they may continue to spread the word about the negative effects of global warming.

Some might wonder whether Gore's film has had a substantial and transformative impact. At the time of writing, the US has yet to ratify the Kyoto Accord, an international agreement aimed at reducing greenhouse gas emissions. This teaching machine, it seems, has its limits. Although it evidently has contributed to shaping the minds and affecting the actions of many among the general public, those in power seem to be the failing students in the class of this particular teacher.

References

BBC News. (2007, October 11). Gore climate film's nine 'errors.' Retrieved October 9, 2009 from http://news.bbc.co.uk/2/hi/uk_news/education/7037671.stm.

Do Something. (2006). SAFE: Student Action for the Environment. Retrieved October 9, 2009 from http://www.dosomething.org/project/a-greener-high-school-experience.

Footnotes. (2007). Framingham State College discovered *An Inconvenient Truth*. Retrieved October 9, 2009 from http://www.asanet.org/footnotes/7.SeptOct07FN.pdf.

Giroux, H. (1995). Animating youth: The Disnification of children's culture. Retrieved October 9, 2009 from http://www.henryagiroux.com/online_articles/animating_youth.htm.

National Post. (2007, May 19) So how did *An Inconvenient Truth* become required classroom viewing? Retrieved October 9, 2009 from http://www.nationalpost.com/news/story.html?id=f7806f79-bf1f-4bd1-8d33-c904feb71047.

media are series such as *Baby Einstein* and *Brainy Baby*, but other examples include the array of educational learning software (*JumpStart, Math Blaster, Where in the World is Carmen Sandiego,* and so on) now available that is designed to improve older students' competencies (Ito, 2008). Some of this media is of course useful, but the problem with these developments is that evidence about the learning value of much of this media remains in short supply (Barbaro and Earp, 2008). Evidence that *Baby Einstein* products were actually harmful to toddlers' development led Disney to pull all products associated with this brand from store shelves in 2009. Perhaps the more important point to keep in mind here, however, is that parents are now under increasing pressure to get their children in front of screens as soon as possible. In many ways, this pressure feeds on adult insecurities about how best to prepare children for life in a socially complex, fast-changing world. In response, the entertainment media industry seems to be suggesting that, if young people don't get in front of DVDs, computer screens, or video games soon enough, they won't develop the right kinds of skills and competencies to succeed in highly mediated, globally competitive societies.

Pressure such as this from commercial media interests on both parents and young people is hardly new. In fact, as we saw in Chapter 2, with the consolidation of child and youth markets in the 1960s in most Western countries, young people (and their parents) have been the targets of intense scrutiny and attention by commercial interests for nearly half a century, though the extent to which this is the case varies depending on national contexts. In Australia, Canada, continental Europe, Japan, and the UK, for instance, traditions of regulation and public broadcasting have tended to mean that young audiences have been protected against some of the most egregious forms of commercial attention. This is less evident in the US, where forms of public regulation and broadcasting have had a more uncertain standing vis-à-vis commercial interests (see Chapter 2 for more detail). Nonetheless, since the 1970s across the Western world, commercial television, branded toys, music, fashion, and now video games and online play environments have come to occupy more dominant roles in kids' lives and their learning experiences (Kline, 1993; Seiter, 1993; Buckingham, 2000, 2007; Oswell, 2002).

These developments have not escaped the notice of progressive educators, activists, and others interested in both developing a critique of these powerful new cultural forms and in using the language of contemporary media itself to promote learning. We have already seen some of the ways educational television has undertaken this work, but at least since the 1970s other strategies have evolved for using commercial media resources for progressive educational outcomes. Perhaps the best examples of this include the use of public service announcements (PSAs), entertainment education, and culture jamming to shape and influence young people's behavior around any number of issues and risk factors today.

Public Service Announcements, Entertainment Education, and Culture Jamming

Public service announcements

Public service announcements are now ubiquitous. They are in schools, on television, online, and at commercial film screenings. They address issues ranging from the dangers of smoking, alcohol, and drugs to concerns about young people's driving habits, bullying in schools, what children are eating, and a whole host of other media-related social causes and health crises. At root, the strategy of PSAs is not altogether different from that of learning programs such as *Sesame Street*. The broad research and learning agenda that informs *Sesame Street* is not often replicated with PSAs, but the idea that commercial media language can be repurposed to influence behavior is common to both formats.

With PSAs, the idea is to use the language of advertising – that is, quick, emotional, and sometimes funny messages that emphasize hard-hitting lessons – and the practices of branding to change people's behavior, identify a specific issue or cause, or encourage youth to get involved with issues shaping their lives. Studies (Winsten, 1990; Singhal and Rogers, 1999; Wakefield et al., 2003; Montgomery, 2009) suggest these strategies can be remarkably effective in influencing young people's behavior. Wakefield et al. (2003), for instance, review a number of studies that show anti-smoking PSAs are useful tools for changing kids' attitudes, especially when combined with school support programs that help youth to quit or avoid smoking.

The very fact that young people now see so many PSAs, however, is among the factors that have encouraged non-profit organizations, foundations, and educators to up the ante with public service campaigns by developing more complex and finely crafted initiatives. Perhaps one of the most revealing examples is the truth® campaign in the US, which began in the early 2000s. Intended to 'de-normalize smoking' and reveal 'the manipulative strategies used by the tobacco industry to snare youth,' the truth® campaign was produced by the American Legacy Foundation as a multiplatform campaign that involved young people in all phases of its design and implementation (Montgomery, 2009, p. 159). Funding came initially from the 1998 Master Settlement Agreement between the four major tobacco companies in the US and 46 state attorneys general, who had sued the tobacco companies for healthcare costs related to the effects of smoking. What is instructive about the truth® campaign, however, is the remarkable range of strategies used in the campaign to engage young people.

Recognizing that children's and youths' mediascapes have changed, the truth campaign was designed from the outset to exploit some of the same alternative marketing strategies the tobacco industry itself has used for years to attract teens to smoking. Most importantly, the campaign rejected efforts to preach at young people about why they shouldn't smoke and instead adopted a savvy media-literate campaign that conveyed 'verifiable information in an edgy and sometimes humorous way that empowers teens to figure out the world for themselves and take control over their own lives' (Healton, 2003, p. 12). To do this, the campaign was designed around a series of hard-hitting PSAs – that is, the 'bodybag,' the 'lie detector,' and 'Splode' – broadcast on cable channels such as The WB (during *Buffy the Vampire Slayer* and *Dawson's Creek*), CNBC, and MSNBC, as well as on mainstream broadcasters such as NBC during high-profile events, including the Super Bowl. In addition, the campaign created a range of digital marketing resources, including a website (www.thetruth.com), branded merchandise, and peer-to-peer on-the-ground (buzz) marketing. The campaign sent 'truth trucks' loaded with teen pop culture paraphernalia to concerts, festivals, and other youth events (e.g., Lil Bow Wow's Scream Tour, the Panasonic Shockwave Tour, and the Warped Tour) to develop brand recognition and offer teens ways of getting involved with the campaign. As a result, by 2005, an independent study published in the

American Journal of Public Health clearly demonstrated that the truth®
campaign had led to significant declines in youth smoking rates (Farrelly et
al., 2005). This study also found that the more youth were exposed to truth
messages, the faster was the decline in smoking (Montgomery, 2009; also see
Montgomery for an analysis of the tobacco industry's efforts to undermine
the truth campaign).

These successes are of course important because they attest to the ways
learning through the media can be nurtured in creative, dynamic, and
effective ways, even in a time when media saturation is a feature of young
people's lives. But a cautionary note is also in order. PSAs have in fact
become so common today that companies are using PSA-like formats to
promote everything from cars to personal care products. The personal
health products company, Unilever Inc., for instance, has been especially
successful with their *Dove Campaign for Real Beauty*. Cutting across online
platforms as well as television and film, the *Dove* campaign has foregrounded the way beauty ads create unrealistic notions about women's
body images. An important message to be sure, at the same time, while
this campaign was underway Unilever simultaneously launched an
equally provocative campaign for *AXE* body products for men. What
stood out in the latter campaign was precisely the opposite message
about women's body images; e.g., MTV ads in fact seem to suggest that
women only matter when they correspond to a rather tired and old set of
stereotypes. This doesn't necessarily undermine the value of the *Dove*
campaign, but it does suggest that the value of PSAs (particularly when
developed as singular learning resources) may be waning as this style of
communication becomes just one more strategy for channeling commercial
messages to kids.

Entertainment education

Educators and media producers working in conjunction with television
networks and film studios have exploited a further strategy to promote
learning through the media. Distinct in some ways from the more explicit
focus of learning television and PSA campaigns, this strategy really takes
advantage of the fact that for some time it has been clear that young people
learn about and negotiate their identities and ideals through popular
media representations. As a result, educators and youth activists have
turned to network programming (e.g. MTV, *Dawson's Creek*, *Glee*) as well
as teen magazines (e.g., *Seventeen*, *Teen People*) as vehicles for developing

storylines and articles that address issues at the very center of young people's experiences.

This strategy – often called entertainment education – has a long and vibrant history in both the global North and the global South (Singhal and Rogers, 1999; Tufte, 2004; Montgomery, 2009). In Brazil, India, Mexico, and South Africa, for instance, popular television program formats such as soap operas and youth dramas (e.g., *Soul Brothers* and *Soul City* in South Africa) have been used to raise awareness and change unhealthy behaviors related to a host of issues, including child poverty, community health, HIV-AIDS, gun violence, and so on. In a related vein, a US organization, the Kaiser Foundation, has been influential in the development of a multinational set of entertainment education programs on HIV-AIDS in partnership with the United Nations. Since 2004, in fact, the Kaiser Foundation has partnered with the United Nations and helped to bring together the BBC, the South African Broadcasting Corporation, Russia's Gazprom-Media, Rupert Murdoch's Star Group Ltd. in India, and more than ten other media companies to develop a Global AIDS initiative. This eventually lead to the integration of HIV-AIDS messages into various programs watched by kids, including shows such as *Indian Idol* in India, a reality series modeled on *American Idol* (Montgomery, 2009).

In the global North, similar strategies have been used. Much like how research and the target marketing of young people (discussed in Chapter 2) have developed over the past quarter century, social marketing through popular television programs, websites, and magazines has become a key way for educators and public health advocates to influence youth behavior and engage youth activists. For some, of course, this will sound counterproductive. In the relentless mediated landscapes young people are growing up in, however, repurposing media – including entertainment programming – for educational outcomes has become a powerful way to teach kids about the issues and problems that are shaping their lives. Indeed, says Montgomery (2009),

> social marketers have crafted their campaigns to mesh with the media habits and journeys of teens and young adults. With the growth of the Internet and the proliferation of teen TV, public-health and social-issue organizations are able to incorporate their messages throughout the youth media culture, reaching their demographic targets. with precision (p. 142)

Working with the Kaiser Foundation in the US, MTV and their teen reality show, *Real People*, have been leaders in this area, developing shows over the years that confront issues of teen pregnancy and sex education. Advocates for Youth, a long-established pioneer of entertainment education located in Los Angeles, has worked with television and film producers and writers to shape programming on abortion, birth control, and lifestyle choices since the 1970s (Montgomery, 2009). Similarly, television series such as the *Degrassi* franchise in Canada and the US have addressed various issues, including family violence, school shootings, mental illness, and questions about sexuality (Byers, 2008). Other series, including *Buffy the Vampire Slayer*, have ventured into similar territory, and, while many educators can be wary of the close working partnership between commercial broadcasters and producers that entertainment education depends on, others note that the very success of this kind of programming demonstrates that media culture can be more than a form of entertainment; it can be a forum of meaningful pedagogy that helps young people engage in real social, cultural, and political debate.

Culture jamming

Fomenting such debate has been the objective of one other strategy used by educators and progressives concerned about media culture. 'Culture jamming' evolves from a long tradition of using media techniques alongside satire and parody 'to draw attention to what may otherwise go unnoticed' in society (Meikle, 2007, p. 168). These antecedents include the Situationist movement of the mid-1950s and 1960s, which sought to undermine what theorist Guy Debord (1994) called the *Society of the Spectacle*; that is, the world of commercial media culture that transforms 'everything that was directly lived [...] into a representation' (Sect. 1). Culture jammers frequently argue that our lives are dominated by multi-modal texts (images, audio, and now hypertext and hyperlinks) and the only way to respond to this situation is to use the design methods (pastiche, bricolage, parody, montage) and genres (advertising, journalism, filmmaking) that characterize commercial media to challenge taken-for-granted experiences and assumptions within contemporary culture (Kenway and Bullen, 2008). Mark Dery (1993) calls this a form of 'semiological guerilla warfare,' which is to say culture jamming is a strategy for fighting back against the status quo by using the principles of media culture to upend the meanings and assumptions operating in this culture.

Perhaps the most common and popular form of culture jamming is the 'sub-vertisement,' which groups such as Adbusters (www.adbusters.org)

have made popular. Sub-vertisements – see www.adbusters.org/spoofads/
index.php for a gallery of examples that target fast food culture, alcohol and
fashion ads, and political communication – use popular references and
techniques in branding campaigns to turn the meanings of logos, branded
characters, and signs (such as the Absolut Vodka bottle) on their heads.
Other culture jamming strategies include the refacing of street billboards in
such a way as to attract attention to key social, political, and environmental
concerns. The Australian billboard-refacing movement, BUGA UP (Billboard Utilizing Graffitists against Unhealthy Promotions) was tackling
tobacco advertising in this manner as early as 1978. In North America, the
Billboard Liberation Front has been executing similar practices in the San
Francisco area since the 1990s.

Other groups, including the Yes Men (www.theyesmen.org), have developed another culture jamming strategy that is based around highly elaborate
spoofs of websites, media interviews, and public announcements. Yes Men's
sharp and politically astute spoofs have lampooned any number of targets,
including Barbie (through the Barbie Liberation Organization), the World
Trade Organization, national governments including the Canadian government at the 2009 Copenhagen Climate Summit, and, perhaps most
famously, the chemical giant Dow Chemicals in an infamous BBC interview
about the Bhopal, India chemical disaster that killed thousands and left tens
of thousands with ongoing health ailments.

In a final example, Reverend Billy and his Church of Earthalujah (www.
revbilly.com) have taken up impromptu, guerilla theatre tactics to raise
awareness about the role of sweatshop labor practices in the manufacture of
consumer media goods (in particular those made by Disney). The idea
behind this and like work is to use fun yet subversive tactics to offer
radical commentary about common images, brands, and ideas that circulate
in our lives.

Bricolage

At the heart of culture jamming, then, is the work of 'bricolage' (Lévi-
Strauss, 1966). To be a 'bricoleur' is to engage in the process of sampling and
piecing together images and signs from various sources in order to create a
new text with new meaning. Culture jammers do this as part of a pedagogical
strategy intended to challenge what media users think they already know
about contemporary media culture. As it turns out, the appeal of this work

as a tool for learning may at least in part be related to the way young people themselves are already using media.

Even without being conscious culture jammers, as we have noted already in earlier chapters, young people are often engaged in sampling and remixing various images and signs from consumer media culture. Angela McRobbie (2000, 2005) has noted this in her research on girls and the way they interact with fashion, music, and other media texts. (See Sarah Barker's sidebar, PRE-TEEN GIRLS AND POPULAR MUSIC, for a discussion of how girls integrate media representations into their everyday lives.) Rebekah Willett (2008) has observed likewise that young people now often 'resist, rework and recreate consumer trends' (p. 52). Adolescents are not thereby culture jammers, *pace* the name. Rather, they are active users of media texts who transform cultural items and references as part of the process of developing their own identities. Think of youths' Facebook pages, for instance. By 'including, omitting, adapting, and arranging' references and images from various sources, young people operate as bricoleurs (if not culture jammers) by recontextualizing media sources as part of 'constructing and performing' a new self-image and identity (Willett, 2008, p. 53).

The model of the young person as bricoleur does not resolve the question of structure and agency posed at the outset of this chapter; rather, it illustrates the concept. Young people work actively within media structures to assure their agency. To recognize the media as a site of pedagogy in the lives of young people, then, is not simply to accept that all media content is illuminating and empowering. Just as we would not accept that all written texts have the capacity to enlighten youth, the media too deserves critical scrutiny and appreciation. In truth, there is much media content that is objectionable and unworthy of focused attention in educational settings. But the reality is that the media plays a central role in the socialization, acculturation, and intellectual formation of young people. It is a pedagogical force to be reckoned with, and we ignore it at our peril. Thus, to argue – as we have in the second half of this chapter – that educationally progressive learning *through* the media is possible does not get around the fact that such learning must be augmented by powerful pedagogical strategies that focus on learning *about* the media. Learning *about* the media and how it operates through and in relation to particular institutions, technologies, texts, and audiences has long been at the center of media literacy. Fostering this project continues to be difficult and exciting work. The aim of Chapter 4 is to examine how it can be undertaken today.

Pre-teen girls and popular music

Sarah Baker, Griffith University

Kate was a member of the all-girl cover band, Lollypop. It was mid-afternoon when I arrived at Lollypop's makeshift studio, and rehearsals were already underway. A small tape recorder, perched precariously on a table, provided the musical accompaniment to the girls' singing and dancing. Kate had clearly been inspired by the 1990s pop group Spice Girls in the construction of Lollypop. Similarly to the members of this British girl group, who each had a character name (Baby Spice, Scary Spice, and so on), each girl in Lollypop had their individual characters: Kate, with her Disney-themed *101 Dalmatians* appliquéd sweater, was Candy-Pop, and the other member present at rehearsals was the blonde, feisty Karate-Pop. On this particular occasion the girls were rehearsing the dance routine for their cover of Aaron Carter's track 'Aaron's Party.' Like the song, the girls' dance was influenced by hip hop and included elements of break dancing. It also incorporated other dance moves that were common in current music videos. However, as Kate explained to me, the dance was quite different from that appearing in the 'Aaron's Party' video. 'We made it up ourselves,' she stressed. While the dancing was taking place, Amelia was hunched over a table busily writing on some colorful paper. I inquired as to why she was present at the rehearsal and Amelia replied, 'I'm writing a contract because I'm their manager.' Previously Amelia had been involved with another girl group but in a different role. She was not a member of the band but, as she told me at the time, she 'helped to organize the make-up, hair-dos and dresses.' Amelia and Kate were nine years old and the playground was their stage.

There are many assumptions that surround young girls' popular music practices. For the most part, girls are seen as passive consumers of pop music, consumers who have been duped into buying a lightweight and worthless commodity of the 'culture industry.' The music listened to by young girls is frequently labeled 'teenybop,' an umbrella term referring to Top 40, commercial music that is distinguished from the serious rock culture of young men (Shuker, 1998). The trivializing of young girls' musical engagement within Western cultures is reflective of the wider trivializing in society of women's popular cultural practices. Pop, conceptualized as a feminine form, became characterized as 'allegedly slick, prefabricated, and used for dancing, mooning over teen idols, and other "feminine" and "feminized" recreations' (Coates, 1997, p. 53). With its focus on the (male) pop idol, pop took its place alongside teen magazines and girls' comics as a 'way in which girls are prepared for entry into heterosexual practices, and, in particular for romantic love' (Walkerdine, 1987, p. 162). In this sense, pop music became intrinsically linked to the learning of femininity.

But girls' engagement with popular music is not as heteronormative as is sometimes suggested. In-depth ethnographic research with pre-teen girls in Australia, for instance, suggests that engagement with pop music is far more complex (Baker, 2004a, 2004b). By teasing out the nuances of girls' musical practices, as the Australian research has done, we can begin to understand the different possible positions that girls can take up within a 'teenybopper culture.' Kate and Amelia provide examples of such possibilities. Kate enjoyed singing and dancing. She was an active member of Lollypop, she performed song and dance routines for her peers in the Millennium Club concert devised by the girls during after-school care, and she would dance to music in the school playground. Amelia, on the other hand, was 'behind the scenes.' She was the manager of Lollypop, the fashion coordinator of the girl group, and although she was a member of the Millennium Club she sat and watched the concert while the other members performed. Kate was the self-proclaimed 'future rock star,' choreographing her own dance routine to Aaron Carter's song, while Amelia remained in the background as manager, organizer of hair and make-up, with a dream of being Aaron Carter's love interest. Even the slightest nuances in pop music engagement can be highly significant in the girls' negotiations of cultural and gendered identity.

Though Amelia, and other girls in the research, did talk about male pop idols as figures of their romantic fantasy, swooning over teen idols was not their primary concern. For example, nine-year-old Rosa wanted to be like the male members of the boy group 5ive, but this was more about fashion approval and *musical* solidarity than straightforward romantic fantasy. When the girls' interests focused on female pop stars, they were often highly critical of the fashion and bodies on display. Much of the time their attention was directed at critiquing the images presented by these stars, who they preferred to be attractive ('pretty'), but naturally so ('without the make-up'); to wear nice clothes ('not 'tight suits' or g-strings – 'yuck'); and to have nice hair (not 'too short' because that is 'freaky'). The girls could also be equally critical of pop stars' musical abilities. As 11-year-old Emlyn said about Britney Spears' song 'Lucky,' 'it's okay, but [it] gets a bit annoying. She can't really sing in it. It shows she has quite a weak voice.'

Ultimately, those who continue to treat young girls' musical practices with disdain demonstrate an ignorance regarding girls and pop. On closer examination, girls' musical activities can be seen to challenge the dominant ideologies that construct their consumption practices as passive and unworthy of analysis. In their play with popular music, girls creatively accommodate consumer culture, utilizing its commodities and technologies to negotiate the terrain of cultural identity and to situate their cultural practices (practices largely devalued by society) within wider cultural contexts.

References

Baker, S. (2004a). Pop in(to) the bedroom: Popular music in pre-teen girls' bedroom culture. *European Journal of Cultural Studies*, 7(1), pp. 75–93.

Baker, S. (2004b). It's not about candy: Music, sexiness and girls' serious play in after school care. *International Journal of Cultural Studies*, 7(2), pp. 197–212.

Coates, N. (1997). (R)evolution now? Rock and the political potential of gender. In S. Whitely (Ed.), *Sexing the Groove: Popular Music and Gender* (pp. 50–64). London: Routledge.

Shuker, R. (1998). *Key Concepts in Popular Music.* London: Routledge.

Walkerdine, V. (1987). Some day my prince will come: Young girls and the preparation for adolescent sexuality. In A. McRobbie and M. Nava (Eds.), *Gender and Generation* (pp. 162–184). Basingstoke, UK: Macmillan Education.

4

Media Literacy 101

Media analysis and critique have been central to the media literacy agenda throughout its history. As a rule, media educators work with young people to help them denaturalize the world around them, primarily by 'deconstructing' the media. What this means in practice is that, through the study of media texts and institutions, media education aims to give young people the conceptual tools to read the media critically. If, as Roland Barthes (1957) said, we have a tendency to mistake culture for nature, denaturalizing the world means recognizing the constructedness of our environments, particularly in relation to social and cultural meaning-making. Through the study of media texts and institutions, youth are encouraged to 'deconstruct' their social and cultural environments. We draw on the term 'deconstruction' from the practical work of media educators (while recognizing its broader meaning in the work of Jacques Derrida). Another term long used by media educators is 'demystification,' which seems more in keeping with the symbolic detective work of young media literacy students. Whether by deconstructing, demystifying, or denaturalizing, the important point to recognize is that a central project of media literacy over the years has been to provide young people with the critical conceptual tools to interpret and analyze media texts and institutions, and hence to read more critically into their social and cultural environments. This act of reading into the fabric of everyday life allows media educators to be historians of the present, to reflect on historical trends and currents as they are unfolding. This historicizing of the present includes not only major world events such as popular uprisings in Iran but

Media Literacies: A Critical Introduction, First Edition. Michael Hoechsmann and Stuart R. Poyntz.
© 2012 Blackwell Publishing Ltd. Published 2012 by Blackwell Publishing Ltd.

also the smallest elements of everyday life, such as trends in teen dating. To recognize the 'soft side' of historical change is to depart from phallocentric visions of history as great men on great dates and to recognize genealogies of social and cultural change. The point here is not to compare the magnitude of historical change wrought from social revolution with cultural changes in teen dating practices but to recognize that macro and micro change – major events and gradual changes – are all historical, and that history is worth studying as it unfolds. This perspective is congruent with a cultural studies approach to media analysis that situates media texts in everyday life practices and recognizes both as worthy of rigorous scholastic inquiry.

As an interpretive scholastic subject, media education shares much with a traditional humanistic curriculum, updated for the twentieth and twenty-first centuries. Given that school subjects such as history and English only emerged in the late nineteenth century from the atomization of what was formerly known as rhetoric – the core subject of the humanities that had encompassed thought, language, and letters – some reconsideration of what is included and excluded by contemporary school curricula is in order. This is, of course, occurring to a certain extent in the many school jurisdictions that are opening up traditional literature curricula to the study of visual media. But the point needs to be made much more forcefully that the present-day curriculum is not set in stone. The inherited curriculum of the twentieth century was and is historically anachronistic, a product of some curricular reorganizations in the modern universities of the late nineteenth century that trickled down to schools in that same period, the epoch of the expansion of mass compulsory schooling. This was a time of libraries, books, and newspapers; a period when literacy was a luxury afforded to the upper classes; and an era when mass communication was the domain of soap box orators and market hucksters. The culture of the time was fundamentally oral, so, for example, in the US if regular folks owned books these were likely books that could be read aloud, such as the Bible or a volume of Shakespeare (Levine, 1988). In the context of a broad oral culture and an elite print culture, it made perfect sense to curriculum developers to craft the school curriculum around print literacy in order to give access to the central (and often hegemonic) ideas of the time. Now that knowledge production and dissemination has dramatically shifted in so many ways, the school curriculum should look forward and back, embracing new modes of communication and reconsidering old ways of interpretation.

A Demand for New Heuristics

What are needed, in other words, are heuristics that allow students and teachers to 'read' the media. One such heuristic is what has come to be called the 'key concepts' model of media education. The key concepts are a set of guiding principles that many would argue young people need to know in order to make sense of life in a media-saturated age. The first articulation of the key concepts is to be found in the resource guide produced by the Ontario Ministry of Education (Canada) in 1989 to support the implementation of media literacy in provincial schools. The authors of the resource guide produced a list of eight key concepts that would be used to structure media education:

(1) All media are constructions.
(2) The media construct reality.
(3) Audiences negotiate meaning in media.
(4) Media have commercial implications.
(5) Media contain ideological and value messages.
(6) Media have social and political implications.
(7) Form and content are closely related in the media.
(8) Each medium has a unique aesthetic form.

(Ministry of Education, Ontario, 1989, p. 8–10)

Since 1989, the key concepts framework has been central to the ongoing development of media literacy training across Canada, and in many countries around the world. A similar list of basic precepts, for instance, arose out of the 1991 statement of the Media Commission of the National Council of Teachers of English conference in the US and has continued to inform the core principles of both the National Association for Media Literacy Education (www.namle.net) and the Center for Media Literacy (www.medialit.org).

We recognize the formative role the key concepts model has had in media education, and yet we contend that what is required today is a blend of the conceptual focus in the key concepts model with a more holistic approach to understanding media culture, one that weaves together an analysis of media producers, texts, and audiences with the broader realities of culture and cultural change. One such heuristic that enables a solid conceptual mapping and a comprehensive paradigm of interpretation is that suggested by Richard Johnson (1986–1987).

Johnson's heuristic for a cultural studies informed approach to media education is one that links questions of production, text, audience, and lived culture in a dynamic tension. Johnson's model is illustrated as a circle, or circuit, with four topoi (places of analysis) resembling the east, north, west, and south points of a compass. The four points of the circuit, each interconnected with the other, are (1) production, (2) textual or material form, (3) audience, and (4) cultural influences on the media and media influences on lived culture. We begin our approach at the bottom of the compass to look at how culture influences the media. Included in this point of analysis are questions of cultural ethos, ideology, and historical legacies. To an extent this is the baggage carried into the acts of media production, the presuppositions and preconditions of media production. Included under the point of production are questions of authorship, complicated and complex matters in an era of corporate media. To tease out the full range of problems associated with authorship in the age of the modern media means looking at the corporate governance and economy of the media industry alongside the agency of the creative personalities involved in media production and the role of technologies, platforms, genres, and modes of media representation. At the site of the textual or material form we analyze the object under study, drawing on forms of analysis from literary and semiotic analysis. At the third site, reception, we recognize the role of the audience in crafting meaning and conduct an audit of audience reactions or readings of a particular text or set of texts. Finally, we examine the influence of the preceding four points of analysis on lived culture to come to an understanding of how culture is reflected and inflected by the phenomenon at hand. As Johnson describes it, each box represents a moment in the circuit, each moment depends on the others but is also distinct, and each is indispensable to the study of the cultural form as a whole. The model demands a holistic mode of inquiry that takes into consideration all four elements. The conceptual framework Johnson lays out does not presume a narrow casting of media 'effects' or media manipulation, but rather situates cultural texts into a set of relationships that enable sometimes contradictory insights to emerge from the same text. In other words, we cannot simply interpret conditions of production, textual forms and practices, and audience readings as resonant sites of meaning without some consideration of the interplay between them and the broader social and cultural contexts in which they are made meaningful. The first and final stages in Johnson's framework thus consider how cultural change feeds back on the moment of production and how the media affect everyday cultural life.

Cultural Life

Every act of representation involves a reflection, a selection, and a deflection of reality (Burke, 1966). There is no neutral ground zero of representation, either synchronically or diachronically (these terms were used by the Swiss linguist Ferdinand de Saussure (1974) to describe the state of the chess board at a particular moment of play (synchronic) and across the whole game (diachronic)). At the synchronic level, one of the great fallacies of our times is that of journalistic objectivity. Journalists seek 'both sides of the story' as if the world were made of protagonists and antagonists, rather than multiple perspectives. More broadly, the inevitability of bias or vested interest permeates all discourse. To paraphrase Claude Lévi-Strauss (1966), the question is: do we speak language or does language speak us? In other words, is there a neutral ground zero of representation or do we all speak from some position that is selective and biased? Bruce Kidd (1987) answers this question in a clever manner: 'Ideology is like sweat,' he says. 'You can't smell your own.' In short, all social actors mobilize meanings and inter-pretations already in circulation in their social and cultural contexts. Whether we are speaking of ideologies, values, theologies, or worldviews engendered by specific conditions (differences based on class, race, and gender; urban versus rural; global North or South; and so on), the reality is that all acts of meaning-making, or representation, mobilize some discourses that are always already specific reflections, selections, and deflections of reality.

At the diachronic level, we all carry with us the seeds sown by our cultural upbringings and our specific biographical experiences. Racism, for example, is an inherited discursive formation. It does not arise spontaneously with each generation, but rather relies on age-old biases. The social reproduction of racism occurs at the intersection of history and biography. It relies on the broader discursive traditions of historical legacies and requires the real-life experiences of social actors to reproduce itself. It is beyond the scope of this book to analyze the formation and reproduction of ideologies, values, theologies, and worldviews through history and personal experience, but we do wish to point out that the many people involved at all levels of media production bring to the table values and ideologies that reflect their social and cultural conditions and their personal experiences. Consequently, the media might best be thought of as a distorting mirror, one that reflects back to a society and culture many of the values and ideologies in circulation in that society. The upshot of this is that, viewed diachronically, the media demonstrates some social changes and also the lack thereof.

For example, if we look at television since the 1960s, we can see changes in the worldviews associated with the family. From *Leave it to Beaver* to *The Brady Bunch*, and then to *Two and a Half Men*, we can see revealed the gradual acceptance in North America of non-traditional family structures. Through those decades we also see the emergence of strong female characters with independence and careers. Yet, alongside this presumably emancipated woman, we also continue to see images of scantily clad women strewn across music videos and elsewhere. On reality television, for instance, we see women and men competing for each other's affections, and in the case of *The Biggest Loser* we also see women very specifically trying to attain an idealized body image. (See Tania Lewis' sidebar, MORAL MAKE-OVERS: REALITY TELEVISION AND THE GOOD CITIZEN, for a detailed discussion of the intersection of individual subjectivity, cultural change, and reality television.) Of course, the media do not set out to accurately portray society, but rather to entertain, to inform, and to generate profits. This reminds us of what Dallas Smythe (1981) said: that there is 'no free lunch' on television; but there are also reasons to believe that the very corporate structure of much of our media shapes the kinds of images of women and other groups we see on screen. Understanding how cultural life appears in our mediascapes is thus at least in part a question of understanding how economic concerns shape media representations.

Production

Taking on this question makes sense because most people in fact recognize that there is a powerful relationship between business or economic life and media culture. After all, we hear about the business side of the media all the time, whether through box office reports about the opening weekend of new Hollywood blockbusters, accounts of the size and economic impact of the gaming industry, or reports about the financial threat posed to media companies (and artists) by downloading. This said, the relationship between media texts and the economic, cultural, and technological environment where such texts are produced is not always well understood. Indeed, a central concern in media education has long been the examination of how media texts are manufactured or produced given the context in which they are made. Questions of authorship or production are

Moral makeovers: Reality television and the good citizen

Tania Lewis, RMIT University

'These twelve people have one thing in common – they're about to change their lives forever!' – so goes the dramatic voiceover for *The Biggest Loser* (*TBL*), one of the recent big success stories in reality television formats. A competitive weight-loss show, the format has captured the imaginations of audiences worldwide, with local versions of the US program being made in Australia, the UK, and even the Middle East (where the show has been rebadged *The Biggest Winner*). While the format has varied somewhat over different seasons and between countries, the basic premise involves a group of overweight people being brought together in a *Big Brother*-style house to compete for a large sum of money by losing the highest percentage of their starting body weight, initially as part of competing teams and later as individuals.

So how might we understand the emergence of a reality television show aimed at helping obese people lose weight with the (not always gentle) guidance of various 'lifestyle experts' and under the gaze of a watching public? One way is to see the show in instructional terms, as 'training' participants and viewers in a particular mode of responsible selfhood or citizenship (Ouellette and Hay, 2008, p. 15). As media scholar Jonathan Bignell (2005) notes in his book on *Big Brother*, the global currency of reality shows suggests a growing preoccupation with 'personal confession, modification, testing and the perfectibility of the self' (p. 40). Such concerns are central to *TBL*'s narrative. The *TBL* journey begins with a 'weigh-in' in which the show's participants are stripped down to the equivalent of their underwear and weighed in front of their peers and the viewing nation, a moment of ritual humiliation that is accompanied by the (usually highly emotional) confessions of the participants as they explain how they have come to this low point in their lives. As Cat, a contestant from the first series of the Australian version of *TBL* tearfully admits as she sees her weight come up on screen, 'I'm just actually *really* ashamed.' The journey the participants then embark on is one concerned with transforming and perfecting the flawed version of the self that has been rather literally 'exposed' at the initial weigh-in. As the host in the first Australian series announces excitedly to the contestants after they walk up the drive to the *TBL* house, 'The walk you've just completed represents your first step towards a new you!'

British sociologist Nikolas Rose (1996) argues that this concern in popular media with renewing and perfecting the self can be seen as part of a broader shift towards an 'enterprise culture' (p. 153). Where governments once looked after the health and welfare of their citizens, the rise of neoliberal politics around the world since the 1990s has seen a growing focus on the responsibilities of individuals to govern themselves. In this setting the increasingly dominant view of the self is one of a go-getting, 'enterprising' individual who takes control of their own life by making strategic lifestyle 'choices.'

The 'new you' depicted on *TBL* in many ways exemplifies this increasingly dominant ideology of enterprising selfhood. Rather than portraying obesity as a product of western lifestyles or as a public health issue, the fat bodies paraded on *TBL* are represented as markers of the failings of specific individuals. The participants in the show buy into this discourse, often admitting that they see themselves as less-than-complete human beings. As Jo, a female contestant on the first series of the Australian *TBL* puts it, 'I thought I had a pretty good life but, you know, I haven't been living at all so it's time to start now.' The journey that the show then takes them on is one that attempts to enable them to become enterprising individuals, to see themselves as flawed 'projects' that need to be tested and worked on in order to attain their full potential.

On *TBL*, experts are central to this process of instructing contestants (and the audience) about how to become slim, streamlined versions of themselves. As I have argued elsewhere (Lewis, 2008), the growing emphasis in contemporary culture on governing through individuals has seen the emergence over the past decade of a whole host of popular experts, or lifestyle guides. On television in particular we have seen the emergence of a range of reality makeover shows featuring experts 'renovating' various aspects of people's lifestyles – from fashion (*What Not to Wear*) and social etiquette (*Ladette to Lady*) to parenting skills (*Supernanny*) and faces and bodies (*Extreme Makeover*). On *TBL* the most highly visible experts on the show are the personal trainers. The well-known Bob Harper and

Jillian Michaels from the original US version are both ostensibly concerned with challenging and transforming the obese bodies of the show's participants. The relentless physical challenges offered up by the experts, however, are underpinned by a strongly *psychological* or therapeutic model of selfhood, with Bob and Jillian often sounding more like life coaches than fitness experts. As Jillian notes (in full-blown 'therapy-speak') in one episode about the members of her team: 'They all have a palpable pain in them and I feel compelled to fix it.'

These strongly psychologized models of self-help again can be seen to shore up an enterprising model of individualism. Crucially on *TBL*, as on makeover shows in general, these forms of therapeutic intervention, while framed in terms of individual freedoms, are done on behalf of the community and in the name of 'good' citizenship. That is, while the emphasis on makeover shows seems to be on individual 'choice' and autonomy, certain lifestyles such as 'choosing' to be thin and exercising regularly are deemed responsible and 'empowering' while other 'lifestyles' – for example, being overweight and eating fast food – are seen as socially aberrant. The lifestyle expertise provided by figures such as Bob and Jillian ironically emphasize freedom and personal fulfillment through the *regulation* of the self. As a contestant on the Australian *TBL* says, 'I need to lose weight [...] to inspire my wife and to inspire my kids.' The participants on *TBL* thus become inspirational 'winners' not through selfish individualism but through embracing self-governance, regulating and reforming themselves on behalf of the family and the nation.

References

Bignell, J. (2005). *Big Brother: Reality Television in the Twenty-First Century.* Basingstoke, UK: Palgrave MacMillan.

Lewis, T. (2008). *Smart Living: Lifestyle Media and Popular Exercise.* New York: Peter Lang.

Ouellette, L. and Hay, J. (2008). *Better Living through Reality TV: Television and Post-welfare Citizenship.* Malden, MA: Blackwell.

Rose, N. S. (1996). *Inventing Our Selves: Psychology, Power and Personhood.* Cambridge, UK: Cambridge University Press.

complicated, in other words. They involve issues of creativity and authorial voice, but, because most commercial media texts are made not by individuals but by groups of people working in highly organized corporate settings geared toward profit generation, it is not enough to think about media production only in terms of authorial intent. Rather, questions of production draw our attention to the way media texts and communication systems are shaped by a whole series of factors and concerns, including the ownership structures within and across media industries; the structures of the market place; technologies of production; government policies and regulatory environments; labor practices and professional codes of practice; and questions of access and participation (i.e., who has access to the media, whose stories get told, and whose stories are excluded from mainstream representation). In considering these issues, a central aim within media education is to understand not only how meaning is produced in contemporary media cultures but also how economic, political, and cultural forces work through the media to shape the exercise of social power in society. Concerns about media production thus raise questions of democracy, including the degree to which contemporary media practices and institutions foster (or undermine) meaningful and equitable participation in public life.

In thinking about the way production settings, technologies, and business practices shape media texts, one pitfall to be avoided is the practice of giving too much explanatory power to any one causal agent. We mean by this that, to understand the structures, forces, and influences that shape how media texts are made and what meanings are produced, it is important to avoid over-privileging any one factor as though it were the sole cause determining what a film, a song, or a website means. For media educators and students of media education, this means developing an ability to examine the production of media in relation to an ecology of forces. Crucial to this ecology is the economic system itself, which in most countries means the particular system of capitalist production under which media goods and services are made and consumed. Thought about the relationship between capitalism and the media has a long history, as we saw in Chapter 3 in relation to the work of Theodor Adorno and Max Horkheimer (1972) and their culture industry thesis. We take from the work of Adorno and Horkheimer and later scholars of the political economy of media that media concentration and economic power can shape what media is produced and how this media effects processes of socialization and acculturation. It is worth remembering this point at a time when global media environments are dominated by powerful media conglomerates (e.g., Disney, NBC-Universal, News Corp., Time Warner, Viacom) that operate across national boundaries and media platforms while producing similar kinds of products that are sold using an increasingly sophisticated array of marketing techniques.

A tremendous amount of all the popular culture (movies, magazines, television, music, etc.) consumed by young people is now in fact controlled by the largest media corporations. If this is telling, the more important point is that the concentration of media power limits the range of cultural objects and ideas young people have access to. This is the case in part because powerful media owners – such as Rupert Murdoch of News Corp. – have a tremendous ability to control and limit how key issues of the day are covered in the news and in entertainment genres. Limits on young people's access to ideas and cultural objects are also evident, however, for more structural reasons.

By 'structural' we mean that the economic conditions under which media conglomerates operate impose their own limits on what is portrayed. Consider, for instance, why scantily clad young women continue to be such a presence on television, in music videos, and elsewhere. Some might suggest that this is a function of consumer choice. Robert McChesney (2008) points out, however, that 'choice' is complicated here. In particular, with mounting debt loads – acquired in the process of merging formerly distinct media companies – media conglomerates are under immense pressure to find simple, inexpensive, and yet familiar images and storylines that will grab and hold audiences' attention. The result is that, in a rich media environment (i.e., one in which there are apparently more and more channels for media production and consumption), we are ironically witnessing an increasingly narrow set of representations of young women (and men, for that matter). Images of scantily clad young women fit this bill, not only because of their shock value as spectacles but because the same images can be repackaged and sold across a range of media, including magazines, websites, entertainment television shows, and movies, which are all too often owned by the same media company. What we end up with, then, is a surprisingly narrow range of representations of young women in a time when some suggest that feminist struggles for diversity and equality in women's media portrayals are part of a bygone era!

As significantly, today's concentrated media environments are marking young people's experiences because the dependence of media conglomerates on advertising revenue has meant that our everyday experiences are increasingly mediatized (converted into mediated experiences) through marketing discourses and practices. This is no more evident than in the case of food, the meaning and appeal of which is increasingly defined for young people through marketing discourses that link high-calorie fast food, soft drinks, and processed meals with movies, celebrities, athletes, and music that are central to young people's identities and social experience. As Montgomery and Chester (2008) show in detail, the development of digital technologies – including mobile phones, social networking spaces, instant messaging resources, and viral videos – has only exacerbated this process, allowing marketing professionals and their media partners to find new and, arguably, more insidious ways to define the meaning and experience of food and health for children and youth. According to the US Centers for Disease Control and Prevention, the result is that

> food and beverage marketing [now] influences the preferences and purchase requests of children, influences consumption at least in the short term, and is a likely contributor to less healthful diets, and may contribute to negative diet-related health outcomes and risks among children and youth. (quoted in Montgomery and Chester, 2008, pp. 179–180)

Beyond the political-economic context that shapes what media is produced and how such media impacts young people's everyday experiences, culture and cultural traditions are also formative frameworks that situate how media producers engage their work. Thinking about how culture shapes the production of media draws our attention to how the social and cultural constructs related to race, gender, class, age, and so on inform the representation of individuals and groups in society. Within media education, debates about stereotypes are likely to be the most common way students are asked to think about who and what we see (and do not see) in the media. However, while important and sometimes useful, especially for younger students, stereotype-spotting can be tedious work, particularly for older youth, who often develop fairly nuanced readings of stereotyping in movies, television shows, and advertising just by participating in this media in everyday life (Buckingham, 2006a). In considering why media producers and authors choose to represent characters and groups in the way they do, then, it is helpful to draw on more sophisticated concepts to explain what we see and hear on screen.

In this regard, Stuart Hall's (1994) observation that 'practices of representation always implicate the positions from which we speak or write – the positions of enunciation' (p. 392) is helpful. By this, Hall means that media representations are never produced in a vacuum. Whenever an artist records a new song, writes a story, or produces a film, their work carries with it the residue of previous representations. Past representations create the ground from which new expressions can be made. But, then, these new expressions always retain or implicate the history from which they develop and from which an artist or producer speaks – what Hall calls 'the positions of enunciation.' One of the implications of this is that an author's voice or unique expression is never entirely her own; rather, all expressions have a history, a past that situates artists in relation to cultural traditions and gives meaning and sense to the songs, images, and stories we consume or produce.

Applied to media analysis, this is a powerful idea because it helps to explain why media producers and artists make certain choices and not others about characters, storylines, or images. For example, some media producers use stereotypes in their work (not to offend but) because stereotypes are a kind of cultural short-hand that calls attention to a history of meaning that requires little explanation for audiences. As such, stereotypes can be an efficient way to tell stories that are not likely to disappear from media artifacts any time soon. At the same time, Hall's point is that practices of media production also implicate or situate the media producer or artist in relation to older patterns and practices of representation. New media representations tell audiences how the producer or artist is responding to past practices; in other words, how they are challenging or changing these practices and how they are not.

For some artists, the legacies of painful and damaging representations of certain groups (for instance women, people of color, the working class, queer youth, etc.) in the media can impose a 'burden of representation' on the way new work is developed (Hall, 1996b; West, 1993; Mercer, 1994). Spike Lee (*Do the Right Thing, Crooklyn, Clockers, Malcolm X*), the most important African-American filmmaker of the past three decades, argues, for instance, that making a film about black men and black communities is never innocent. Rather, showing African-Americans on screen necessarily evokes a painful history of racism and racist imagery. The burden felt in his work is thus to challenge this history and to provoke social awareness through any number of strategies, including the melancholic style of his Hurricane Katrina documentary, *When the Levees Broke: A Requiem in Four Acts* (2006) or the satire used in *Bamboozled* (2000) to criticize Hollywood for not giving African-American artists the chance to make films and be recognized for their work. In other words, media producers and artists never work in a cultural vacuum, and so for media educators and students of media education this means developing an ability to examine how specific media texts have been shaped by and in response to the cultural traditions from which they emanate.

In addition to the political-economic and cultural contexts of media production, attention must also be paid to how the specific technologies and media of representation play a role in meaning making. Technologies of media production (e.g., cameras, mobile phones, digital editing software) are not just objective tools for storytelling and journalism; rather, the technologies we use shape the nature of the messages that are produced. Broadly speaking, this is what the Canadian media scholar Marshall McLuhan (1994 [1964]) meant when he wrote that 'the medium is the message.' For media educators, beyond looking at the messages on screens, this means we also need to ask how the medium of communication itself shapes those messages. How, for instance, does television change the nature of political debate in contemporary cultures? Or, how does digital technology change the meaning of participation in the public life of mediated cultures? We know, for instance, that digitization is providing more and more opportunities for young people to cut, paste, and distribute their own stories, images, and music. But, if digitization also makes it easier for corporations to target, track, and strategically manage consumers because of the information and data trail we leave behind when we participate online, questions need to be asked about whether and how our involvement with digital media and online spaces contributes to or undermines democratic participation in contemporary public life.

How media texts are produced thus has a tremendous influence on what such texts mean. But, of course, the context of production is not the only factor shaping how media texts communicate meaning to audiences. In addition to production contexts, what also matters are the specific strategies and content of representation present in the texts we consume and produce. Making sense of these strategies brings us to the next set of conceptual issues in Richard Johnson's heuristic for mapping the circuits of cultural production.

Text

A media text is any cultural phenomenon, including a song, a movie, a billboard, clothing, the design of a shopping mall, a website, or an advertisement, that is intended to convey meaning. Texts employ multiple modalities (visual, aural, or written) to communicate with audiences, and in fact are most likely to convey meaning by working simultaneously across various communication modes. For example, whatever meaning is meant to be conveyed by the average billboard or by the design of a department store (such as Ikea or Target) or clothiers (such as American Apparel, French Connection, or Hollister Co.) is typically produced through a cross-section of images, sounds, and words that are woven together into a particular idea. As we mentioned in earlier chapters, this is in part why literacy now refers to more than communication through the written or spoken word. In highly mediated cultures, communication comes at audiences through complex texts that use visual, aural, and written modes. To be literate in contemporary cultures thus requires that we are able to read and analyze texts that deploy multiple languages of representation.

At the same time, making sense of how any text represents an idea, an experience, or a person is complicated. As Celia Lury (1996) points out, for instance, it is increasingly the case today that the production of consumer goods and experiences is subject to a process of stylization. 'Consumer objects have become increasingly aestheticized: like art objects, it is as often as not how something "looks" that guarantees that it will sell, not what the object actually does or is used for' (O'Brien and Szeman, 2004, p. 124). This has happened in response to the increasing diversity and complexity of consumer cultures. The result is that the principles of fashion have been applied to an ever-expanding array of products. Indeed:

> The availability at any one time of numerous models of Nike running shoes, of sleek modernist household appliances designed by architect Michael Graves for Target stores, and of trendy clothing created by designer Mossimo for Zellers all point to ways in which style and design have become essential elements of the production process, if not the essential element in the design of products for end-users. (O'Brien and Szeman, 2004, p. 124)

A central task in media education is thus to make sense of how texts communicate and determine what it is they say. To understand how media texts convey meaning requires learning to read and analyze the language of media representation. Thinking about the language of media representation draws on semiotic traditions in which the term 'language' is used loosely to refer to the familiar 'codes' and 'conventions' media texts employ to produce meaning. The codes used in media texts refer to all those signs, including music or sound in a horror movie or pictures in a car advertisement, that are used to tell a story or portray an event. In this sense, codes can be fairly simple or quite complex (e.g., formal languages). What is important to remember is that the codes used in media texts come to represent reality for us. As noted earlier in the chapter, we never encounter reality in its bare factuality. We always experience the world through its representation. Another way to think about this is that reality is encoded for us as a particular cultural phenomenon.

Our appearance, for instance, is never simply a bare fact. Rather, our dress and behavior are culturally encoded; they operate through the mobilization of various gestures, colors (of our clothes, for instance), tonality (in our voice), and expressions (such as slang) that produce the 'reality' of our selves for others. Similarly, where electronic and digital media are concerned, technical codes, including shots, lighting, sound, textual layout, and editing are used in particular ways to produce certain effects. For instance, a close-up shot in a film is used to suggest intimacy; a slow and evocative violin sequence in a movie might be used to suggest romance or sadness; the color green might be used to suggest warmth, beauty, lushness, as in a number of sequences on the world of Pandora in James Cameron's *Avatar* (2009). Codes are thus the material resources through which stories, ideas, and reality itself are represented.

Conventions refer to the familiar ways codes are used in specific cultural settings. So, for instance, music is typically used in horror movies to create shock or surprise. Conversely, nature is often used in car ads to convey a sense of peace, escape, or tranquility – an odd practice given that cars are so often thought to be the source of noise, pollution, and danger in the first place. There are also conventions (often associated with genres) for the representation of heroes (for instance, s/he is often shot from below so as to look larger than life), for the representation of television news anchors (full lighting with a medium headshot, which suggests rationality and trustworthiness rather than intimacy or distance), for the way narratives work in certain films (for instance the use of narrative closure in children's stories), and for the way stories about youth are represented in tabloid newspapers (typically with large headlines that highlight episodes of violence or moral decline). Many of these conventions are difficult to see or hear, because we become so used to their role in media that they appear 'natural,' the way things (including reality itself) 'should be.'

A central task of media education is thus to 'make the familiar strange' by constructing a history of the present. This is done by revealing how different codes and conventions are used to produce *realism*, which is to say the *experience* of reality (which is different from something like reality itself). One of the best ways to do this is for educators to use media that challenges or upsets the 'rules of representation,' otherwise it can be difficult to see the conventions described above because they are too familiar to us. Sometimes youth-made work can be the most effective for this purpose. Youth videos or web spaces can be used to discuss the success (or failure) of a student's efforts to work with more conventional languages of representation or to show efforts by students to meaningfully break these rules. Certain movies (e.g., *The Fog of War*, 2003; *Syriana*, 2005; *The Hurt Locker*, 2008) and television shows (i.e., *The Simpsons*, *The Wire*) also attempt to break with the rules of media representation, particularly within certain genres, and these too can be helpful for developing an understanding of how media texts construct the idea of war (*The Fog of War* and *The Hurt Locker*), the politics of oil in the international community (*Syriana*), or a sense of reality itself (*The Simpsons*).

As evidenced in these instances, whatever media languages are used in a text, these languages are also the bearers of values or normative claims about how things *ought to be* in our world. In other words, media texts are not only tools for telling stories but are also the means through which ideologies, values, and ethical positions are articulated, defended, and contested in our culture. For this reason, to understand the circulation of meaning through cultural phenomena, media educators and students of media education need to learn how to read media texts *and* to develop an understanding of the dominant value frames embedded in these texts. Within communication and media studies, two primary methods have evolved to do this work.

Content analysis, or counting the pictures

Content analysis is a systematic way of looking at media representations that involves analyzing media by breaking down texts into their constituent parts in order to detect common patterns or tendencies (Casey et al., 2008). The point is to look at the frequency of words, images, or categories used across a range of related media to assess the values or effects that might be contained therein. The most common way for students to do this work in media education classrooms is to come up with a set of criteria – or a coding frame – to use to look at a selection of related media. The coding frame is then applied to media texts, and once the various elements have been counted they can be analyzed for trends or patterns that suggest what values or biases are being propagated.

For instance, students might decide that their coding frame is a question, something like: What kind of people are typically used as 'experts' in news coverage? Using this frame, students could examine television news reports on a given station for a week in order to chart who it is that is relied upon to provide expert interpretations of key issues of the day. In fact, we know from work by communication researchers that most of the experts used in news broadcasts are people who already occupy certain positions of power in society – for instance, politicians, police officials, or business leaders – whereas others who have access to key information – including researchers in the academy or people who work with public agencies or non-governmental organizations – are typically ignored in news coverage (Lewis, Cushion, and Thomas, 2005). Those interested in content analysis would argue that this tells us something about how knowledge and truth are produced in culture. To be more precise, these results suggest how the value of certain figures of authority (i.e., police chiefs and 'captains of industry') is maintained and what might be required to shift the structures of authority in society.

At the same time, drawing these kinds of conclusions simply by counting the number of times people appear as experts in the news is, for some, dubious. In particular, media scholars have argued that content analysis can tell us something about how often certain images or people appear in the media but cannot really tell us what these elements mean because such analysis does not dig deep enough into the complex ways that media texts such as television, music, or online forms of representation actually work. For instance, while we know that politicians and police officials are more likely than not to be put forward as experts about key issues of the day, to know how credible their messages are we not only need to know *that* they are on television but also *how* they are portrayed in the story and *how* audiences interpret this portrayal. How a politician is represented in relation to a news story – as believable, trustworthy, or suspicious – provides a context or an impression for understanding the message they are delivering. This context, in turn, establishes what scholar Teun van Dijk (1991) calls the 'local coherence' of a message. For many, 'our understanding of narrative structure, visual imagery and the many textual elements that create moods and impressions – such as editing techniques to the use of music – gives us access to forms of understanding and appreciation that are difficult to reproduce' simply by counting words or images (Casey et al., 2008, p. 55).

Because of this, scholars interested in content analysis have evolved more sophisticated ways of examining what is represented in the media.

Cultivation analysis is one such model. Developed by the late George Gerbner of the Annenberg School of Communications, at root, cultivation analysis addresses what values are contained in media texts. Rather than just assuming that these values are taken up by audiences, however, this model focuses on the attitudes media viewers actually develop in relation to the media they consume. Working at the intersection of lived reality and mediated realities, cultivation analysis seeks to understand what people believe and from where they learned it. The model moves the work of content research forward, then, by conducting content analysis in conjunction with survey research about viewers' worldviews. In assessing these worldviews, Gerbner made distinctions between heavy and light viewers of media in order to develop a more refined understanding of how media messages are actually interpreted and used by audiences. We talk about this model more in the following section, but suffice it to say here that Gerbner's work points to the way students of media education can develop more sophisticated readings of what is represented in the media by examining both what is in media texts and how these texts are understood by audiences.

Semiotics, or learning to read the production of cultural meaning

If sophisticated forms of content analysis can help media educators, it is also clear that semiotics has long dominated cultural analysis in media education classrooms. One reason is that semiotics has been part of literary studies, and English and language arts programs have typically been key curricular areas where media education is taught. Perhaps more importantly, semiotics focuses attention on interpreting how different elements in media texts construct cultural references and meanings for audiences. As such, semiotics draws our attention to the complicated ways cultural myths and ideologies are produced and reproduced.

We have already introduced some ideas from semiotics above in talking about how codes and conventions operate in media texts. Here we note that the key idea semiotics brings to the interpretation of cultural phenomena is the notion that media texts only have meaning in relation to the contexts in which they appear. This is also true for the codes that appear within a media text. They too are only meaningful in relation to other codes and to the larger social, cultural, and historical contexts in which media texts operate. As we saw above, for instance, the meaning of a car in an advertisement is entirely dependent on the other codes (including color, lighting, sound, and so on) that are used to situate and define what a car means. Likewise, a business leader may be represented as a figure of high esteem and power or a figure of suspicion and greed, depending on how s/he is portrayed and the social context in which this portrayal occurs. Financial crises across the global economy, for instance, have altered the context for thinking about business people and corporations. Consequently, what business leaders signify is more ambiguous today. Do corporate tycoons represent the 'smartest guys in the room' or the greediest guys on the floor? How one answers depends on the context in which the signification takes place.

To capture this flexibility in the way codes and media texts operate, it is useful to discuss the basic 'grammar' of semiotics, beginning with the concept of the 'sign.' A sign is a composite of a 'signifier' and a 'signified.' The signifier is the word, object, image, or sound that exists outside our heads in the material world. The signified, conversely, has no material presence in the world. It is the feeling or thought a signifier suggests. So, for instance, an image of a car (or the word 'car') is a signifier and the signified is the idea this image (or word) creates in our minds. Taken together, these two elements constitute the sign 'car.' Of course, we don't experience cars in this way – in fact, as soon as we see a car we are usually quick to associate an idea with this image. In this sense, the division semiotics makes between the signifier and the signified is theoretical. Nonetheless, this division is important because it highlights the fact that words, objects, and sounds can mean different things depending on how and where they are used.

In thinking about how context shapes meaning, semiotics also helps media educators to understand that the meaning of media texts (or codes) is formed by a process of association and difference. Where ideas of rationality, physical strength, and control are often associated with the meaning of the word 'man,' for example, this association only works within a process of differentiation in which the word 'woman' is taken to mean emotional, physically dependent, and vulnerable. Similarly, a number of scholars of race and postcoloniality point out that the meaning of 'black' in the media is only constituted in relation to its difference from the meaning of 'white.' Moreover, because white is not typically seen as a color in Western cultures, it comes to operate as a kind of invisible norm against which black-ness is defined as different and/or exceptional.

If we think about how this process of association and difference works, attention is drawn to another key concept in semiotics: 'discourse.' Discourse refers to the meaning frames that operate in a culture that enable certain meaning opportunities while restricting others. So, for instance, there is a 'gender discourse' in Western cultures within which the image of a man comes to signify one thing while the image of a woman signifies something else. The same is true in regard to race. Key for media educators is understanding which discourses – about gender, technology, the law, the environment, class, and so on – are being mobilized in a media text, how they are defining the use of specific media codes, and for what ends. While discourses develop in specific historical contexts, they are central to the way power relationships are constituted and reproduced in our culture. For this reason, understanding how cultural values are being used in media texts tells us a great deal about how the former are developing and changing.

Finally, semiotics also draws attention to the way levels of meaning operate in media texts. Denotative meaning refers to the literal meaning of a word or an image – what we might call the dictionary meaning. When we talk about the denotative meaning of a print ad, for instance, we are typically referring to a description of the things we see in the picture – the specific colors, the words, the positioning of people in the picture, and so on. On the other hand, connotative meaning refers to the symbolic or metaphorical ideas that are associated with the literal things we see in an ad or news story. So, for instance, if we see a group of people engaged in a political protest, does this connote an idea of freedom or a sense of fear about unruly mobs in the street? Does an image of an athlete suggest strength and endurance or greed and untrustworthiness? In thinking about these kinds of questions, media educators and students enter into the space of cultural analysis and cultural politics.

The French philosopher and semiotician Roland Barthes demonstrated that we should seek to go beyond surface meanings of media images because, at root, these are texts that articulate and reproduce cultural myths. Barthes meant by this that, at the most abstract level, media texts tell us about the dreams and ideals of our culture. This does not happen through logical argument. Rather, it happens (particularly in advertisements) through the juxtaposition of products and things with those ideas we hold in high regard. So, for instance, bottled water is marketed to us not as a product to satisfy our thirst but one that offers us a form of purity and freedom. Nike shoes are not just useful for running; they are a form of technological liberation. And a Blackberry isn't just a smart phone; it is a whole new way of being you.

Of course, as media culture has become more and more complex, reading the intended meaning of movies, television shows, advertisements, and online spaces is made more and more challenging. Indeed, especially in those media texts targeted at young people, there is often a complex set of intertextual references to other films, songs, or cultural moments that can be challenging to read and interpret, depending on one's media experience. That said, making sense of how and what meanings cultural phenomena constitute is crucial given the rich and complex semiotic worlds we now inhabit.

Audience

The two strategies of textual analysis presented above depend on a static or singular reader, an omniscient 'I' who can be counted on to respond exactly the same way to each act of media consumption. Of course, we know the truth is much more complicated. In fact, not only do we react differently to particular media from, for example, our family members and friends, but each one of us is capable of distinct readings of a media text, depending on fickle elements such as our mood or the context of consumption. We know the drill. The same television melodrama that brings us to tears one day looks trite and silly the next. The same movie that one of our friends absolutely loved is offensive to us. Or, an experience may change our viewing perspectives. The Philippine immigrant to America realizes that the US is not like it is portrayed by Hollywood. The American youth who works in a Mexican community for a summer comes home and finds portrayals of Mexicans and Latinos in the media prejudiced and loathsome. If experience, context, and mood can change our viewing experience and media interpretation, how do the fundamental differences that exist among us impact media consumption? How do Afro-Britons react differently and distinctly to images of black people in the media? How do Asian-Americans respond to the common portrayal of them as restaurant, laundry, or grocery store owners? Being a Mafia boss might be portrayed as kind of cool, but how many Italo-Canadians are tired of the stereotype? And, when male and female teenagers view bikini-clad babes gyrating and swarthy dudes swaggering on music videos, how do their reactions differ? Evidence shows that insecurity over body image affects both genders but is more acute among girls. The two most basic reactions to the 'perfect' bodies portrayed in the media are emulation and self-loathing. Given the near impossibility for most people to become one of those stylized beautiful people, depression is a common response. And this can lead further into eating disorders, steroid use, and even suicide. These observations hardly scratch the surface, but media theorists and media educators have developed complex conceptual tools for analyzing the role of the audience in media meaning-making. We will describe these in relation to three broad categories: (1) the active audience, (2) media effects and cultivation models, and (3) reception theories.

The active audience

There are two main trajectories of scholarship that have contributed to the formation in media studies of the concept of the active audience, one in sociology and the other in literary studies. In sociology, there was a series of transitions in the twentieth century that led to the robust theory of an active audience, which moved media education away from the simplistic hypo-dermic theory of media effects (see below). The first innovation was the two-step model, which suggested that 'opinion leaders' who have an appropriate level of media literacy and a critical understanding of society and history would interpret media and then share their informed perspectives with a wider mass audience. The second innovation was the 'uses and grati-fications' model, which asserted that people use the media for such functions as diversion, information, identity, and relationships (often substituting television viewing for family life). These early transitions in a theory of audiences led to a more subtly inflected reception theory (see below).

Media reception theories also share a genealogy with developments in literary studies. Literary studies draws deeply from the well of humanistic traditions through the millennia. In particular, the early work in rhetoric included highly sensitized theories of audience. Like modern media, the orator had to size up the audience and use a highly sophisticated series of strategies to tailor the delivery and content of a message, changing it midstream if necessary. Similarly, through the ages, literature has been changed by authors to adapt to audiences. Indeed, it was only in certain periods (often totalitarian) that readings became predetermined and fixed. Despite the bloom of democracy, the late modern period was one such period, meaning that the inherited tradition of literature in the early twentieth century was one of authorized readings by expert literary critics of the New Criticism.

By the mid-twentieth century, this practice began to change. In partic-ular, Louise Rosenblatt (1938) was a pioneer in developing a theory of transactional reading that led to the development of reader-response criticism. For Rosenblatt, the act of reading is unique because the reader brings their own biography, beliefs, and knowledge to the process. As such, there is a transactional relationship between the reader and text, a give and take that ensures a text is read differently by everyone. Rosenblatt also categorised the rationales readers bring to the act of reading, positioning these rationales on a continuum between aesthetic and efferent (from appreciation/pleasure to research/information seeking).

Since Rosenblatt's work, there has been much written on reader-response criticism and the active audience in literature. Here, however, we want to point to one other key intervention from literary theory that has informed how media educators think about active audiences. The term 'intentional fallacy' was developed by New Critics to counter the fallacy of authorial intention (Wimsatt and Beardsley, 1946). The argument here is that, once created and in circulation, a text dissociates from the intentions the author had for it. Thus, it is freed from the restrictions of meaning that might have been intended for it and is made available for alternative interpretations. Roland Barthes (1977) would later refer to this as 'the death of the author,' arguing that the text should be free of the author's ascribed meanings and intentions. On the one hand, this is easy to see in media studies: most television shows are received as authorless texts. Moreover, programs are produced and distributed by media corporations but they are, for the most part, received as ready-made texts. On the other hand, in film and popular music, the author is still important. The interpretive turn taken by Barthes and others is to free the text from the tyranny of that author and allow its much more polysemic (multiple meanings) attributes to be foregrounded. This is crucial to the concept of the active audience, which plays a role in determining the meaning of a media text, and to the emergence of the critical interpretive reception theories described below.

Media effects and cultivation models

An important element of audience studies is the critique of what is called the media effects model. This model of media analysis, also referred to as the hypodermic model (above), is based on the assumption that the media can affect behavior in some predictable manner. This idea continues to linger in the popular imagination, appearing in the mainstream press any time there is a troubling incident of transgressive youth behavior that can be attributed to media consumption habits. Most recently, it has been used to explain famous incidents of school shootings, with a link conspicuously drawn to video gaming. Much evidence has been offered to demonstrate the unpredictability of the media's influence on behavior, and, where such research has come up short (see Chapter 3 for a more extended discussion of these failures), notions of predictability still resonate as a form of popular common sense. As much as media researchers seek to debunk the media effects model, in other words, it survives through anecdote and conjecture in everyday life. Ultimately, however, there is no simple pattern of predictive behavior associated with media consumption, and it is important that media educators know that. (See Shakuntala Banaji's sidebar, CHILDREN'S MEDIA ENCOUNTERS IN CONTEMPORARY INDIA: LEISURE AND LEARNING, for a detailed discussion on media effects and children's lived experience with media).

Of course, it is also important that media educators are aware of the complex yet subtle ways in which media is consumed by audiences. Media effects are produced more like a lottery than a church; in other words, for some young people, some of the time, the media may provoke particular behavior. This is to say that, while it is very difficult and almost impossible to prove that long term exposure to media violence – *in and of itself* – provokes violent behavior, it is not so difficult to prove that long term exposure to images of thin models can provoke body image problems leading sometimes to eating disorders. In both cases, however, the many people who are not negatively affected by the media exposure prove the impossibility of the idea of a direct theory of media effects. And, where violent behavior is concerned, the opposite tendency should be considered. If someone is troubled enough to consider mass violence as a solution to their problems, should we be surprised if their media diet includes inappropriately violent content? Given this, the most compelling case for media effects we can agree on is in relation to the promotion of consumption itself, which is one of the guiding principles of media messaging, but even that effect is not guaranteed.

A more subtle version of the effects model is found in cultivation analysis, which evaluates the effect of long term media exposure on the world views and opinions of heavy viewers (and media consumers in general). We discussed this model above, and so suffice it to say here that the cultivation analysis work produced by George Gerbner and his colleagues suggests that heavy media users typically overestimate the amount of crime in their neighborhoods and tend toward middle-of-the-road political beliefs. Moreover, cultivation analysis researchers have found that the media tends to propagate and maintain political values already in circulation, hence serving

Children's media encounters in contemporary India: Leisure and learning

Shakuntala Banaji, London School of Economics
and Political Science

The media environment surrounding children in the metropolis of Bombay, India has altered almost unrecognizably since the 1990s. Several hundred national and international cable and satellite television channels, broadband Internet, video, and mobile phone cameras have entered middle class homes. Even in India's rural areas, the dispersal of satellite and Internet connections is growing. Nonetheless, the media environment of millions of children growing up in most small towns and villages across the country remains limited – some radio or magazines, little access to television, no access to cinema or the Internet, rare sightings of a computer in a village school or non-governmental organization center, and no chance to discuss or experiment with media-making. In this context of highly uneven access to media resources, discourses about children and media have remained monolithic and stagnant, falling into one of two paradigms. The first is a 'hypodermic' effects paradigm, which focuses on content in a negative or, occasionally, a celebratory manner. The protectionist stance that sees 'Western' media as dangerous and having negative effects on 'Indian' ethics and culture is one example. The second paradigm ignores content and views all developments in Indian media and communications as socially beneficial because they make India, apparently, more 'modern' and 'competitive.' While a host of other positions do exist, these are rarely articulated.

To make some sense of contemporary media environments for children in India, I conducted a small-scale interview-based study. The study – involving 12 Bombay children (aged 10–12), a similar-sized group of children (aged 10–13) in a village (Barsu) in the Himalayan foothills, and a larger focus group of children (aged 10–14) in a small town (Palakkad) in Kerala – aimed to disentangle some of the rhetoric about values, global skills, and ethnic identity from the realities of young people's media, family, and social experiences.[1]

The children interviewed in Bombay were of lower middle class backgrounds and had the most diverse experience of media of the groups. Most of them had been on the Internet, looking up sporting websites, playing games on the Disney and Fox Kids websites, or researching for school, and some had occasional unfettered access to the Internet. Computers, usually situated in communal spaces of the home, were seen by parents as necessary for giving kids skills for the modern economy. Television remained (by and large, and with the exception of trips to the cinema) the favorite form of entertainment. Everyone in the sample agreed that they loved to watch television, particularly unsupervised. The kinds of programs watched varied from Hindi films, chat-shows, comedy programs, and serials (with quite grown-up themes) to films in English and dubbed American, Canadian, European, and Japanese programs: *Peppa Pig, Dora the Explorer,* and the Indian version of *Sesame Street* appealled to younger siblings, while *Hannah Montana, That's So Raven,* and *The Sweet Life of Zach and Cody* were favorites with older girls. The boys claimed to prefer to watch cricket and films.

My discussions with parents confirmed that television was variously seen to compete with doing housework, looking after younger siblings, and playing outdoors, but the most common complaint about it was that it made children lazy about their 'studies.' For these Bombay children, who were subjected to dull, conformist school environments for much of the day, the colonization of their television-viewing time by homework was their single largest bone of contention. The parents' and teachers' focus on rote learning of facts and skills for apparent future economic gain, and their sense of media as 'insidious,' discouraged the learning that children did from television and negated children's pedagogic justifications of viewing. Equally, the concept of children having leisure time in which to relax was understood as something 'negative' picked up from despised Western programs.

In the village and small-town environments sampled, where film and the Internet were notably absent, children enjoyed looking at pictures in occasional vernacular magazines or listening to songs on the radio. Given that many of the children had never been to the cinema or used the Internet, and that some lived in such poverty that the mid-day meal provided by the school was their only source of nourishment during the day, occasional unsupervised television viewing was highly valued. Ironically, learning – about literacy, 'good' behavior, and life skills – was linked more to television than to school. Several of the children referred to television's potential for teaching 'different languages' and 'about nature' as pedagogic justifications they used to persuade parents to allow them to watch non-vernacular content.

This brief description of environments and findings leaves room for wider debates about media, family life, and education in India. It suggests that media education, for most adults, is a low priority, while media censorship – which for many campaigners and academics is such a high priority – might do with far less attention. This snapshot also points to painful gaps and absences in the lives (and in writing about the lives) of children in India. These children are frequently homogenized into the figure of the urban, media-savvy, or media-endangered child consumer, or treated as victim statistics. This study emphasizes the need for including detailed views and concerns of children *from different classes and locations* in any debates about the spread of mass media and media literacy across the country.

Notes

1. The data in Barsu and Palakkad were gathered by local researchers. The author acknowledges her gratitude. More detailed discussions of these research findings appear in a chapter in Banaji (2010).

Banaji, S. (Ed.) (2010). *South Asian Media Cultures*. London: Anthem Press.

to reproduce the social order. Cultivation analysis thus recognizes the media as a key socializing and enculturating institution, but not one that works in a vacuum. Rather, this approach recognizes the ideational influence of the mass media and accords to the media its appropriate position as a dominant force in people's lives. In this sense, cultivation analysis allows us to agree that, yes, the media does affect the young people in our classrooms; they do have attitudes cultivated by media exposure. At the same time, to develop a more finely grained understanding of the relationship between media and audiences requires that we turn to other resources.

Reception theories

In contrast to cultivation analysis and media effects models, reception theories start from the premise that the reader (or viewer, listener, etc.) is capable of critical reflection. As such, these theories call into question the perspective of children as innocent victims of media messaging, as well as perspectives that rest on ideas of mass media manipulation (such as cultural imperialism, culture industries, and so on). Rather, drawing on the work of Stuart Hall, and in particular his article 'Encoding/decoding' (1980), what is proposed instead is a tripartite scheme of media reception. Here, the idea is that any media text is susceptible to at least three kinds of interpretation: dominant (or preferred), oppositional, and negotiated. A dominant reading is that which is intended by the author/producer; an oppositional reading rejects the central meaning intended within the texts; and a negotiated reading lies somewhere in between. After watching Christian Bale and Heath Ledger push the limits in the Batman-franchise movie *The Dark Knight* (2008), for example, one viewer may find it 'cool' and exciting, another may see it as senseless and offensively violent, and another may view it as a cult classic with troubling issues. Arguably, most of us negotiate our media viewing most of the time, but there is also a pleasure of viewing that is compromised by being constantly critical. Media theorists have the handy term 'guilty pleasure' to reconcile watching lowbrow cinema or other such cultural forms without having to analyze it or simply reject it out of hand. In this sense, Hall's theory is a handy conceptual tool, but it is important to recognize that his three categories are very fluid. For example, a given viewer might read a media text differently depending on the context of viewing (screening *The Dark Knight* in the classroom would likely cause a young person to view it differently from when alone with peers). Moreover, watching television advertisements, a viewer might see three ads in sequence and have a different reaction to each that reflects the three reading positions noted above.

It is also important to remember that, ultimately, the perspective of the viewer is to a great extent affected by factors external to media viewing that are brought to the act of viewing. Because of this, a key component of audience studies has been ethnographic research, which involves studying audiences in action. In his research on varying audience reactions to the video game *Grand Theft Auto: San Andreas*, for instance, Kurt Squire (2008) tells the story of one young player who described his engagement with the game differently depending on who he was speaking with. Alone with Squire, this 12-year-old African-American boy described his interest in automotive design and tricking the game by using a wide variety of cheats to play more effectively. Once with peers, however, the youngster spoke of the game 'as a space for performing impressive (often violent) feats, pulling off stunts, driving erratically, or "capping" people' (p. 175). Other youth interviewed by Squire spoke of the freedom the game offers to make your own story and of the impressive collection of music that can be listened to on the car radios. While that first group of young people scoffed at the issues of racism and violence that so many of the game's adult critics have voiced concern over, two other groups of youth did consider these issues important. A group of white, working class 14- and 15-year-olds expressed concerns about how 'crazy kids' might react to the game, and they demonstrated a sophisticated analysis of racial and cultural stereotypes in the game. The third group, an older teen group of working poor African-Americans, felt the violence in the game was of less concern than the violence in their own neighborhoods. They also argued that white kids might get unrealistic impressions about black people as upwardly mobile when their own experiences of racialized poverty in the US stood in stark contrast. Ultimately, differences in cultural and economic backgrounds afforded these groups of youth a variety of resources with which to read and use the game very differently from the way anticipated in the moral panics that characterize public debates on video gaming and violence.

The upshot of this is that deep insights can emerge from audience research that demonstrate the complex nexus in which the media reside. That said, the cumulative impact of audience theories has been to demonstrate the multiple perspectives from which, and through which, we consume and live with media.

Cultural Life

The trickiest work of media interpretation is to take the next step forward, from audience reception to an evaluation of how media impact everyday cultural and social life. What becomes apparent from the research and theorizing on audiences, in other words, is that we can talk about models of *limited effects* and *effects without guarantees*. If, as Kenneth Burke (1966) says, however, attitudes are incipient actions, then there is a powerful effect associated with heavy and long term media exposure. This is not anything as simple as a direct, causal impact on behavior, but it is not a stretch to see media viewing habits and practices as a concomitant variable in actions, practices, and behaviors. Further, the model of effects without guarantees refers to what we named above as the lottery effect: some people, some of the time, can be impacted by media experience to the point of it directly affecting their behavior or actions. Thus, while we agree that youth transgressive behaviors are often unfairly attributed to media consumption and that resulting moral panics prove little more than the fact that adults have a tendency to desperately seek simple answers for complex youth behavior, we cannot deny that media consumption has a powerful set of effects on youth consciousness, behavior, and practices that is experienced uniquely and contextually.

At the same time, the impact of the media on the lives of young people goes far beyond the feelings, actions, and attitudes of the individual. The stories and tropes circulated by and through the media have a broad impact on cultural life and culture has a reciprocal impact on what stories and tropes are circulated through and by the media. If this feedback process is not new, the major historical innovation in our time is that the generation and circulation of stories has been amplified by the modern media, both in terms of frequency and reach. Drawing on Richard Johnson, we suggest that assessing the cultural echoes of media consumption, including the way such consumption influences the development of future media, is a key goal in media education. The study of media allows us to find points of convergence with school curricula, particularly in matters that are historical (not limited to the study of history but encompassing the historical elements buried in all curricular domains, including, for example, the study of literature). The ways in which cultural motives impact on how and what can be expressed in the media have their echoes in other modes of cultural expression. Thus, the representation of women and racialized minority persons in the media enables a broader historical discussion of the same matters across time. The same can be said of how work and leisure, school and church, society and culture are represented. The point here is that media texts, like other forms of representation, reflect back something of the cultural ethos of the time, even while (often) distorting it. Consequently, an opportunity arises from the careful study of media to make sense of the worlds in which students live and the historical lineages that have brought them to these brave new realities.

The vast majority of our students are consumers and fans of at least some media texts, and these texts are sites not only of pleasure and entertainment but also of learning (as noted in Chapter 3). Commercial media texts are produced for the most part by a media industry that relentlessly researches its audiences and that produces a great bulk of material for those demographics that are seen to mobilize spending power in the marketplace.

Discussing the cycle of symbolic exchange that leads to youth media consumption, Paul Willis (1990) states that 'commerce keeps returning to the streets and common culture to find its next commodities' (p. 19). What he means by this is that commerce does not manufacture youth consciousness but attempts to harness it. This is how and why Michael Jordan and Nike shoes became so madly popular near the end of the twentieth century. Michael Jordan was, or is, an imaginary version of real social and cultural selves at a particular historical moment of economic and cultural globalization – a distorting mirror to be sure, but one that also tells a story about the state of our culture(s) at the time:

> That moment in history – when globalization, media culture, the fetishization of Afro-American culture, the marketing and popularity of the sneaker, the growth of a new global corporation (Nike), and the need in the United States for a squeaky clean black role model coalesced – will be forever Michael's. (Hoechsmann, 2001, p. 269)

It is not Jordan the person who is consumed, in other words, but rather his carefully staged image. And these images are drawn from, and correspond to, contemporary conditions as experienced by youth. Thus, media 'moments' such as those represented by Michael Jordan provide powerful synchronic snapshots or points of view of history as it is lived and felt by young people. (See Sonja Cunningham's sidebar, THE SIMPSONS: NOT SUCH A DUMB SHOW AFTER ALL!, for a detailed discussion of *The Simpsons* as historical artifact and classroom resource.)

Today, a related example is lonelygirl15, or Bree, as she was also known. The story of YouTube's lonelygirl15 stands out as a testimony to amateur celebrity in the age of participatory media, but it also highlights the way that celebrity is imbricated in and through a corporate media culture forever on the lookout for new ways to engage and commodify youth experience. Perhaps most interestingly, however, it also suggests how youth themselves are coming to terms with this culture. Here is what we mean.

In the Web 2.0 era, a webcam, some editing software, and a high-speed Internet connection are all that are needed to make anyone a star. And, with over 10 million channel views (the total number of viewers of lonelygirl15 videos) and over 90,000 subscribers (dedicated viewers) in 2007, lonelygirl15 was an early YouTube star. Like many girls who participate in social media, lonelygirl15, or 'Bree,' would sit in her bedroom and speak languorously about her everyday life, occasionally joined by her boyfriend

The Simpsons: Not such a dumb show after all!

Sonja Cunningham, Simon Fraser University

As the longest-running American sitcom, with over 450 episodes and 20 seasons to its credit, *The Simpsons* has encountered its fair share of criticism, praise, and controversy. The series began as a collection of shorts by cartoonist Matt Groening and producer James L. Brooks that were aired as part of the *Tracey Ullman Show* in 1987. After three seasons, it was developed into a full half-hour prime-time show and picked up by Fox for the 1989–1990 season. Classified as both an animated series and a family-based situation comedy, *The Simpsons* popularized a new hybrid genre that appealed to both adults and children. Kids were at once attracted to the show's occasionally crude humor as well as to the devious anti-hero Bart Simpson. This has often been a source of concern for parents, particularly during the early 1990s, when shirts emblazoned with the slogan 'Underachiever and Proud of It!' were popular among schoolchildren and consequently banned in many schools. During its first five years of production, the show was often critiqued as having a degrading influence on families and society, exemplified by then-President George H. W. Bush's proclamation that 'we're going to strengthen the American family to make them more like *The Waltons* and less like *The Simpsons*.'

To viewers' delight, Bart himself responded within an episode of the show, stating 'we're just like *The Waltons*, we're praying for an end to the depression too.' Despite popular (and political) critiques, many pundits argue that *The Simpsons* provides both a realistic, if tongue in cheek, depiction of the average American family and an astute and often multi-layered commentary on American life. During a monologue on *The Tonight Show* in the early 1990s, Johnny Carson observed that *The Simpsons* provided a more realistic depiction of American families than programs such as *The Cosby Show*, which presented an idealized version of American life. The geographically ubiquitous city of 'Springfield' emphasizes the show's appeal to the average American family, complete with flawed parenting styles, belligerent children, and inept authority figures. In addition to this emphasis on realism, *The Simpsons* also involves, and is perhaps characterized by, a parodic nature that often draws on a variety of cultural, political, and social references that vary from the base (slapstick violence) to the sophisticated (i.e., allusions to classic films, literature, history, and so on). In fact, these references are so abundant and often so subtle/brief that they frequently require repeat viewings in order to appreciate the level of connotation at work, as devoted fans will attest. The show itself has evolved into a cultural artifact in its own right, as lines and quips from episodes have been integrated into popular lexicon – from Homer's infamous exclamation 'd'oh!' to the popular expression of apathy 'meh' and Nelson's signature 'ha-ha!' As such, *The Simpsons* has become an influential touchstone of popular culture.

One of the hallmarks of the show, aside from its parodic nature, is its ongoing hyper-reflexivity and self-awareness, which allow for its success as both a satirical social commentary and a popular source of televised entertainment. Matt Groening has stated that the essential message of the show is that authority figures are not necessarily the idealized figures they are often represented to be. Popular targets of the show's satire include incompetent teachers and school administrators, corrupt political officials (particularly Mayor Quimby, a parody of Ted Kennedy), and bumbling Police Chief Wiggum. One of the most common themes is the critique of capitalist/consumer society, typified by the all-powerful and nefarious corporate boss, Mr. Burns. The fictional setting of Springfield also provides a complete social microcosm in which the writers parody 'real-world' issues: Homer's job at a nuclear power plant allows for commentary on environmental concerns; media channels (journalism, television, films, and newspapers) in Springfield all serve to satirize the entertainment and news industry; and Lisa and Bart's school provides a rich site for examining controversial issues in education. In one episode, for example, School Superintendent Chalmers and Principal Skinner discuss test scores:

SKINNER: So, what's the word down at One School Board Plaza?
CHALMERS: We're dropping the geography requirement. The children weren't testing well. It's proving to be an embarrassment.
SKINNER: Very good. Back to the three R's.
CHALMERS: Two R's, come October.

As a result of its insightful and often controversial commentary on American society, in addition to its entertainment value and mass appeal, *The Simpsons* can be effectively used to illustrate sociological themes and encourage critical thinking in a pedagogical setting. English teachers have found success in using the show's parodies of classic literature and films to engage their students, while social studies teachers find that the cultural reference points and satire provide ample opportunity for deconstruction and reflection on these themes. While some still view *The Simpsons* as just another 'dumb' cartoon show, since its beginning it has proved itself a site of insightful and at times scathing commentary on American cultural life.

For further reading and lesson plans, see:

- Scanlan, S. J. and Feinberg, S. L. (2000). The cartoon society: Using *The Simpsons* to teach and learn sociology. *Teaching Sociology*, 28(2), pp. 127–139.
- Wright, J. (n.d.). Lesson plan: Exploring satire with *The Simpsons*. *ReadWriteThink*. Retrieved May 21, 2011 from http://www.readwritethink.org/lessons/lesson_view.asp?id=811. (*ReadWriteThink* is a language arts literacy organization.)
- *Media Awareness Network*. (n.d.). Television dads: Immature and irresponsible? Retrieved May 21, 2011 from http://www.media-awareness.ca/english/resources/educational/lessons/elementary/stereotyping/tv_dads.cfm. (This lesson plan encourages students to critically reflect on stereotypes in television sitcoms and includes an analysis of *The Simpsons*' Homer.)
- *Media Awareness Network*. (n.d.). Teaching television: Critically evaluating television. Retrieved May 21, 2011 from http://www.media-awareness.ca/english/resources/educational/lessons/elementary/television_radio/teaching_tv_evaluating.cfm. (One of another set of lesson plans from the *Media Awareness Network*. It aims to make kids critically examine television products.)

Daniel. Her tone was monotonous but cute. Bree played up the role of a naïve but spirited teenage girl. Indeed, the classic lonelygirl15 pose was a close-up of her face, leaning on one knee pulled up tightly to her chin. On her very first v-log, viewed by over 2.7 million people, she included a written comment that contextualized her as just another DIY (do it yourself) youth videographer: 'So, I finally got a webcam and got it working (ugh, harder than I thought...). Hope you like it:).'

Bree was very good at producing v-logs, a media production within the limitations imposed by webcam technology. Ironically, however, and as we found out later, lonelygirl15 was everything that the usual webcam user is not – she auditioned for the part, read from scripts, and was produced professionally with proper lighting, camera, and editing. It turned out, in fact, that this girl was not lonely at all but was surrounded by a production team. Moreover, she wasn't 16, as she had claimed, but rather a 19-year-old actress named Jessica Rose, hired to create a new online franchise. Despite, or because of, the notoriety of being outed by her audience, however, lonelygirl15 was chosen as a spokesperson for the United Nations Millennium Campaign to fight global poverty!

This seemingly contradictory development may be confusing, but we contend that the story of lonelygirl15 is instructive because, while standing up against global poverty might not have been the outcome the lonelygirl15 organizers had bargained for, it suited their goals of creating and sustaining her brand identity. More importantly, as a peculiarly helpful lens on the life of contemporary youth, lonelygirl15 reveals the tensions that mark out this experience. We mean by this that Bree's appeal for a time was the fact that she seemed to signify every girl – someone working through her turmoil and problems online in a manner familiar to other teens. That she was in fact an intentional brand construct may have been disappointing, but this also evidences the way new amateur media networks are imbricated with corporate protocols and appeals. Some – including the international news and online forums that reacted with shock when lonelygirl15 was outed – may regret this fact, but it is instructive that, when it was revealed that lonelygirl15 was a hoax, the backlash was ultimately modest. Moreover, it receded quickly, making it possible for Bree to become a United Nations spokesperson. From our perspective, this is telling because it suggests that while many young people are wary of corporate media influences in their lives today, many are also increasingly sanguine about this fact. Said otherwise, the story of Bree suggests that the needs of lonelygirl15's audience for an affective alliance with a reliable YouTube regular was greater than their wariness about corporate shenanigans in the shaping of this alliance. This of course will be frustrating for those of us weaned on the bottle of independent media, but the historical moment we now face is different. It is a time when the cultural life of young people is evolving through new and complicated forms of participation enabled by media technologies that constantly risk cooptation by corporate ambitions.

Educators like to style themselves as 'in the know,' sensitive to and aware of the spheres of influence young people have to contend with, but of course they lack the resources mobilized by the media industry for extensive grounded research into the lives of young people. This, however, is where taking media texts seriously as windows into the lifeworlds of our students is one of the great potentials of media literacy. Windows such as those presented by lonelygirl15 open up revealing portraits of the world young people will inherit. Children and youth are now growing up in a historical period with no easy answers, an epoch of cultural and economic flux, where contradictory worldviews are a reasonable response to the social, cultural, and economic conditions present today. Regardless of how educators mobilize cultural life to illuminate the analysis of media texts under consideration, it is always necessary to foreground the question, 'how does this media text or phenomenon respond to the world of my students?' The analysis of cultural life moves away from screens and into the living rooms and street corners where kids hang out. In these times of interactive media, it also takes us to the new cutting rooms of contemporary youth media production. In Chapter 5, it is to this world of interactive media and youth media production with media education that our story turns.

5

Media Production and Youth Agency

There have been times in the history of media education when media production has been cast as the playful yet less important cousin of a conceptually sophisticated analytic project that places reading texts (images, sounds, fashions, etc.) at the center of media literacy. The reasons for this are many. At root, the distinction between the creative work of media production and the analytic work of media education draws on a bias in the Western cultural tradition that privileges the work of the mind over the work of the hand. In Ancient Greece, Plato drew on this idea to condemn the public influence of artists and poets, who operate in the realm of the senses, the physical world of creation, arguing that it is only in the realm of reason and the mind that truth and real understanding are achieved. Today we may be suspicious of this claim, but cultural stereotypes persist in reinforcing the idea that thinking is more important than doing. Consider, for instance, the way stereotypes are used to distinguish carpenters and artists from bankers and lawyers. Some may find the first group more trustworthy or interesting, but those in the second group, who work primarily with their minds, are often thought the more successful and significant.

Where these stereotypes have become part of media education, the mental labor of reading or analyzing media texts, institutions, and experiences has been thought more important than the creative work young people do with these texts and resources. In some instances, this has led to suspicion that media production should be considered as distinct from media education. We argue, however, that the rich and complex practices that characterize young people's media production are inseparable from the development of media literacy. In fact, it is our contention that the

Media Literacies: A Critical Introduction, First Edition. Michael Hoechsmann and Stuart R. Poyntz.
© 2012 Blackwell Publishing Ltd. Published 2012 by Blackwell Publishing Ltd.

boundaries between the analytic work of media education and the creative work of media production are porous. One supports the other and, in many ways, thinking of media literacy outside of the way young people articulate their ideas and experiences through creative work makes little sense.

At least one reason for this is that the last decade of the twentieth century and the first of the twenty-first have witnessed an explosion of youth media production practices in informal (private) settings, in schools, and among not-for-profit arts organizations and community groups. Research from UNESCO also tells us that this growth is hardly limited to the so-called developed world. In fact, programs such as the *Little Masters* national magazine in China, the video production project *Cámara! ahi nos vemos* in Mexico, *Youth Broadcasting* in Somalia, *Bush Radio* in South Africa, the *Young Journalists Group* in Vietnam, *Trendsetters* magazine in Zambia, and many community-based media production programs in Australia, Canada, the UK, and the US indicate that young people today are producing creative work across a range of textual modalities. What's more, these practices address a cross-section of purposes, goals, and objectives – some more ambitious than others but all indicative of a vibrant world of creative youth expression now emanating from all corners of the globe. (For an extended discussion of contemporary youth cultural production in the context of today's creative economies, see the sidebar YOUTH CULTURAL PRODUCTION AND CREATIVE ECONOMIES by Miranda Campbell.)

In this chapter, while not attempting to address all these practices and initiatives, we provide a map outlining what media production adds to the project of media literacy. To do this, we begin by parsing the meaning of production and linking this with Paul Willis' (1990) discussion of youth experiences as creative consumers of popular commercial media. In the second half of the chapter we then examine how media production has been understood to nurture young people's agency. Here we address four constructs that suggest the value and contribution creative work can have for children and youth, noting the limitations and possibilities for young people's agency that arise in each framework.

What Creative Work Adds to Media Education: Production as Praxis

When young people engage with media, they learn about themselves and the social world that shapes their lives and is in turn shaped by youths' own

Youth cultural production and creative economies

Miranda Campbell, McGill University

From bedrooms to classrooms to studios, dark rooms, and green rooms, youth are increasingly producing creative works, and scholars are beginning to take note of this 'wildfire of youth cultural production' (Hoechsmann and Low, 2008, p. 6). Cultural production is increasingly becoming part of school curricula, and, while creative work has long been taught in a variety of fields (e.g., art class, music class, creative writing in English class), media educators now suggest that 'multimedia "digital creations"' (Sefton-Green and Sinker, 2000, p. 2) should be taught across the curriculum rather than in one isolated subject. Other research suggests, however, that the home is where youth are gaining skills in cultural production: Henry Jenkins (2006), for instance, suggests that it is Internet-based affinity spaces rather than schools that are fostering and nurturing young people's creative media work today.

Whichever is the case, there is little doubt that the increase in youth cultural production is a result of the accessibility of digital technologies. David Hesmondhalgh (2002) comments that digital technologies, including samplers, sequencers, and MIDI, have had a substantial impact on music-making since the early 1980s. Where this suggests that 'digitalization [has] allowed "ordinary" consumers more easily to become producers,' statistical and anecdotal evidence also indicates that similar trends are underway in a variety of creative industries, including film and photography. Nurturing these developments, community-based youth arts programs have seized the moment to dismantle the traditional barriers between production and consumption and have turned to cultural production as an increasingly important tool of engagement for at-risk youth.

Youths' engagement with creative activities not only undermines traditional distinctions between the roles consumer and producer but also breaks down distinctions between work and leisure, as youth are increasingly seeking out careers in the creative industries. While some nations have begun to seize this trend more than others (e.g., see the UK's Department of Media, Culture and Sport's new 'Creative Britain: New talents for a new economy' policy document), this trend has socio-economic ramifications that are only beginning to be grasped by scholars. Angela McRobbie (1999) notes, for instance, that youth are involved in creative economies in self-generated and small-scale ways. She tracks the 'the growth in self-employment' among youth in the creative industries, and she characterizes this trend as 'the future of work in the creative sector' (p. ix). Her research thus takes up an investigation of 'small scale cultural economies and livelihoods upon which so many people now depend for a living' (p. x). While David Hesmondhalgh (2002) characterizes the core creative industries as advertising and marketing, broadcasting, film, Internet industries, music industries, print and electronic publishing, and video and computer games, McRobbie looks at youth activities that may have once been characterized as leisure activities ('cooking, gardening, sports, rambling, "Internetting," producing fanzines, etc.') and notes the need to research the 'sprawling sector of micro-economies of culture' in which youth are self-employed as 'stylists, make-up artists, or [...] [producers of] dance tracks [...] in their bedrooms' (1999, pp. 26–27).

British census data, used to compile a Cultural Trends survey, also suggest that youth are taking up cultural work in ways that are markedly different from their parents' generation. Discussing youth cultural producers in the British context, for instance, Leadbeater and Oakley (1999) characterize young people in the cultural industries as 'the independents' who often actively pursue work away from major organizations. Drawing from the Cultural Trends survey, they (1999) report that 'about 34 percent of people working in the cultural sector are self-employed, compared with an average of 15 percent for the economy as a whole' and that this workforce is 'disproportionately young' (p. 21). Further, the 'rate of self-employment is much higher in younger, newer sectors of the cultural industries and is lower in the subsidized and public cultural sectors, such as museums and galleries, which tend to have an older workforce' (p. 21). While Oakley (2004) notes that the British government's uptake of the creative economy has been largely for political gains, many other governments have yet to fully grapple with the growth of the creative industries. Moreover, there is an absence of attention to youth activities in research in the creative industries, even if youth are those who are newly entering into the field and shaping its direction. Youth register most loudly in discussions of creative work when youth are seen as a social problem. Youth cultural production takes place largely at home, however, in front of computers, guitars, cameras, and sewing machines. While the field of education recognizes that youth bring skills from home into the classroom, it does not put enough stock in the fact that these skills return home after graduation. These bedroom economies need to be taken seriously if we want to get an accurate picture of youth life pathways and of economic trends, and this warrants more empirical attention regarding how youth navigate and negotiate multiple streams of work and grants in order to generate income while engaging in personally meaningful activities.

References

Jenkins, H. (2006). Confronting the challenges of participatory culture: Media education for the 21st century. An occasional paper prepared for the MacArthur Foundation.

Hesmondhalgh, D. (2002). *The Cultural Industries*. London: Sage Publications.

Hoechsmann, M. and Low, B. (2008). *Reading Youth Writing: 'New' Literacies, Cultural Studies and Education*. New York: Peter Lang.

Leadbeater, C. and Oakley, K. (1999). *The Independents: Britain's New Cultural Entrepreneur*. London: Demos.

McRobbie, A. (1999). *In the Culture Society: Art, Fashion, and Popular Music*. London: Routledge.

Oakley, K. (2004). Not so cool Britannia: The role of the creative industries in economic development. *International Journal of Cultural Studies*, 7(1), pp. 67–77.

Sefton-Green, J. and Sinker, R. (Eds.). (2000). *Evaluating Creativity: Making and Learning by Young People*. London: Routledge.

agency and activities. Within this relationship, at its best, media production operates as a powerful form of praxis, a way of learning by doing. Production is fundamentally about the way creative work acts as a pivot point through which dialectics of 'doing' and 'analysis' merge (Buckingham, 2003a). Thinking of creative media work in this way focuses attention on how expressive acts afford young people opportunities to locate themselves in larger social worlds, not simply by acquiring a set of ideas about how the media shapes our lives but in the way youth make sense of these ideas through creative expressions.

Thinking of production work as a form of praxis is not new. In the 1930s the critical theorist Walter Benjamin drew attention to the way acts of creative expression can form the basis for transformational experiences. Rather than just being 'armed' with ideas about how the press works, Benjamin (1986) proposed that the best way for readers (or media consumers) to take control of their lives is under conditions that make way for 'the reader [...] to become a writer, that is, a describer, but also a prescriber' (p. 225). How one takes on this role is less important than that fact that 'the forms of expression [...] channel the [...] energies of the present' (p. 224). Benjamin meant by this that the mode of expression (writing, audio or visual representations, etc.) is less important than the fact that this mode be common and familiar to those undertaking creative work. When this is the case, Benjamin argued, conditions are ripe for media consumers to become the producers of cultural expressions that matter in their lives.

The educational challenge posed by this idea is significant. On the one hand, the implication is that it matters that media educators do more than just 'arm' young people against the media environments we face daily. On the other hand, it also matters that educators move beyond 'writing and speech as the weapons of choice' for teaching children and youth about media culture (Goldfarb, 2002, p. 66). While valuable and necessary modes of communication, writing and speech are just two of the forms of communication common in young people's lives. They may not even be the most familiar or ready-to-use forms, and so what matters is that educators explore other forms of expression, including media (e.g., film and video, the Internet, and social networking platforms such as Facebook and Flickr) that mix together visual, audio, and textual modalities. Such media are now a common feature of adolescent lifeworlds and what has become increasingly apparent is that young people's very familiarity with these modes of representation is the ground from which interesting and expressive 'energies [in] the present' (Benjamin, 1986, p. 224) can be loosed upon the world.

At least part of the reason this is the case is the range of learning possibilities offered by creative media work. David Buckingham captures these possibilities when he (2006a) writes: 'Media production requires an ability to access and manipulate technology, and an understanding of issues such as media language and representation, as well as an awareness of one's audience' (p. 24). (For an extended discussion on the role of writing in the assessment of students' learning through media production, see the sidebar ASSESSING LEARNING FROM PRACTICAL MEDIA PRODUCTION AT AN INTRODUCTORY LEVEL: THE ROLE OF WRITING by Sara Bragg.) Production of new media never

Assessing learning from practical media production at an introductory level: The role of writing

Sara Bragg, Open University

It is widely accepted that being media-literate includes the ability to *produce* media alongside accessing, understanding, and analyzing them. But what does making media achieve in the media education classroom?

Students generally enjoy and are motivated by practical work although pleasure alone may not seem a sufficiently academic rationale. In introductory-level courses, specific vocational skills training is rarely a central aim – not least because some learners may be more confident with key software and tools than are their teachers – although the production process may develop generic competences, such as 'working with others,' 'communication,' and so on. Primarily, the intention is that students learn *from* rather than *about* media production, coming to understand and question key concepts of their course (such as audience, representation, institution) more deeply than they would through only studying existing texts. To produce media, students must draw on the knowledge they have unconsciously imbibed as audiences, which therefore – it is argued – makes it available for reflection and analysis. There is a social justice aspect to this, too. Other school subjects take little account of literacies beyond the print-based or of learning from low-status media (rather than more highly valued cultural forms), whereas practical production can recognize such expertise, sometimes even substantially rewarding it through formal assessment. In this way it may benefit 'non-traditional' students in particular.

Although being able to generate intelligible and appropriate media texts in itself arguably demonstrates understanding, educators tend to ask that more explicit evidence of learning is submitted alongside the product, in the (usually written) form of an evaluation, reflection, or commentary. Yet such assignments often prove unsatisfactory: they are unpopular with students, while teachers complain that students fail to relate key concepts to the product, that they are descriptive rather than analytical, or that they make claims about the product reflecting obdurate wish-fulfillment rather than cool and detached appraisal. In addition, the essay format may help academically confident students compensate for weak products but unfairly penalize those who struggle with academic conventions, whatever their creative talents – an issue partly addressed by diversifying the range of permitted media (video, audio) and genres (blogs, commentaries).

The problem, I suggest, is not that students are deficient, nor that writing is unnecessary and unimportant; it may instead lie in the assumptions made in the framing of tasks and the guidance given to students.

For instance, first, media production is sometimes conceived as 'putting theory into practice' and begins only after instruction in media theory and techniques for textual analysis. Students are expected to use this material in their own productions – and in their writing to recount (in effect) how helpful their teachers have been. But this epistemological model surely overestimates the contribution of explicit knowledge to learning and action, and it is insufficiently interested in what other, unexpected and varied, frames of reference might in fact be relevant to students. It would be better to ask students to discuss in detail how their own texts relate to existing media genres and forms with which they are familiar, and how they have selected, combined, and shaped material to their own interests. Provided students are reassured that such 'bricolage' is creatively legitimate (rather than scholastically criminal 'copying'), they can be surprisingly eloquent on such matters. And what they reveal may in turn help teachers appreciate their students' personal media passions and how they might build on them pedagogically: learning in the classroom should not be only one-way.

Second, students are commonly asked to write about 'why' they worked as they did – that is, to illuminate the reasons behind their actions, how they planned the work, and how their 'intentions' were 'realized' in the final product. It is hardly surprising if they then fabricate improbable stories about how masterful and in control they were, how they bent technology to their will and manipulated the world to achieve their predetermined grand plan. Perhaps they are merely being polite in not wanting to expose the delusion embedded in the very demand for explanation – that we can capture the understandings implicit in our practice, in a complete way, within a rational framework. Historically, the modernist institution of school has invested heavily in the ideal of the self-knowing, autonomous subject for whom this would present no challenge. But students know well how disjointed and ad hoc media production processes really are; how they improvise (can we make this garden look like a jungle?), are limited by circumstances (the battery on the camera runs down, editing time is short), have to work with what is possible rather than what they want (no car chases…), and must rely on others (to turn up, to act, to comment) in ways that both help and hinder them. In so doing they are more, not less, creative, but we do not always help them tell us this.

John Shotter's description of a 'knowing of the third kind' (1993) is helpful here: it refers to knowledge derived from one's circumstances that is neither abstract (knowing that or knowing why) nor technical (knowing how); it is practical in that it enables us to act 'appropriately,' but it is a background knowledge that one thinks *out of* in order to act *into* a situation. If media-making mobilizes such knowledge, no wonder students struggle to explain 'why' or realize their intentions – because they respond to and negotiate with circumstances, events, and other people; because their understanding shapes their practices but in ways that at the time may feel simply instinctive.

To foreground and validate such ways of knowing, teachers could ask students to discuss how they worked in practice, and about their tactics for overcoming the frustrating limits of technology and circumstance – perhaps during the production process in class presentations designed to share ideas and generate collective solutions and further questions. The accounts that emerge may be narrative or descriptive, but these are not inferior to 'analytical' academic genres and indeed may be more accessible for many students and so should be valued and assessed appropriately – for example for how clearly they outline the dimensions of problems encountered and solutions found.

What is implicit in students' texts can also be explored through 'reception' studies using 'real' audiences, as educators have long known. Work can now, of course, be showcased online, although local audiences may be more motivated to respond and more aware of cultural reference points. However, evaluation – saying how 'good' texts are according to ill-defined criteria – is at most gratifying and is rarely illuminating. Audiences *describing* the texts – what they are about, what they think they mean – may more effectively help students to appreciate their work from the perspectives of others, realize that they have created unintended meanings, and understand what impact these might have on others, therefore becoming 'accountable' for their representations in retrospect rather than in advance. If teachers too eschew value judgments for description using the specialized vocabulary of media analysis, they may return students' knowledge to them in a form in which they can take pride and for which they can be accredited.

My comments here imply at most only minor adjustments to existing practice: nonetheless, I hope they might help generate more meaningful writing from students and stimulate reflection on our theories of knowing, learning, and creativity.

Shotter, J. (1993). *Cultural Politics of Everyday Life: Social Constructionism, Rhetoric and Knowing of the Third Kind.* Toronto, ON: University of Toronto Press.

involves just the application of a set of technical skills, in other words. Rather, even when schools focus solely on the development of such skills or when students are asked to ape advertisements or music videos they have seen on television or YouTube (for example), the work of production moves one to address and think through questions about the meaning of different visual and audio languages (shot selection, editing choices, sound effects, and so on). In addition, young producers are faced with questions about how their representational choices will impact the meaning of their work. This in turn can lead to thinking about one's audience and the way different audiences read certain aesthetic choices and use texts given their own interests, backgrounds, and needs. Again, these latter issues may not be taken up in all learning environments, but they are present in an oblique way, even if educators and students fail to explore them.

Making clear some of the learning possibilities offered by production work draws our attention to the way these practices involve young people with questions of agency. That is, in an important way, creative compositional acts position youth as actors in the world. Rather than being positioned as victims or even the site of a series of 'effects' thought to emanate from an omnipresent and all-determining commercial media system, a focus on media production addresses the complex ways youth become agents in their lives and the lives of others. From the perspective of researchers, this offers a qualitatively different insight into how kids make meaning in relation to media culture (Sefton-Green, 2006). This is important because, as we note throughout this book, media educators are learning that young people are hardly dupes or blindly willing consumers of media (McRobbie, 2000, 2005; Weber and Mitchell, 2008; Willett, 2008). In fact, production work is telling us that children and youth have a complex relationship with the media they consume, a relationship no doubt shaped by the formative influence of media institutions and representations and yet one that is also open to playful re-imagination and change. As Buckingham (2006a) has noted, it is for this reason that

> It is [now] widely accepted by media educators that the experience of media production is valuable both in its own right, as a means of promoting self-expression and communication skills, and also as a way of developing a more in-depth critical understanding. It is seen to provide a more participatory, 'hands-on' approach to pedagogy, which students generally find more motivating than approaches based solely on discussion and writing. (p. 44)

The very popularity of media production among young people raises a series of other important questions, which we address later in this chapter. At this point, however, it is helpful to take a step back and examine more specifically what it is we mean by 'production work' in the first place.

What does Production Mean?

The salience of this question stems from the fact that media scholars, educators, and youth have increasingly become attentive to the many ways young people creatively use the media they consume. We noted this in Chapter 3 and Chapter 4, but Paul Willis (1990) and Angela McRobbie (1994, 2000) have been especially influential in addressing the role of 'creative consumption' as an aspect of the way youth digest and involve media texts and experiences in their lives. At root, creative consumption refers to the ways kids remix the meaning associated with consumer media culture in the process of bringing this culture into their lives. This is not to say that youth are free-floating agents able to make whatever sense they want of the television shows, websites, and movies they watch. Rather, creative consumption focuses attention on youth as bricoleurs who remix the narratives, signs, and meaning of fashion, music, magazines, and so on as part of their everyday use of such resources. For Willis, conceiving of youth as bricoleurs focuses attention on the processes of symbolic creativity that are part of how teenagers use media texts. Such creativity is neither trivial nor inconsequential; rather, '[i]n conditions of late modernization, [...] [symbolic creativity] can be crucial to the creation and sustenance of individual and group identities, even to [the] cultural survival of identity itself' (Willis, 1990, p. 2).

Various researchers have picked up on this idea and identified what we might call an intermediate form of production that youth engage in as part of the consumption process. Julian Sefton-Green (2006) points to this work, noting a study by Ben Rampton (2006) that shows how pieces of music and pop culture phrases are reworked and remixed as part of the daily talk heard among youth in urban school classrooms. Adding to this, Anne Haas Dyson's (1997) research shows the way media texts can become resources for identity work among children asked to write classroom stories about their lives.

> Studies of children and young people's writing (within conventional curriculum areas) have [in fact] begun to acknowledge how media-determined narratives and texts [...] can be absorbed, internalized, and then re-'written' by young people and how these narratives and texts now need to be considered as central to children's changing imaginative and textual universe. (Sefton-Green, 2006, p. 294; see also Willett, 2008)

These sorts of observations are tremendously important and need to be taken into account when designing learning possibilities across educational curricula. For our purposes, however, we are also interested in distinguishing this intermediate form of production from a more explicit kind of production that has long been part of media education practice.

Historically, creative work within the field of media literacy has been associated with institutionally mediated projects and practices (developed in schools, community groups, art institutes, and so on) that are intended to develop young people's expressive possibilities and agency through various forms of media practice (including written journalism, radio production, video-making, web design, and so on). Distinguishing this work from the everyday forms of creativity youth engage in with media is not a perfect science. In fact, as evidenced in Chapter 7, the more recent development of robust and complicated remix cultures is making it more and more difficult to sustain the division we propose here. At the same time, production work is not an abstraction but rather a series of historically created practices that have developed in specific circumstances since the 1960s, if not earlier. Many of these practices have developed through intentional efforts to nurture youth writing, production, and design in schools and other learning environments. As such, while the situation may be becoming less clear today, there still seems to be value in drawing a distinction between intermediate forms of production and institutionally mediated projects and practices. At any rate, we believe this to be the case, and so in the remainder of this chapter we explore how institutionally mediated forms of youth production in schools, universities, and community settings have contributed to the project of media education.

How is Production a Form of Agency?

Within schools and less formal learning environments, production has been broadly understood as a potent means for enabling youth to become actively involved in their worlds. This vision is not wholly different from how analytic practices in media education have been thought to serve youth, and yet a number of different constructions and concerns have arisen that make clear the specific contributions creative work is thought to bring to media literacy. In this section, we outline four pivotal sets of concerns that make up a continuum of key issues embedded in the youth media production process – vocationalism, youth voice, democratic participation, and pleasure – that are always already present in youth production projects, whether they are explicitly addressed or not. Of course, we acknowledge that the continuum of key questions in youth media production will play out differently across distinct contexts.

Technical skills development and vocational training

Perhaps the most common view of production work in media literacy is that it is an ideal way to develop the technical skills and competencies young people need to function in a highly media saturated world. The notion that media production can serve this role actually begins quite early. As far back as the 1930s, in fact, the first school- and film-club-based production programs developed in the UK (Sefton-Green, 1995). The idea was to help youth learn the grammar of filmmaking – that is, how shots work, the meaning of lighting styles, different editing strategies, and so on – so that they could better figure out how the technology operates. To this end, students were not asked to complete whole films; rather, they were given exercises derived from the work of Soviet filmmaker and montage theorist V. I. Pudovkin that were meant to teach the language of cinema (Sefton-Green, 1995; Buckingham, 1999).

From this interesting beginning, more recently the idea of developing young people's technical skills has been justified as an aspect of vocational training within media education. Since at least the early 1970s, learning how to produce a radio show, write a newspaper article, or use a camera have been thought ideal ways to prepare young people for job markets. In this sense, the dialectic of learning by doing mentioned earlier in this chapter is taken up, but largely in functionalist terms. Learning how to work with editing equipment, light a scene, or record an interview is not about thinking critically about one's world; it is about developing strategies for job-readiness.

The appeal of this notion of media production as skills development has been particularly strong in programs targeted at kids who do not perform well in more academically oriented learning streams. Broadly speaking, media production programs inside and outside schools have often been targeted at low-income or otherwise marginalized youth. At least in part, the idea has been that schools and/or community-based programs can put a dent in what is now called the 'digital divide' by giving low-income kids access to technologies they might not otherwise have. Learning skills is thus a kind of equalizer in socio-economic circumstances and an enabler for those not succeeding in academic streams.

British educators Ian Connell and Geoff Hurd (1989) extend this argument a step further and argue that media production as skills development is best understood as a form of critical vocationalism (Goldfarb, 2002). Connell and Hurd mean by this that for some students – particularly those who have fewer opportunities, for combined reasons of class, race, gender, or assessed intelligence – skills development is a necessary step in gaining access to employment and the means of production. They suggest that learning how to critically read the media is something of a luxury, suited mostly to those who already come from middle or upper class families and are headed to university. Conversely, for kids who are not succeeding in the mainstream school system, a technical orientation in production work provides something everyone needs: a way to survive (Goldfarb, 2002).

Of course, there is a great deal of truth to this argument. At the same time, though, the idea of targeting production classes and programs at less-well-off students has added an important class dimension to the way production work as skills development has evolved. In fact, the long history of association between vocational training and students with poor academic records has cast a shadow over the idea that skills development should form the basis for including media production within the project of media education.

One reason for this is that, by framing media production in relation to instrumental ends, creative work has sometimes come to be seen as merely imitative. That is, in arguing that institutionally mediated learning can develop young people's job-ready skills, the notion of skills-based learning has been interpreted as merely learning how to imitate the styles and practices of the media industry itself. Media education is meant to develop one's critical understanding of the media industries that operate in our lives, however; and so, if all media production does is lend itself to imitative behavior, then many, including Len Masterman (1985), have been correct to express doubt about production work as a means for developing media-literate youth.

This claim is interesting because in many ways it touches on sensitivities that arise whenever young people get their hands on media. The worry is that it will only lead to copycat behavior, or perhaps mindless play with new toys. What we are learning, however, is that imitation is neither mindless nor includes straightforward acts of mimicry.

On the one hand, learning any new media form always and necessarily involves some kind of imitation. This is how young people learn about technical equipment and the relationship between this equipment and the sedimented practices of visual, audio, or textual representation that are invoked whenever one plays the game – any game, critical or otherwise – of media production. One cannot expect new media producers to simply invent novel visual, audio, or written languages when they pick up a pen, choose to use a camera, or decide how to design a webspace. Rather, learning how to write a magazine article, produce a video, or craft a digital media space involves a process of learning media conventions: how media languages have been used, how these languages relate to specific technical resources, and what expectations media producers and audiences have about the use of specific representational codes. In this sense, imitation is not something to be avoided; it is a necessary and unavoidable step in learning how to produce cultural expressions in the first place.

Further, evidence also suggests that when young people imitate other work – a music video, an advertisement, or a film genre, for instance – they rarely if ever simply reproduce what they see, read, or hear (Grace and Tobin, 2002; Buckingham, 2003a). Indeed, it is increasingly apparent that teenagers usually alter or rework the meaning of the texts or genre language they are working with. As many educators will attest, this process of reworking is often laden with a sense of parody or irony that draws explicit attention to the very codes or conventions of representation youth are being asked to work with. Reports from classrooms and community-based practices suggest in fact that, when youth imitate other media practices, they undertake a mode of dialogic communication (Bakhtin, 1981) that leads to the production of new texts that contain evidence of the conventions and codes of representation that youth have learned, but also evidence of some repositioning or reimagination of these codes.

If the foregoing discussion brings some comfort to those who promote media production in relation to skills development, many youth, educators, and researchers argue that technical training still does not capture the full richness of learning possibilities available through creative work. Indeed, many of the people who develop youth media programs – particularly in community-based, not-for-profit settings – are aware of this fact, and only foreground skills development as part of funding applications because this goal is what governments and foundations want to hear to justify funding decisions. Where skills development is part of fostering young people's agency, however, the full sense of what this agency might involve is not addressed if we only imagine production practices in terms of instrumental ends that are dictated by economic circumstances and needs. Many would suggest in fact that broader questions emerge through youth media production that relate to issues of youth expression and voice, participation in public life, and the role of pleasure and play in young people's media work. We thus turn to these issues in the next sections.

Creativity, expression, and youth voice

The second framework for thinking about media production in relation to the development of media-literate youth has been especially popular with school- and community-based arts educators. At root, the idea here is that, while media production may allow for skills development, it is also a tremendous vehicle for developing young people's voices and self-identities. In this sense, youth media projects often describe what they do as helping young people to 'find their voice' or as aiding '"silenced voices" by providing teenagers with the skills and access needed to express their stories' (Soep, 2006, p. 198). When expressed in this way, the implicit claim is that media production fosters youth agency by providing a means through which creative self-expression can be materialized and shared. This in turn is thought to provide the ground on which one can come to understand oneself and, as importantly, manifest this self or voice to the world. Again, like the notion of media production as skills development, this idea too has long had currency in the history of youth production.

In the 1960s in the UK, for instance, this sentiment found expression in Douglas Lowndes' book *Film Making in Schools* (1968). Lowndes' text came about in response to changes in thinking about the role of media (and film, in particular) in classrooms that arose during this period (see Chapter 1 for a longer discussion of these developments). Adding to this work, Lowndes argued that filmmaking offered a unique learning possibility, especially for working class urban kids, whose issues and experiences were often repressed through disciplinary regimes and practices in school. In contrast to attempts to simply marginalize tough kids, Lowndes argued that film offered 'new and different ways of seeing' (Sefton-Green, 1995, p. 85). Practical work provided students with a wider range of resources – in particular, the visual resources of the shot and the well-edited scene – to tell their stories. Lowndes suggested that, by fusing vision and expression and allowing young people to depict their lives, filmmaking offered a form of counter-practice to traditional academic work. This in turn offered a promising way for working class and other youth to take control of their lives. Creative expression thus became a means for self-actualization and, in the best-case scenario, a new way to control one's life.

This idea continues to carry a great deal of weight, not least because it draws on embedded assumptions in the West about what it means to be an artist and what creativity means in relation to art practice. Since the earliest days of modern art, the artist has been envisioned as someone capable of manifesting a unique and distinct vision of the world. This vision in turn has been thought the objective articulation of a creative individual force emanating from inside the artist-genius. As such, creativity has often been interpreted as having a mysterious and even mythic quality. In a sense, creative voice has been cast as the conduit through which an authentic expression of the true nature and identity of the artist and his or her experience might reveal itself.

Where creative youth production is concerned, this notion has been appealing, especially for art educators. Youth composition in text, audio, or visual formats has been cast as a vital means through which students' real experiences and identities can reveal themselves. The degree to which this is true is of course a crucial question. Research does tell us that creative practices are a powerful means for students to explore their emotional investments in the media (Buckingham, 2006a). It also offers a space for young people to showcase how they feel and think about popular television shows and movies while providing an important context to examine how these emotional investments relate to teenagers' identities. In addition, as the work of Goodman (2003), Charmaraman (2006), Soep (2006), and Hoechsmann and Low (2008) tells us, students gain a good deal of confidence through production work. In part, this comes about because of the competencies developed in the act of creation; in part, self-esteem benefits accrue because, once complete, students' work is typically circulated to audiences beyond classroom peers or close friends.

Beyond psychological benefits that help young people to find their voice, production work also fosters youth agency by nurturing those silenced voices that otherwise go unheard in contemporary culture. This has been especially important among educators and artists who work with young people of color, women, and working class or gay, lesbian, and bisexual youth. Deirdre Kelly (2006) points out, however, that young people in general 'do not participate equally in the making of culture in the everyday world or in public spheres' (p. 35). This contributes to their subordination because there are 'few youth-generated self-representations to counter dominant images of children as violent and irresponsible [or] [...] brainless consumers of fashion' (p. 36). In schools, and more markedly within the community-based youth media production community, this has led to the development of programs that put cameras and computers into the hands of young people. For some the benefits have been significant.

In a study of a summer youth media program in Vancouver, Canada, for instance, Poyntz (2008) shows that the creation of such spaces is itself empowering for teenagers. Today, youth-centered public spaces are on the decline, especially in poor, urban communities. If this situation is common across national settings, Elizabeth Soep (2006) reminds us that

The 'street' remains a potent symbol [...] [that] young people themselves use in reference to a whole constellation of styles, circumstances, and modes of behaviour [...] Yet the physical street itself – the paved one young people [...] walk along and across everyday en route to school, home and other places – is increasingly a site of surveillance and regulation. (p. 36)

The result is that public space unencumbered by the most egregious forms of control and regulation is diminishing. Youth media production programs are thus more valuable as a result. A young female participant in Poyntz' study noted as much, suggesting that such programs create a place for youth expression that seems increasingly hard to find:

> Young people have such interesting stories to tell and such important things to discuss. [They] have so much potential to contribute to their communities by producing art and engaging in conversation. [...] Allowing people to have these conversations and articulate what they're thinking is so important [...] [At the same time,] there needs to be more opportunities where youth can [...] [engage with each other and adults] in a really free, unrestricted, uncensored way. (quoted in Poyntz, 2008, p. 230)

These spaces are increasingly rare, but, the student continued, they allow time for teenagers to 'try to articulate things we're thinking and philosophizing about' (quoted in Poyntz, 2008, p. 231). As such, media programs can operate as a youthscape, an environment shaped by social, political, and cultural forces that simultaneously nurtures the perspectives and points of view of new creative voices. (For an extended discussion of using video for social change see the sidebar YOUTH AS KNOWLEDGE PRODUCERS IN COMMUNITY-BASED VIDEO IN THE AGE OF AIDS by Naydene DeLange, Claudia Mitchell, Relebohile Moletsane, and Jean Stuart about youth media production in South Africa.)

While media production can foster and develop youth voice and agency, there are at the same time good reasons to think that the celebration of voice is hardly trouble free. David Trend (1997) notes, for instance, that media producers who work with marginalized youth often overstate the benefits of such projects for young people. At root, the problem is that many community-based media producers hold to the modernist assumption that all self-expression is always liberating. The problem with this assumption, however, is that it fails to acknowledge the way self-expression can itself be a limiting or disempowering act. Mimi Orner (1992) has noted this problem and argued (as paraphrased by Soep, 2006) that 'celebrating student voice can backfire, by positing a fully egalitarian environment where none exists, thereby obscuring rather than unsettling uneven distributions of power' (p. 201). Video, in particular, is tricky in this light because it holds an appeal as a resource for marginal communities and is often thought to offer a form of communication to which young people have a natural affinity (Messaris,

Youth as knowledge producers in community-based video in the age of AIDS

Naydene DeLange, Nelson Mandela Metropolitan
University; Claudia Mitchell, McGill University;
Relebohile Moletsane, University of KwaZulu-Natal;
and Jean Stuart, University of KwaZulu-Natal

> Unless youth are given a more significant voice in creating and distributing public messages, HIV programming and other programming directed at youth sexuality organized by adults, donors and so on are doomed to failure. (Ford, Odalla, and Chorlton, 2003, p. 112)

How can youth be protagonists in their own learning in rural South African settings hard hit by HIV and AIDS? How, as 'knowledge producers' (Pattman, 2006; Mitchell et al., 2010), can they become resources to themselves and to the community? How can video production become central to mapping out challenges and solutions? These are some of the questions that have framed our work with young people in community-based video.

The essence of community-based video can be found in the words of a member of a rural community who, upon viewing a video created by other members of the community commented, 'it is easy to understand a thing if it means you sit with him/her and talk about the matter [...] rather than standing in front of them.' This equaling of power relations creates a space for dynamic interaction around topics that have often been kept silent in rural South African communities ravaged by HIV and AIDS, and where communication at various levels, as well as between generations, has been difficult. Video has been used in various ways in social science research, and a distinction between collaborative video and participatory video (which often overlap) is necessary. Sarah Pink (2001) and others refer to collaborative video as a process where the community worker or researcher works with a group of participants to create a video production, while in participatory video the process involves a group of participants primarily constructing their own video texts with only minimal assistance from the research team. In our work with young people and video, we see community-based video as encompassing at different times both collaborative and participatory forms and, indeed, following from the work of Nair and White (2003) and Mak (2006), we include in our consideration of community-based video the idea that participation refers not only to the ways in which community members are involved with creating the video narrative as part of the production process but also to the ways in which the video text itself can function as a catalyst or trigger in post-screening discussions with other members of the community.

Beyond the obvious participation of youth, we also highlight in our work the participation of adults such as teachers in the community. Teachers often have not had exposure to human rights frameworks that support the rights of children, and may not realize how significant the voices of youth could be in combating violence in and around schools, in participating in classroom management (as an alternative to corporal punishment, for example), in addressing HIV and AIDS, and so on. We are seeing the value of creative and participatory approaches (Mitchell et al., 2005; Mitchell, 2006; Moletsane et al., 2007; de Lange, 2008). These strategies involve those methods that have a strong media base such as photography and video, including indigenous media, as well as those that draw on other arts-based and participatory approaches such as drama and role play, writing, and the uses of literature.

How do youth knowledge producers work within a community-based video framework? In our video-making projects, participants work in small groups of five to seven. The process itself is broken down into several parts:

(1)   'In my life' brainstorming: what are the issues that we see as critical to address in our lives?
(2)   Choosing democratically which topic or issue to focus on for the video.
(3)   Direct instruction on the use of video cameras, storyboarding, and what we call the 'NER' (no editing required) approach.
(4)   Storyboarding and planning-out seven or eight scenes for a short video in small groups.
(5)   Shooting the video (with all members having opportunities to perform and operate the video camera).
(6)   Reviewing the final product (and reshooting if necessary).
(7)   Public screening to other groups.
(8)   Follow-up discussion and reflection on the process and the issues.

There are a number of critical processes that contribute, we argue, to the overall engagement of young people in interrogating identity and taking action: reflexivity itself; constructedness and the idea of constructing a story line and resolution; and collectivity and the role of group processes (particularly in the context of addressing the social determinants of HIV and AIDS – gender inequalities, poverty, and so on).

An additional component to our research with community video is to work with a videographer to produce more extended composite videos that are made up of the short videos made by the participants plus some footage and analysis that offer a context for various community members to view and respond to the issues. Throughout, the focus is on the process, on community engagement, on dialogue, and ultimately the possibilities for social action.

References

de Lange, N. (2008). Women and community-based video: Communication in the age of AIDS. *Agenda*, 22(7), pp. 19–31.

Ford, N., Odalla, D., and Chorloton, R. (2003). Communication from a human rights perspective: Responding to the HIV/AIDS pandemic in eastern and Southern Africa. *Journal of Health Communication*, 8(6), pp. 111–117.

Mak, M. (2006). Unwanted images: Tackling gender-based violence in South African schools through youth artwork. In F. Leach and C. Mitchell (Eds.), *Combating Gender Violence in and around Schools* (pp. 113–123). Stoke-on-Trent, UK: Trentham Books.

Mitchell, C. (2006). Taking pictures, taking action: Visual arts-based methodologies in research as social change. In T. Marcus and A. Hofmaenner (Eds.), *Shifting the Boundaries of Knowledge* (pp. 227–241). Pietermaritzburg, South Africa: University of KwaZulu-Natal Press.

Mitchell, C., de Lange, N., Moletsane, R., Stuart, J., and Buthelezi, T. (2005). Giving a face to HIV and AIDS: On the uses of photo-voice by teachers and community health care workers working with youth in rural South Africa. *Qualitative Research in Psychology*, 3(2), pp. 257–270.

Mitchell, C., Stuart, J., de Lange, N., Moletsane, R., Buthelezi, T., Larkin, J., and Flicker, S. (2010). What difference does this make? Studying Southern African youth as knowledge producers within a new literacy of HIV and AIDS. In C. Higgins and B. Norton (Eds.), *Language and HIV/AIDS*. Clevedon, UK: Multingual Matters.

Moletsane, R., de Lange, N., Mitchell C., Buthelezi, T., Stuart, J., and Taylor, M. (2007). Photo-voice as an analytical and activist tool in the fight against HIV and AIDS stigma in a rural KwaZulu-Natal school. *South African Journal of Child and Adolescent Mental Health*, 19(1), pp. 19–28.

Nair, K. and White, S. (2003). Trapped: Women take control of video story-telling. In S. White (Ed.), *Participatory Video: Images that Transform and Empower* (pp. 195–214). Thousand Oaks, CA: Sage Publications.

Pattman, R. (2006). Making pupils the resources and promoting gender equality in HIV/AIDS education. *Journal of Education*, 38, pp. 89–115.

Pink, S. (2001) *Doing Visual Ethnography*. London: Sage Publications.

1994). What Orner draws our attention to, however, is the fact that some instances of self-expression or youth voice can work to merely reinforce older, entrenched forms of power. Nicole Fleetwood's (2005) study of a youth video program highlights this point.

For her study, Fleetwood spent time working with a racially diverse group (although most were African-American) of young women in a summer media-production program in San Francisco, California. The video the youth were to produce was 'decidedly about youth and was to be shot from youths' perspectives' (Fleetwood, 2005, p. 155). This goal is hardly unique and in fact, as Fleetwood (2005) explains, 'similar to mass media and popular culture in the United States, youth-based media arts organizations share a common goal – a drive, that is – to document an authentic urban experience from the perspective of racialized youth' (p. 156). In working on this project, however, what Fleetwood discovered is that, when young people are invited to produce so-called authentic representations about their lives, the results can be problematic. More often than not, what youth produce is not authentic as much as it is a reproduction of the racialized stereotypes and identities that are used to categorize and isolate specific young people in contemporary culture. As Elizabeth Soep (2006) summarizes, 'media projects have a tendency to pursue the fantasy of "authentic" youth experience' but this goal often ends up producing 'sensationalized portrayal[s] of racialized urban youth' (p. 201). The problem with this is that the work then ends up reifying entrenched social inequalities, even if the youth media program intended to undermine these very inequities.

Further to this problem, Sara Bragg (2007) has demonstrated that an emphasis on youth voice can have a disciplining role on young people.

What Bragg means is that the call to have young people pursue their own self-expressions can be a way of managing youth conduct. The push to have young people become spokespersons for themselves and for their lives can in a sense become a way of governing (in Michel Foucault's sense) youth behavior. After all, Bragg points out, when we invite students to take responsibility for their own stories and to tell these stories to the world, we are, in an important way, asking them to become certain kinds of 'enterprising subjects.' The danger this creates, Bragg (2007) notes, is that in calling for youth to act this way educators are instilling 'norms of individualism, self-reliance and self management, which resonate with new configurations of power and authority under neo-liberalism' (p. 343). The call for youth to develop their own voices can mask a more subtle form of regulation – one that does not enable youth agency as much as it manages that agency in a way that fits with the needs of a global information economy.

Fleetwood's and Bragg's studies point to some of the social, cultural, and political forces that intervene whenever young people engage in creative work. The need to pay attention to these forces has led educators, youth, and others to look beyond questions of voice in thinking about how production practices foster youth agency. Inevitably, this has raised questions about the dialogic nature of production and the way creative practices relate to normative questions, including the relationship of production to the participation of young people in public life. In the next section, it is to these issues that our discussion turns.

Media production, dialogic experiences, and the making of public life

The idea that media production can contribute to young people's agency by fostering an analysis of power relations and the social conditions that shape kids' lives has a powerful appeal among media educators. At least in part this is due to the fact that production practices themselves seem to position young people dialogically in relation to the larger social world in which we live. In other words, creative practices place youth in conversation with others and with the sedimented social discourses and cultural practices that shape our experiences. Creative work is not so much the vision of an isolated artist, in other words, as it is the result of an inherently social process.

In practical terms, the social nature of production is probably most apparent because group work dominates the way zines, videos, and other media are made in institutionally mediated youth programs. This is the case for two reasons. First, group work helps to leverage limited technical resources to give a greater number of kids access to the means of production. Second, group work tends to encourage attention to the process of production as much as to the final product. From the perspective of educators, the advantage is that this encourages youth to engage with others, to discuss why certain choices are being made, and quite possibly, to discuss what aesthetic and socio-political implications these choices have in relation to one's audience or to youths' social positioning as gendered, raced, and class-bound subjects. Of course, these questions do not always arise. Most often they are the outcome of a process of analysis and questioning initiated by educators working with young people (Drotner, 2008). It is of note that research also suggests that group work may not always be beneficial to youth producers (Goldfarb, 2002; Buckingham, 2003a; Buckingham, Niesyto, and Fisherkeller, 2003; Poyntz, 2008). The most common problem is that, while group work may be necessarily social, it can lead to compromises that produce flat, generic storytelling that has little to do with meaningful and rich dialogue about the social, political, and cultural dimensions of kids' lives.

Beyond group work, Elizabeth Soep (2006) has offered a somewhat different explanation for why creative practices situate youth in dialogic relations with others. Soep's study draws on data and experiences gathered over a decade of working with youth media arts programs. In contemplating her experience, Soep notes that what often goes unrecognized in thinking about media work is the way youth speak in 'double-voiced discourse' throughout the production process. The notion of double-voiced discourse comes from the work of the Russian literary critic Mikhail Bakhtin (1981). What Bakhtin wanted to draw attention to with this idea was the way the words of others 'enter a speaker's utterance in a concealed form' (Soep, 2006, p. 202). When we speak, Bakhtin argued, our own voices are formed in and through our inclusion of the voices of others. In this sense, our own voices are mediated by multiple voices. One voice is never singular but is actually an articulation of many voices. Using this idea, Soep (2006) goes on to analyze a youth media program, showing the way young people inevitably 'weave various voices into their own utterances, particularly as they prepare and assess their own creative projects' (p. 202). Youth are often unaware of this process; nonetheless, what one hears in their voices is a kind of 'crowded talk,' an intertextual form of speaking woven through a mixing together of one's own words with the words of others. Crowded talk refers to the way teenagers' own words are always a kind of remix, one that is made possible by kids' relations with others. Soep concludes from this analysis that production work is profoundly social, even if these social relationships and their effects on youth participants are not always addressed explicitly (see also Weber and Mitchell, 2008).

The work of developing production pedagogies that explicitly address the social and political concerns that arise through creative practices is complicated. Community-based media programs have shown some real success in leading this work. In fact, the idea that media production can contribute to young people's agency by fostering an analysis of the power relations and social conditions that shape kids' lives has been a dominant preoccupation in community media programs. There are various reasons for this. (For a discussion of how one such program has facilitated young people's involvement in public life, see the sidebar YOUTH RADIO by Elisabeth Soep.)

In general, community-based media initiatives around the world are united in the belief that media can be localized. Radio and television, newspapers and magazines, or, now, electronic communication networks can be appropriated by amateur producers to tell stories about the places and issues that shape our lives (Jankowski, 2002). In the history of the community video movement in Canada and the US, this has led to important visions about the ability of local media producers to challenge the power and authority of mainstream commercial and public broadcasters. By taking advantage of portable video and now digital media, the idea has been that students, artists, and social activists can 'participate in the production of images that [...] shape their culture. [...] Through [this], the mystique of production [is] shattered' and video is turned into a 'vehicle through which the social world [can] be [...] documented' and the public sphere remade (Berko, 1989, p. 289). Between the 1960s and 1980s in the US, this sentiment fed the development of the first 16-millimetre film production workshops for inner city teenagers at Buffalo's Channel of Soul and the Film Club in New York. Later it would inform the development of production workshops for young people at non-profit video centers and cable access television stations, such as Appalshop in Appalachia in the Eastern US and Downtown Community Television and the Paper Tiger Television Collective in New York. In Canada, the sentiment further influenced the development of the National Film Board's Challenge for Change program between 1968 and 1980 as well as the creation of various youth media programs developed by film institutes, local community arts groups, and other organizations throughout the 1990s and 2000s (Kline, Stewart, and Murphy, 2006; Poyntz, 2008; Stack, 2008).

Youth Radio

Elisabeth Soep, Youth Radio

Someone is always on a deadline at Youth Radio, a Peabody Award-winning youth-driven production company headquartered in downtown Oakland, California, with bureaus and correspondents in every region of the US and around the world. But, even by the newsroom's busy standards, the first few weeks in January 2009 were especially intense. Youth Radio's reporters and producers range in age from 14 to 24 and come into the organization primarily from resource-strapped and rapidly resegregating US public schools. Recruitment targets young people who have been marginalized from digital privilege and social capital. They begin with introductory multimedia classes and advance through specialized courses and eventually into paid positions as peer educators, engineers, and media-makers working across platforms and delivering content to local, national, and global outlets.

During the first month of 2009, Youth Radio's newsroom was producing three series that were simultaneously coming to a head. The first, based in Oakland, centered on an unarmed young black man named Oscar Grant who had been shot by a white police officer at a public transit station on New Year's Day. The shooting unleashed street protests that led to young activists' arrests before the officer himself was charged with murder. The second series, with its center of gravity in Washington, DC, culminated in the inauguration of Barack Obama as President of the US. Obama made it to the White House riding a wave of energy and organization from young voters, who supported him in record numbers. The third series, based in the Middle East, featured dispatches from young Palestinians and Israelis reporting from the front lines of an Israeli assault that kept many Gaza residents cloistered with family members in the safest rooms they could find in their homes, though several walked the streets daily to document evidence of danger and devastation. Youth Radio's newsroom delivered multiple stories on each of these themes to outlets including National Public Radio, *The Huffington Post*, Public Radio International, MTV News, and iTunes, as well as to popular culture blogs and social media sites across the Internet.

The three series, while vastly different in history, scope, scale, stakes, and character, had some important elements in common. In each one, young people were the main characters in the central action and its aftermath. The stories, in this sense, highlight the often-overlooked roles young people play in global matters of civil rights and citizenship. In all three, young people used media production tools both to *carry out* the events and to *report* on their experiences for massive audiences. They pulled out cell phones to videotape the police officer shooting a restrained Oscar Grant in the back, and soon anyone with access to the Internet could watch the incident from multiple angles on YouTube. Young people fanned out across polling sites in swing states and used open-source platforms to upload interviews with first-time voters on the day of Obama's historic election, extending this kind of coverage through inauguration and beyond. In the Gaza story, when regular phone coverage was spotty at best, young people relied on Skype to record testimonials from bombing sites and shared first-person accounts of what they saw, heard, and felt in real time through blogs read by global audiences.

As a senior producer at Youth Radio, I collaborated with young people on these three stories and, as the organization's research director, I have joined with adult and youth colleagues using ethnographic techniques to analyze our learning as a form of collaborative production. In both of my roles, I have been struck again and again by how young people are redefining and reconfiguring public space through their media production. They tell their stories as they live their stories, integrating digital documentation as a matter of course into a role of witness/participant they define and assign for themselves whenever they see that need and have the requisite tools and skills at their disposal. In the process, they leverage a mediated public space at the same time that physical streets and open places are increasingly over-run, monitored, policed, and militarized.

It is not that action does not unfold in the more conventional public spaces we associate with young lives – street corners, parks, school yards – nor that these contexts for social gathering are any less important today than they once were. Rather, at the same time that more and more of these environments are locked down, they are also opened up to outside onlookers and eavesdroppers by virtue of the digital tools young people carry with them wherever they go. The separation between online engagement and on-the-ground realities blurs, as does the distinction between private and public, between living and transmitting, and between documentation, which implies simply capturing what happens, and provocation, which means telling a story to elicit a response. By deploying media production to blur these boundaries and issue these provocations – for justice, for change, for freedom – young people are creating new through-lines that run across disparate places. They are connecting sites such as a subway station in Oakland, California, a public plaza in Washington DC, and a living room in Gaza to other places of upheaval and potential across the US and around the world.

Of those many initiatives that have developed, the Educational Video Center (EVC) in New York is widely regarded for its work developing programs that involve young people in public life. As a non-profit media organization, EVC aims to help young people investigate how power relations (especially in regard to race, class, gender, sexuality, and ability) shape community deficits, identity relations, and social life (Goodman, 2003, 2005). The group's central goal is 'to build students' skills in documentary production and media literacy while nurturing their intellectual development and civic engagement' (Goodman, 2005, p. 207). It does this most often through a pedagogy of critical literacy that is developed over the course of an 18-week after-school documentary workshop.

In this program, students work together researching, shooting, and editing a film on a community-based social problem of their choosing. Learning to deconstruct media is a key part of the process, so time is given to the analysis of stereotypes in news and youth media and to examining how audio and editing codes, as well as visual, linguistic, and spatial conventions, produce meaning in still and moving images (Goodman, 2005). Students make sense of these conceptual resources by creating videos and applying 'the analytic concepts they have [...] learned' (p. 211). In conjunction with this, EVC has also developed a key set of teaching practices called 'continuous inquiry.' This approach gives 'students the opportunity to move between the personal and public spheres, starting with the self-referential and then reaching beyond themselves to study their community at large' (p. 215). Dialogue-based teaching organized through small group work, alongside opportunities to pose questions, conduct interviews, and challenge adults in positions of authority empower students as they learn to imagine how the world might be otherwise than the way they found it. Clearly student-centered, EVC's production pedagogy demands reflection through a portfolio assessment and exhibitions that 'offer a rich portrait of what students are capable of knowing and doing. They give students an opportunity to publicly show their best work and talk about it with members of the community, including parents, other students, teachers, principals, researchers, producers, and artists' (p. 222).

This model facilitates civic engagement by showing student video-makers how 'to use media as a tool to educate, inform, and make change' (Goodman, 2005, p. 207). Where students' democratic habits of mind are nurtured, it is not by freeing youth from the effects of consumer media culture. Rather, in John Dewey's words, it is by supporting youth to be 'a civically active "articulate public" that has the intellectual capacity to engage in collective dialogue and inquiry into the most pressing social problems' (Dewey quoted in Goodman, 2005, p. 226). Of course, there is also a therapeutic dimension to EVC's programs. This is noted by Goldfarb (2002), who further argues that EVC uses video as 'a means for working through the social and psychological issues that play a role in [...] students' ability to make it through the school system and life' (p. 72). But EVC-produced documentaries are used to facilitate public forums on issues such as school funding, neighborhood violence, and homeless teenagers. The work of EVC students has also reached larger audiences through broadcast on PBS. Thus, from our perspective, EVC highlights how creative youth work can nurture youth in multiple ways, including helping teenagers to become more fully engaged in their communities.

If EVC offers one model that demonstrates how production practices can foster youth agency, other researchers have explored additional strategies for linking creative work to issues of citizenship. Michelle Stack (2008) focuses on youth–adult collaborations as the context for making videos that explore both the pleasurable aspects of media culture and those aspects that need to be 'critically analyze[d] and challenge[d]' (p. 117). Stack's study reports on a unique university media education course she created in a mid-size Canadian city that brought together teenagers from a lower middle class high school and university students, most of whom were training to work as teachers, counselors, or child and youth care workers. Both the high school students and the university students engaged in media literacy discussions before working in small groups (with at least one teenager and one university student) to make videos that explored the role of media consumption and production in their lives. The students' backgrounds with media literacy no doubt influenced their approach to this broad topic (Stack, 2008, pp. 118–119). But Stack notes that the collaborative production process itself created an important opportunity for participating teens to situate their work in a public context.

On the one hand, collaborating with adults forced the youth to define what they meant by a 'youth issue.' Initially, the adult participants did this and listed concerns such as 'eating disorders, drugs, alcohol, and unprotected sex' (Stack, 2008, p. 120). To the high school students, this list represented the 'stuff [they hear about] all the time' in school (quoted in Stack, 2008, p. 121). As such, these were not understood to be youth issues as much as schooling issues. In response, the youth proposed a different set of concerns, including the environment, the war in Iraq, and consumerism. What is interesting about the second list (and the videos that evolved from it) is not that it is necessarily more public or political than the first; rather, the point is that the collaborative working relationship created an opportunity for teenagers to define their understanding of the public issues that matter in their lives. Through this, they not only challenged stereotypes that suggest youth are largely apolitical today; they also began to articulate how politics fits in with their lives and their vision of the future.

On the other hand, production work itself allowed the youth to explore ways of knowing that moved beyond traditional versions of adult (or teacher)–student relationships. Video-making (and other media production practices) typically does not involve information transfer or the kind of fact-based learning that still dominates in many schooling environments. Rather, it allows youth to engage in multiple ways of learning, 'including the artistic and the aesthetic' (Stack, 2008, p. 121; see also Drotner, 2008). What Stack found is that, because of this, teen participants in her study took seriously the power of video as an alternative knowledge source. The appeal of this source, in turn, led 'the youth [to see] themselves as playing a vital role in [...] discovering and generating new knowledge [...] that would lead them and others to a better understanding of the issues they explore in their videos' (Stack, 2008, p. 121). In this sense, the dynamism of media production itself opened up new opportunities for learning, a process that, in turn, led participating youth to take on roles as public actors capable of representing the issues that matter in their lives.

In Poyntz' (2008, 2009) study of a youth media program in Vancouver, Canada, he highlights one further way youth media programs can contribute to young people's democratic participation. Peer-to-peer mentoring has been a feature of informal, community-based youth media production programs since the 1970s. Surprisingly, however, there has been little written about how peer mentorship impacts mentors themselves (Goldfarb, 2002; Charmaraman, 2006). What we do know tends to be focused on psychological or vocational changes that result from mentoring experiences. But peer-mentoring less-experienced media-makers can also have a profoundly democratic influence on how youth see themselves and their social futures.

In Poyntz' year-long ethnography, he followed a group of teenagers hired to mentor less experienced video-makers in a summer media institute. Summer Stories is designed to give low-income kids opportunities to become more actively engaged with contemporary media. Developing creative voices while fostering young people's sense of competency, belonging, and power is a part of this process. So too is promoting media literacy, which is done in Summer Stories by nurturing youths' critical viewing and production habits. Alongside these broader objectives, the role of youth mentors in the program is to support, challenge, and guide novice participants over the course of each production cycle. Mentors are typically former students of the program, ranging from 16 to 20 years of age. Symptomatic of the global influences shaping Vancouver today, the mentors also represent a cross-section of educational levels, socio-economic backgrounds, and cultural and ethnic diversity.

Importantly for our purposes, what Poyntz' study suggests is that peer mentoring is an important way youth begin to see themselves as social beings, as actors whose lives are bound up in a set of contestable relationships with the media environment in which they live. Mentoring demands that young people listen to other youth. It tends to draw attention to the way commercial media scripts insert themselves into the ideas and self-identities of all media producers, but especially those new to any media form. Identifying this process in turn can help mentors understand their own social positioning and how they might respond to this through their work. In this sense, mentoring can foster youths' democratic habits of mind by nurturing a form of thinking and doing that is responsive to others, to the fact that we are all part of a shared world (Arendt, 1968).

For many, media production fosters youth agency by helping youth to see themselves in light of the social, political, and cultural forces that shape and enable experience. The hope is that this will lead to a critical examination of our world and how we act and engage with it now and in the future. The goal of nurturing a critical perspective on contemporary worlds has also been taken up by those interested in media production for less rational ends. Indeed, in the next section, it is to the question of pleasure that we turn our attention.

The problem of pleasure/play and critique

The problem of whether and how to address the thorny nexus that links together adolescence, pleasure, and popular culture has long been a challenge in media education. Where media production is concerned, the stakes have only seemed to rise as more young people have gained opportunities to produce their own work. In part this is because the easy pleasure young people often find in popular media culture has been cause for suspicion within educational discourses. Anything that easy to consume can't be good for you, many argue. Of course, this sentiment has been around for some time and, if it is beginning to wane, pleasure itself – whether linked to media or not – remains a challenge for educators. This is so because pleasure immediately raises questions about the body and thus sexuality. It raises concerns about transgressive behavior that pushes beyond the bounds of 'proper decorum,' and issues about what it is appropriate to address in institutionally mediated learning environments. 'Schooling has traditionally been defined largely in instrumental terms. Along with the explicit goals of imparting knowledge, skills and information, the school has also been implicitly mandated to transmit the norms, language, styles, and values of the dominant culture' (Grace and Tobin, 2002, p. 206). Consequently, questions of pleasure can seem to open a messy and contestable can of worms, pushing many media literacy practitioners, researchers, and scholars to avoid this terrain altogether.

Perhaps because of this, some educators and theorists have been drawn to the challenging role of pleasure in youth media production. At root, this interest revolves around questions about how agency is enabled and fostered when young people explore and leverage the relationship between pleasure and play in media culture and their own identities and possible social futures. More centrally, this work tends to be motivated by larger questions about how our identities are constituted in the first place.

The whole question of identity is complicated and yet central to youth media production, as we saw earlier in this chapter. To begin unpacking this problematic question, it is worthwhile to note that our identities involve personal, social, and cultural dimensions. More, given that our identities are shaped by our personal biographies *and* our relationships with others, including other things (like the artifacts and practices found in consumer media culture and the media produced by youth), we can say that none of these dimensions of our selves is ever really static. Rather, as the relationships between our selves and our social and cultural worlds change, our identities also shift. This does not mean that we never achieve periods of relative stability in our self-identities. It just means that our identities are never ultimately fixed. They are in a sense always becoming. They are enacted in and through the social conditions, cultural relationships, and political imperatives that situate our lives and position our personal biographies. Our personal biographies, or what cultural theorist Stuart Hall (1996b) calls our self-narratives, are not, however, merely a reflection of the social and cultural worlds we inhabit; as our self-narratives develop, they too afford us with a sense of direction, a sense of agency about how to engage with and shape the worlds we encounter in our lives.

A nice way to summarize this idea is to suggest that our identities are not things at all; they are – to borrow a phrase offered by Sandra Weber and Claudia Mitchell (2008) – 'identities-in-action' (p. 27). Identities are really a set of practices and 'story-ings' that take shape through our activities and histories with others, including other things such as the commercial media that surrounds our lives or the creative media kids produce. Where the role of pleasure in youth media production is concerned, this idea of identity is important, because with it space is opened to consider how the aesthetic dimension, including play and fun, constitutes and is involved with young people's production.

Of course, pleasure is almost always an aspect of youths' relationships with media. It is often what draws kids to certain media texts and that which has a deep bearing on how youth approach making media. Because of this, Leander and Frank (2006) argue that a key part of understanding media production as a social practice 'involves understanding how individuals relate to images aesthetically – as pleasing, stylish, "cool," beautiful, or tasteful' (p. 185). In a sense, the aesthetic, or the pleasurable, is a kind of glue that binds together the affective relationships between media production and kids' personal, social, and cultural lives. For many media educators, this point is beyond doubt. In fact, in a very practical sense, we have known for some time now that the pleasures of creative work – that is, the appeal of collaboration; the possibilities of sharing work with one's peers; opportunities to dress up, make jokes, or just have a laugh; and so on – are a significant part of the appeal of media production in education (Buckingham, 2003b). But pleasure is more than just a motivating force in production work. As evidenced in a study by de Block and Rydin (2006) examining the production and exchange of a series of videos made by refugee and migrant youth, for instance, certain forms of pleasure can also function as codes of belonging among diverse groups of youth.

In the European project Children in Communication about Migration, six media clubs were set up for children aged 10–14 in six European countries (Germany, Greece, Italy, the Netherlands, Sweden, and the UK). The clubs met weekly after school over a year, producing videos and exchanging them over the Internet on themes such as education, peer relations, families, and intercultural communication. Among the productions was a subset of rap videos. In examining these productions, de Block and Rydin (2006) note that the youth found pleasure working in this genre not only because they liked rap 'fashions, language, dance, graffiti, videos and [the] associated technology' (p. 300). The pleasures found in these resources were also related to the way they functioned as codes of belonging that linked together 'the feeling of social exclusion among immigrant boys from very diverse backgrounds' (pp. 299–300). In other words, pleasure was not only tied to personal appeal; additionally, to know and love rap was a sign of social awareness, an indication of shared experience and respect that bound kids together who were otherwise separated by geography, language, cultural heritage, and history. Pleasure was not just bait in the production process, then, but a kind of glue that bound together the social and political lives of disconnected immigrant youth.

In the context of global consumer cultures and the ongoing commodification of hip hop, it is of course possible to over-romanticize the relationship between rap and youths' meaningful social engagement, as de Block and Rydin (2006) note in their study. At the same time, their work offers a sense of how the dimensions of pleasure and play are important in fostering youth agency in media production. This theme is taken up more explicitly in a study by Grace and Tobin (2002), which looks at how children's agency might be furthered by allowing elementary students to create videos according to their own tastes and interests without the usual restrictions on content that is common with school projects. The intention behind the project was to assess how video production could help foster children's literacy practices in the context of a child-centered pedagogy that challenged typical classroom hierarchies between teachers and students.

For Grace and Tobin (2002), what this exercise served to demonstrate is that video production can become a powerful means through which 'students can play with the boundaries of language and ideology and enjoy transgressive collective pleasures' (p. 196). With fewer constraints over what could be imagined, this approach gave the students freedom to explore and parody the meanings and messages within popular culture, as well as to experiment with and celebrate their own sense of joy at the physicality of being on camera, performing gestures, facial expressions, and sound effects. 'Fueled by the desire to surprise, amuse, and entertain, the content of some of these videos was [of course] of questionable taste, including depictions of drool, burps, blood, [...] violence, and occasional severed body parts' (Grace and Tobin, 2002, p. 200). But, as Grace and Tobin note, at root the young producers were also mobilizing forms of parody and taboo associated with what Mikhail Bakhtin (1984) called the 'carnivalesque.'

For Bakhtin, the carnivalesque describes instances where laughter, bodily pleasures, and bad taste are used as expressions of freedom, pleasure, and desire. Bakhtin argues such expressions have been historically important among those with little social power. With few other resources, the bawdy and the body become sites of contestation, a way to challenge systems of order or figures of authority by those on the outside of power. In a like vein, Grace and Tobin (2002) suggest that we see 'the parodic, the fantastic and the horrific, the grotesque, and the forbidden' in the children's videos as an affront to the normal hierarchies and restrictions that govern students' lives in the classroom (p. 201). The excessiveness and silliness of the children's videos is thus an expression of agency, a transgressive challenge to the learning environments where kids spend so much of their days. Of course, Grace and Tobin are aware that foregrounding pleasure in children's media production work can generate unwanted consequences, including harmful language, racial caricatures, and forms of cruelty that are inappropriate in any context. The challenge their study raises, however, is where media educators should draw the line around the role of pleasure in production work.

In the past, a modernist assumption that media education necessarily involves rational, conceptual understanding demonstrated through distanced, critical analysis of texts has carried the day. What we are learning more and more, however, is that young people's relationships with media culture and media production are never only rational. Media relationships are always embodied and involved with questions of desire, pleasure, and play. These dimensions filter through the affective intensities we all feel toward certain media texts and production practices. This does not mean that we should excuse the morally and ideologically objectionable practices and representations that can come about when young people produce their own media. It means that 'attempting to assess such work merely in terms of what it tells us about students' conceptual understanding is inevitably reductive' (Buckingham, 2003b, p. 324; also see Bragg, 2000). Pleasure fosters student interest and student understanding. It knits together our self-identities with our social, cultural, and political lives. As such, it cannot be ignored, but must be made susceptible to a kind of understanding, not only in terms of how it nurtures youths' social engagements but in the way it fosters youth identities and learning.

If media production has long been cast as a derivative practice in a media education project that favors the work of critical reading, analysis, and conceptual understanding, it is increasingly becoming clear that this positioning will no longer do. Long on the fringes of media literacy, today creative production work fosters a range of literacies, including competencies that allow young people to express themselves through modalities that extend beyond the written word. Production work is a vital way through which youth come to understand themselves and their social and political worlds. As we move more fully into the new millennium, such work is at the center of creative youth practices, inside schools and throughout the rest of young people's lives. In Chapter 6 and Chapter 7 we examine what this means in terms of digital literacies and new forms of knowing and learning that are at the core of media education today.

6

Literacies: New and Digital

What does it Mean to be 'Literate' Today?

Definitions of literacy have varied through the centuries, but they have for the most part included some combination of the capacity to read and/or write. In the contemporary era it means, at minimum, the ability to read and comprehend simple texts; thus, 'functional literacy' – as coined by the US army – is the ability to interpret and respond to written instruction. But what does it mean to be 'literate'? In one context, this may mean having read and appreciated Charles Dickens. In another, it may mean having the sufficient scribal skills to escape a Dickensian nightmare. In other contexts, it could be a means to empowerment and critical consciousness for individuals or communities. And in yet another, it may be a child's first day of reading. Given that we would not refer to a preliterate child as 'illiterate,' it is clear that literacy has not been a value-neutral term. While literacy may be a means to empowerment, in other words, it has also been a regulatory force, a marker of, and a means to social status.

While literacy has primarily referred to reading and writing print texts, it has also morphed into a catch-all term for various cultural 'competencies,' such as those the terms financial or emotional 'literacy' suggest. Our use of the term 'media literacy' in this book does not imply an association with this competency-driven open-ended use of the term. Rather, we see the legacies of literacy (Graff, 1987) as including a trajectory of communication and reasoning tools inherited from primarily oral cultures and now overlaid with the legacies of print literacy, the modern communication media, and the new digital media. Our focus is on the latter two.

Media Literacies: A Critical Introduction, First Edition. Michael Hoechsmann and Stuart R. Poyntz.
© 2012 Blackwell Publishing Ltd. Published 2012 by Blackwell Publishing Ltd.

Media Literacy 1.0 is the pedagogical response to the era of modern communication, an era stretching from the mid-nineteenth century to today (although in modified form) that includes technological developments such as the telegraph, the photograph, the electric light bulb, the daily newspaper, film, radio, and television, as well as cultural developments such as modern advertising, department stores, movie theatres, and in-home entertainment. The legacies of that era live on into the present, and we are keenly aware that a Media Literacy 2.0 does not supplant a Media Literacy 1.0, but rather both augments and transforms it.

Given that much of the cultural impact of modern communication was in the realm of leisure, school systems have for the most part resisted viewing media literacy as a necessary corollary of a traditional print literacy curriculum. Exceptions have existed, as we acknowledge in our brief history of media education programs in Chapter 1, but it is nonetheless the case that, until recently, media literacy has mainly been a marginalized, add-on component of school curricula. With the arrival of digital media, however, there is a new impulse in schooling systems to incorporate communication technology into the curriculum and into classroom pedagogy. We argue that the urgent implementation of pedagogical and curricular adoptions of digital technologies into schools has everything to do with their rapid adoption into both professional and leisure communication practices, though primarily the former. The conception of literacy that has been mobilized in public discourse in most eras or contexts has been intimately related to the needs of workplaces, to produce citizens that can be productively integrated into working lives. And it is no different today, as schools strive to enlarge the agenda of literacy to include the digital domains.

This development presents an opportunity for media education to expand its parameters into the center, rather than the periphery, of schooling and to articulate a Media Literacy 2.0 that is central to the formation of children and youth. Teaching the new media presents a particular challenge, however, for, just as young people experience new media in an immersive media environment, many adolescents are immersed in new media learning outside of school walls. To some extent, teaching Media Literacy 2.0 in school is like teaching agriculture in a farming community; in other words, many of the students in the classroom are learning about the subject in their everyday lives and need new perspectives, not new basics. To go forward with a vision of Media Literacy 2.0, then, we need to develop a deeper understanding of the everyday

practices of youth with new media and to contend with expanded definitions of literacy. We also need to be attentive, however, to the formative and
still substantial role educators can and must play in developing young
people's media literacies. One problem today may be that there is uncertainty over what role schools and other learning institutions can play in
nurturing what we call Media Literacy 2.0. To address this, in this chapter,
we look at the rethinking of literacy that has been ongoing since the 1980s.
We then situate the development of new media literacies in relation to the
ongoing role learning institutions must have if the full potential of Media
Literacy 2.0 is to be achieved.

Expanded Literacies

While there are a wide variety of approaches to the implementation of media
and technology in schools, some of which draw on media education
traditions and some of which do not, there are also widely differing
discourses in scholarly circles on what constitutes 'literacy' today, each
of which has radically distinct implications for how media, technology, and
literacy are considered and taught. Here, we wish to address digital literacies,
largely in relation to a discussion of new literacies. Taken together, these
discourses will form the basis for our vision of what we call Media Literacy
2.0. To historicize this new conceptual model, we need to begin with a brief
introduction to the history of literacy.

Literacy, as construed up to the very recent past, has typically referred to
the capacity to read and write the written word. Sometimes, the term has
also been used to invoke a quality of writing or a depth of appreciation, as
the use of the adjective 'literate' can imply (e.g., 'this highly literate
interpretation of Shakespeare's *The Tempest* moved the audience to tears').
Other times, and perhaps more frequently in the late twentieth century,
literacy has been used to describe the lowest common denominator of
participation in a literate culture (as in the use of the qualifier 'functional'
literacy on the part of adult learners and 'early' literacy on the part of
children). Each of these uses of the term assumes that literacy is a normal
condition, a way of being and a set of abilities toward which all should strive
and from which we can interpret cultural competence. And indeed, there is
no doubt that cultural participation and cultural capital are realized
through various levels of literacy competency. It is indicative of this that
the United Nations has published literacy benchmarks for international

development for years, suggesting that countries will raise their GDPs (gross domestic products) based on the literacy levels of their populations.

While these kinds of indicators seem to make intuitive sense, we note that literacy in and of itself cannot guarantee much for individuals. The notion that it can forms the foundation of the 'autonomous' model (Street, 1984), an approach that treats literacy as a skill or technique that can be analyzed apart from situated practices and everyday life. On the other hand, as proponents of New Literacy studies have argued, literacy depends on a social context in which the competencies and skills of literacy are understood as useful and meaningful (see Lankshear and Knobel, 2006, p. 16). The ability to read and write (or to engage in other forms of literacy) only matters, in other words, in relation to a social environment where these competencies are valued and can be used. Outside of such environments, such literacy skills and competencies have little bearing. Literacy, in this sense, has a fundamentally social dimension. It depends on the acquisition of skills and access to and participation in social settings where those skills allow one to do certain kinds of highly valued things. As Lankshear and Knobel (2006) state: 'Literacies are bound up with social, institutional and cultural relationships, and can only be understood when they are situated within their social, cultural and historical contexts' (p. 12; see also Gee, Hull, and Lankshear, 1996). Thus, to be literate means to practice meaning-making under certain conditions and in relation to particular social worlds. Once we begin to think of literacy in this way, it is a short step to conclude that literacy is also linked to social identities – to being the kind of people we are and hope to be. For instance, it is difficult to separate the meaning of 'illiteracy' from the social class or social group connotations it carries (Lankshear and Knobel, 2006).

Of course, if literacy involves social relationships, there is also a longer history of its ascendance in scholarship and education that is relevant to new media literacies. This story traces a Eurocentric lineage through the development of so-called Western culture. The significance of tracing literacy's genesis is not one of choosing sides, nor of giving too much value to the cultural contributions of particular cultures. In fact, certain key moments in the genealogy of literacy that have been attributed to classical Greece or pre-Renaissance Europe were coproduced by other cultures, in particular cultures centered in the Islamic world. The story of literacy that brings us to modern and postmodern writing systems, however, tends to be traced back to the invention of the phonetic alphabet in ancient Greece. For many scholars and historians, the quality of the phonetic alphabet that enabled its

ascendancy was its economy. A limited number of symbols, which represented sounds rather than objects, could be used to represent an infinite
number of mental concepts, material things, and those elements of language
that enable fully articulated sentences (i.e., words such as 'this,' 'and,' 'of,'
'because,' and so on). A stable textual language system such as the Greek
alphabet also allowed scholars to write down epic stories and emerging
theoretical arguments (early philosophy) that began to evolve as an emerging
record of human thought, endeavor, and stories. In this sense, the alphabet
enabled the cultural system from which emerged the archive and the library.
As Jack Goody (1977) remarks, this 'frozen speech' enabled critical analysis,
or what he refers to as the 'scepticism of scepticism.' Rather than the circular
and performative nature of oral communication, where repetition and
the use of 'tropes' (i.e., key words understood by the audience to represent
a series of pre-existing premises) were drawn on to persuade people of
the veracity and/or value of what was being said, 'frozen speech' developed
new benchmarks for what should be taken seriously.

Characteristic examples of these benchmarks include: the authority of the
written word (i.e., the faith in written and signed contracts and the
presumption that what has been published by reputable sources, such as
in *The New York Times* or by Cambridge University Press, is true and
accurate); the cultural centrality of linear narrative (in which stories and
treatises are constructed with a clear beginning, middle, and end); the idea
that knowledge is a limited resource (the specialty of authors, teachers, and
experts); and the notion that social and economic participation depend on
at least 'functional' literacy. Of course, it is of single importance that *none of
these benchmarks require actually having to read or write*. Rather, they speak
to culturally embedded notions about the value and values of literacy that
have formed over time. The benchmarks of print literacy are, in other words,
a mind-frame – a lay literacy that is a 'fall-out from the use of the alphabet in
Western cultures [. . .] [They are] a distinct mode of perception in which
the book has become the decisive metaphor through which we conceive of
the self and its place' in the world (Illich, 1987, p. 9).

New Literacies and New Ways of Thinking and Doing

Recognizing the characteristics of a book-centered mind-frame is important
because it is precisely this form of literacy that is in transition today, given
the various new 'literacies' that are emerging. The new literacies are part of a

developing cultural ethos being shaped by a changing ontology of meaning production:

> To say that 'new' literacies are ontologically new is to say that they consist of a different kind of 'stuff' from conventional [that is to say, print-centered] literacies we have known in the past. It is the idea that changes have occurred in the character and substance of literacies that are associated with larger changes in technology, institutions, media and the economy, and with the rapid movement toward global scale in manufacture, finance, communications, and so on. (Lankshear and Knobel, 2006, p. 24)

On the one hand, the stuff of new literacies refers to the new social practices that are developing given the increasingly central role of digital tools across all the significant areas of our lives, including work, education, politics, and entertainment and leisure. At the center of these social practices are new skills and new ways of producing and distributing meaningful cultural texts and experiences through digital code.

To put this in perspective, consider the kinds of digitally enabled practices that typify the new literacies today. Many would include at least some of the following: playing a first-person shooter video game, finding a bus schedule online, watching and 'favoriting' a video on a social media site, making a budget using spreadsheet software, posting and tagging a photograph on a social networking site, writing an essay using embedded tables and graphs, purchasing a book online, developing a software application for sharing or sale, sending an e-mail, writing and maintaining a blog, participating on a fanfiction site, searching the Internet for images of attractive people, selling t-shirts online, using mobile media to communicate, texting friends, downloading and listening to music, editing videos, checking sports scores on an online newspaper, or checking the authenticity of someone's writing on a plagiarism filter site. Some of these practices are obviously more important than others, but the point is that they speak to the range of relationships, technologies, and institutions that are involved with digitally mediated experience today.

On the other hand, the stuff of new literacies also includes forms of participation with new communication technologies that are independent of keyboards, mouses, and joysticks. These forms of participation have to do with a newly developing lay literacy (Illich, 1987); a cultural ethos that is not a material communicative practice but is related to what Lankshear and Knobel (2006) call the insider 'mindset' (p. 34). The insider mindset is distinguished from a newcomer mindset, which is reserved for those with limited or no experience in '"post-typographic" forms of text and text production' (p. 24). Some of the new lay literacies or mindsets that are evolving in conjunction with the increasing use of digital technologies include: the assumption that many perspectives are better than just a few (Tapscott and Williams, 2006); that you can learn the new literacies in part on your own if you are motivated to do so (Gee, 2003); that culture is co-created (Lessig, 2008); and that, in the era of two-way media flow, grassroots voices can challenge the mainstream media (Jenkins, 2006a).

While there is a compelling case to be made for new lay literacies or mindsets, and for the power of the new technologies to transform our lives, some caveats are in order. In this era of dazzling new machines that facilitate the creation, distribution, and discovery of multimodal texts, we are easily tempted to confuse certain surface changes with much more substantial shifts in our social and cultural realities. According to the cultural historian Paul Ceruzzi (1986), the computer as defined today did not exist in 1940: 'Before World War II, the word computer meant a human being who worked at a desk with a calculating machine, or something built by a physics professor to solve a particular problem, used once or twice, and then retired to a basement storeroom' (p. 188). In the intervening years, the computer has emerged, first as a bit player in university basements and increasingly, by the dawn of the new millennium, as a ubiquitous technology in all social and institutional realms of advanced economies.

Increasingly, the discourse of digital futures is used as proof that we have changed, socially and culturally. As Kevin Robins and Frank Webster (1999) point out, 'the idea of technological revolution has become normative – routine and commonplace – in our technocultural times' (p. 1). Arguably, it is the speed of change that so mesmerizes us in the present day (Virilio, 1986); we are, to a great extent, overwhelmed by the quantity of changes as much as their qualitative effects. Where a strong dose of hyperbole pervades some discussions around new technologies and new literacies, however, it is undeniable that they have changed the way we inhabit our lifeworlds (as discussed throughout Chapter 2), particularly in relation to how we communicate with one another and how we access knowledge (Castells, 2001; Barney, 2004; Bakardjieva, 2010). As a result, literacy, whether new or multiple, digital or traditional, has assumed a place of importance in public and educational debates worldwide. It is a competence that is indispensable in the twenty-first century, yet its very qualities are the subject of intense contestation and uncertainty in educational and governmental circles.

Digital Literacies and 'Top-Down' Approaches

Where digital literacy is concerned, the importance of student work with digital technologies was conveyed to schools as far back as the 1980s, when children's early fascination with computers suggested that digital technologies would be ideal for cultivating active learners. This approach received further impetus through efforts by most Western governments to make digital literacy a national objective during the 1990s (Tapscott, 1998; Kline, Stewart, and Murphy, 2006). What came out of these efforts was a broad if shifting consensus that training in digital video and multiple literacies are a necessary part of preparing all young people for life in the new information economy (Cazden et al., 2000 [1996]; Luke, 2000, 2002; Goldfarb, 2002; Kline, Stewart, and Murphy, 2006). For instance, in 2006, the Department for Education and Skills in the UK argued:

> Technology is an essential and inescapable part of 21st Century living and learning. All aspects of school life are enhanced and enabled with technology. Technology is crucial to making sure that each individual maximizes their potential through the personalization of their learning and development. (quoted in Livingstone, 2009, p. 23)

In Australia, North America, the UK, and New Zealand, these sorts of observations fuelled an increase in information technology courses – in graphic design, website authoring, and digital video production – in schools (Luke, 2000; Livingstone, 2002; Goodman, 2005; Buckingham, 2006b, 2006c). While this development is encouraging, less evident is whether this uptake of digital literacies in schools has nourished richer and more meaningful learning environments (Gandy, 2002; Goodman, 2003; Sefton-Green, 2006).

What we do know suggests otherwise, and in fact Julian Sefton-Green, Helen Nixon, and Ola Erstad (2009) tell us that most government policy having to do with digital literacy is designed around 'top-down' approaches that establish particular goals for learning without necessarily taking into account how young people are developing quotidian forms of digital literacy in their everyday use of computers, social media sites, and other digital resources. As a result, while digital literacy is the most widely adopted term in public discourse, the term seems to have a logic of its own. If we drill down a bit, however, the meaning of digital literacy becomes much less evident. In fact, as Lankshear and Knobel (2007) argue, 'digital literacy is actually digital literacies [...] we should think of "digital literacy" as shorthand for the myriad social practices and conceptions of engaging in meaning-making mediated by texts that are produced, received, distributed, exchanged, etc., via digital codification' (p. 11). Complicating how we define and understand digital literacy, however, is the reality that many young people have done most of their digital learning outside of school contexts in a just-in-time manner (learning new skills in the context of completing a task), either in a DIY fashion or with peer assistance. As a result, increasingly, young people are coming into schooling contexts with capacities, skills, and knowledge that far exceed those of their teachers.

Given that many top-down approaches to fostering digital literacy are initiated by politicians and opinion leaders, downloaded to ministries of education or school boards and then trickled down to schools, there is often a disconnection between policy and practice. To a great extent, in fact, the advocates of top-down approaches to digital literacy retrace the footsteps of those who campaigned for universal print literacy, promoting the new tools as essential for citizenship engagement and economic growth. A vision of education for a greater good that promotes economic and/or social participation informs these perspectives, but more often than not they lack direction or a sense of informed outcomes.

One area where 'top-down' initiatives have drawn significant public attention concerns citizenship education, particularly the realm of ethics and questions about cyberbullying. Cyberbullying refers to the use of new media to circulate hurtful or abusive texts about or images of others, and covers both the act of bullying and the circumstances of victimhood. The discourse of cyberbullying seeks to protect young people from the impetuous or retributive actions of others, and to harness the tendency of the bullies to use media to hurt and humiliate others. The broadest definition of cyberbullying encompasses both widely circulated online hate messaging, usually directed at a social grouping, and the more narrowly targeted messaging directed at individuals. Drawing on their survey of youth online behavior, Kaveri Subrahmanyam and Patricia Greenfield (2008) found that 'the anonymity of the Internet produces a disinhibiting effect on [...] racist behaviour' (p. 136). One result is that the most dramatic cases of online racism often 'occur on hate sites targeted to children and teens' (p. 134). At the level of more narrowly targeted incidents of cyberbullying, an extraordinary amount of attention has been given to the online interpersonal transgressions of young people. Drawing attention to these incidents is tremendously important, but we also wonder whether issues of cyberbullying risk turning young people's abusive acts into a problem specific to the online world, when it is clear that these practices reflect longer-established and more entrenched issues of power in our culture. In other words, the problem of bullying and racism did not wait for Web 2.0 to arrive to expose itself, and, while the presence of these practices in online environments requires the attention of educators, this is also part of an ongoing struggle against the kind of abuse that happens across youth social spaces, including sports fields, locker rooms, and street corners.

Perhaps a more common dimension of top-down approaches to digital literacy concerns the economic imperative, which is reflected in the widespread adoption of training in computer skills in school curricula. Here, the goal is to teach young people how to use some of the major workplace-oriented software packages and computer platforms, but in a manner that often limits training to learning soon-to-be redundant basic – or functional – computer skills. Meanwhile, school districts are under intense pressure to purchase ever more sophisticated equipment in good repair and add new resources, even while training initiatives for teachers lag behind the demands of new curriculum initiatives. The upshot is that, while schools are, in many ways, responding to the challenge to teach and integrate digital technology into the school experience, we often see a clash of perspectives between a utilitarian ICT orientation and a creative media education approach (Luke, 2002). Consequently, good teaching in the new technologies is often the luck of the draw: an inspired teacher, a privileged school, or an innovative program for at-risk students. At worst, where digital literacy refers only to schooling practices that allow young people to use their own resources to produce PowerPoint reports for assignments or generate videos and other media as alternatives to written assignments, it becomes just another exercise that privileges the cultural (and economic) capital of middle and upper class kids.

The Role of Learning Environments in Relation to Digital Literacies

In response to this situation, we find Kirsten Drotner's (2008) assessment of the role educational institutions and organizations can play in nurturing young people's digital literacies to be helpful. Drotner, like many of us, argues that it would be a mistake to conclude that schools and other institutional learning environments have no role to play in fostering young people's digital literacies just because kids are learning digital competencies beyond classroom walls. Indeed, she, like us, contends that educators have a profound role to play in shaping the competencies and conceptual knowledge young people need to develop to live full and rich lives in digitally mediated worlds. This is especially true given the fact that – as noted in Chapter 2 – young people are often not as creative with new media as we sometimes think. Moreover, the fact that significant disparities continue to sustain digital divides, not only within nations but between nations and regions around the world (Seiter, 2008), means that schools, after-school programs, and other community-based learning projects remain crucial in helping young people to learn the 'myriad social practices and conceptions of engaging in meaning-making mediated by texts that are produced, received, distributed, exchanged, etc., via digital codification' (Lankshear and Knobel, 2006, p. 11).

In many countries, schools continue to be 'the central social institution in which individuals come together with the specific purpose and possibility of pursuing sustained, joint learning processes' (Drotner, 2008, p. 180). Many know this, but our point is that learning institutions are instrumental for developing young people's concrete experiences of digital media into more conceptual forms of knowledge. This matters because, as Drotner (2008) argues,

> [conceptual knowledge is] needed in order to make abstractions – a key competence that is required to handle complexities and that is therefore in great demand in late-modern societies. Abstractions are also at the core of critique, which is to do with making connections between different problems and with drawing conclusions across seemingly different discourses and practices. (p. 180)

The role of learning institutions is thus both to level the playing field of digital access and to ensure that young people are developing a critical understanding of the technologies and practices they encounter in network societies. Andrew Burn and James Durran (2006) nicely summarize this project in arguing that educators must occupy an 'interstitial space' today, between the domestic use of camcorders and other digital media and the use of these technologies in schools in a way that widens 'the expressive and communicative repertoires of our students to include the variety of [screen] practices and cultures so important in their lives and ours' (pp. 274–275).

Framing the challenge of media education in this manner recalls a key distinction developed by the Soviet psychologist Lev Vygotsky (Vygotsky and Cole, 1978). In recent years, Vygotsky's work on the social conditions shaping children's education and development has been influential, especially among those concerned with socio-cultural approaches to literacy and learning. Vygotsky drew attention to the fact that learning is a fundamentally social enterprise. As Buckingham (2003a) notes in summarizing Vygotsky's position, learning 'depends upon the linguistic (or, more broadly, semiotic) tools and signs that mediate social and psychological processes. Learning is, in this sense, a matter of the acquisition of symbolic codes, which are socially and historically defined' (p. 140). Learning these symbolic codes and concepts is not a matter of simple discovery or spontaneous growth; it is a function of the way children's current knowledge and understanding is situated in relation to new challenges and scaffolds that help young people to develop higher-order concepts. The role of educators in this process is to help scaffold young people's learning so they can develop more complex readings and conceptions of the world and eventually take possession of these conceptualizations as their own.

To capture this process, Vygotsky spoke of a movement between *spontaneous* concepts and *scientific* concepts of knowledge. For media educators, what matters about this distinction is that the former might be understood to refer to the knowledge, understanding, and concrete experience of media culture, including digital technologies, that young people develop by living and acting in media-saturated societies. Scientific concepts, on the other hand, are developed with adult intervention and are meant to allow distance, generalizabilily, and reflection on the nature, practice, and ethics of our media culture. If this distinction is useful, a few cautionary notes are also appropriate.

Perhaps most importantly, while Vygotsky recognized the role of social experience in shaping children's spontaneous knowledge and in positioning teachers to scaffold children's learning, his notion of scientific concepts is also surprisingly asocial. It fails to acknowledge the social interests involved in any production and circulation of knowledge, including 'the relationships between language and social power, or the social functions and uses of language in everyday situations – including classrooms' (Buckingham, 2003a, p. 142). Scientific or key problematics in media education (including those four problematics central to Media Literacy 1.0 noted in Chapter 4) should not, in other words, be understood as objective lenses from which to view the world, nor should a full understanding of media culture be thought of in entirely conceptual terms. After all, as noted in Chapter 5, the affective dimension, the world of play, is crucial to how certain media shapes children's (and our own) lives, including young people's interests in media production.

This said, Vygotsky draws our attention to the key role educators can play in developing young people's understanding of and participation in contemporary media culture. At root, this role is essentially dialogic (Bakhtin, 1981). That is, educators are charged with the task of acknowledging the situated experience and understanding young people bring to a discussion and analysis of media (Cazden et al., 2000 [1996]), and yet, at the same time, their role is to trouble what children and youth think they know about media culture. This includes introducing ideas and concepts that have to do with the technical and design elements of digital media, and asking our students to step back from the technology and/or project at hand to denaturalize it and situate it critically in relation to its social and cultural implications. Through this, the point is to enable young people to interpret media texts and institutions, to make media of their own, and to recognize and engage with the social and political influence of media in everyday life. Ultimately, the goal of this work is to generate what the New London Group (Cazden et al., 2000 [1996]) of literacy scholars call 'transformed practice.' This is a practice or praxis (practice informed by theory and vice versa) that connects young people's out-of-school technological practices with a questioning and reflective approach that recognizes the social and cultural implications of the technologies, institutions, and texts that shape and are part of our lives.

In order to work with, rather than against, emergent mindsets associated with an expanded conception of literacy's evolution in the digital era, we have to learn more about what young people are learning and developing in their spare time. Through this, the intent is to enable young people to develop critical conceptual tools that will help them to interpret media texts and institutions, to make media of their own, and to recognize and engage with the social and political influence of media in everyday life. The concomitant responsibility of educators is thus to develop a nuanced appreciation of how young people are interacting with digital technologies on an everyday basis. In Chapter 7, we examine more closely youth cultural practices in the digital era. Specifically, we present the seven 'C's of contemporary youth digital practices – consciousness, communication, consumption and surveillance, convergence, creativity, copy-paste, and community. Each of these issues is linked to the way media education's key problematics – production, textual form, audiences, and cultural life (discussed in Chapter 4) – operate in relation to the digital media environments young people now inhabit. For each 'C' we offer key ideas about pedagogical practices that can aid in unpacking and exploring these issues with children and youth.

7

Media Literacy 2.0: Contemporary Media Practices and Expanded Literacies

A group of teenagers dances to the wildly popular *Dance Dance Revolution* (*DDR*) video game at an arcade in Los Angeles, California. One takes a picture of this activity with a cell phone and sends it to a friend in Tokyo. This friend includes the image in a mashup video that mixes elements of anime, the original *DDR* song soundtrack, images of herself playing *DDR* at home, and screen shots of Google Earth that demonstrate the distance across the Pacific Ocean between Tokyo and LA. The mashup is later uploaded to YouTube and a link is made to the friend's home page on a social networking site. Subscribers to this person's home page send the link to others and before long a viral audience of thousands have viewed the video. A viewer in Cape Town recognizes an old friend dancing in the video. She looks up the dancer's name on a voice over protocol service and phones the person in Los Angeles. The two old friends smile and laugh over their webcams as they trade stories and catch up on each other's lives. The friend in Cape Town downloads the *DDR* song ringtone for her cell phone to be reminded on a daily basis of this rekindled friendship. The friend in LA looks up background information on anime on the Web and finds a description of this Japanese animation genre on Wikipedia. Later she updates her blog with this story of global communication and hybrid cultural exchange.

This fictional passage tells a story that is not at all implausible in the new media environments that many of the world's young people inhabit. With new tools at their disposal, young people today have the capacity to become more easily what Alvin Toffler (1980) called 'prosumers,' both producers and consumers of media content. And, not only can they create media, but they have broadcast (or 'narrowcast') and distribution possibilities

Media Literacies: A Critical Introduction, First Edition. Michael Hoechsmann and Stuart R. Poyntz.
© 2012 Blackwell Publishing Ltd. Published 2012 by Blackwell Publishing Ltd.

previously unheard of. As well, they have access at their fingertips to a staggering array of information resources, of which the above-mentioned Wikipedia is but one widely heralded example. And they have the use of sophisticated software that can enable them to produce complex texts by creating or copy-pasting. Further, they have the capacity to play interactive games alone, in the presence of others, or virtually with friends or strangers from around the world. Young people can also produce, play, and consult media on the go with mobile devices that enable the capture, distribution, and consumption of media resources on the street, on the bus, or in the home. Finally (as noted in Chapter 2), many youth live in 24/7 interpersonal communication environments, hooked into social networks with peers and strangers and connected with their inner circle of friends and family via instant messaging, texting, and telephone. The implications of these developments are many for social, cultural, and educational interactions, and they create both challenges and opportunities for media literacy.

Clearly, media literacy needs expanded parameters to contend with a new media environment that has dramatically shifted the terms of the field. Youth today experience media as actors in an immersive environment, not just as external spectators of entertainment and information. While Hollywood and Madison Avenue – the old 'mass media' – continue to exert a dominant force in shaping the meaningful narratives of the day, increasingly youth are making media and shaping media flow. Not only have the cultural conditions of growing up changed, in other words, but also the changed nature of communications holds implications for social and economic life in general.

To frame an educational response to these conditions, we focus on seven key conceptual problematics that are at the core of Media Literacy 2.0, and that we have developed based on what we know about how young people are using and interacting with digital media today. We view each in relation to the four concerns – production, textual form, reception, and cultural life – we drew attention to in our heuristic for Media Literacy 1.0 in Chapter 4. We contend, however, that the connection Johnson (1986–1987) saw between the four points in his heuristic for understanding media culture has become more fluid today. Consequently, while we maintain that students of media literacy will be better prepared to encounter and explore the seven problematics we list below once they have developed a clear understanding of how production, textual form, reception, and cultural life operate in and through media culture, we see the following concerns as posing novel remixes of

Media Literacy 1.0 concepts. As such, what follows forms a new set of concerns that result from changes in media technology and shifts in the way media is experienced and used today. Our goal is to map each problematic and offer ideas and resources educators can use to foster young people's meaningful participation and engagement with contemporary digital spheres.

Media Literacy 2.0: The Seven Cs of Contemporary Youth Media Practices

Consciousness

Identity formation is at the heart of young people's biographical trajectory of growing up. As noted in Chapter 5, a consciousness of self in relation to others, and of cultural and subcultural belonging, is intertwined with young people's experiences of communication, consumption, and creation. Indeed, performing and positioning one's identity in real time through material, semiotic means in online environments is a central preoccupation of many youth today. It is the way their 'becoming' unfolds, because increasingly young people are wearing their status on their cyber skins, updating their profiles on social networking sites and managing their status through instant messaging and cell networks. The process of identity performance on the part of young people still includes residual cultural practices associated with fashion and pop music, but it now also involves a rich set of multimodal and textual practices online and on cell phones. Online social networks are in fact complementing and even displacing youth subcultures as vital nodes of youth identity. Digital media have thus become key modalities through which young people are exploring 'the me that is me' (Buckingham and Sefton-Green, 1994, p. 98).

Many educators won't be surprised by this figure, but, to get some scale of young people's level of involvement in online social networking, consider that as of May 2009 one sixth of Internet users worldwide were connected to Facebook, the world's fourth most visited site. According to Alexa Internet, the largest demographic on Facebook is the 18–24-year-old age group (www.alexa.com/siteinfo/facebook.com#), but it is important to note that Alexa Internet does not include under-18s in its demographic profile. Like other popular social networking sites, Facebook allows users to create an online profile, basically a home page that draws on the user-friendly functionality of a Web 2.0 interface. The upshot is that creating one's own web portal is no longer the province of techies. Anyone with Internet access can participate and register their identity in the virtual world. Here, in real time, people can update their 'status,' a double entendre for sharing information and showing off. The identity performances enable the writer to represent themselves in place and time ('I communicate, therefore I am') while allowing the reader to imagine a sense of belonging to a virtual community. The importance of these sites to contemporary youth is enormous. As danah boyd (2007) found in her ethnographic work on kids who use Friendster and MySpace, the rewards of participation stand in contrast to the terror of non-participation. Said one 18-year-old interviewee: 'If you are not on MySpace, you don't exist' (boyd, 2007, p. 1).

For educators, what matters about these developments is that digital media spaces allow young people's cultural identities to materialize in concrete ways. To borrow a concept again from the British cultural theorist Stuart Hall, online spaces such as Facebook facilitate a kind of symbolic 'articulation' that links inner feelings and ideas with the external world. As Drotner (2008) explains in glossing Hall's term, 'we have no direct access to other people's thoughts and emotions, but symbols such as words and text, image and sound offer a means of expressing inner states so that they may be shared by others' (p. 174). Articulation refers both to utterance and making linkage, and, in the latter sense, articulating self-identity and group identity in relation to a broader sense of culture. (The metaphorical root of the linkage is British: the cab and trailer of a lorry, or truck, are 'articulated' together.) To say digital media enable a form of symbolic articulation thus means that they provide spaces where the relationship between our socio-cultural selves and our individuated selves becomes apparent. After all, it is through such spaces that 'identities are constructed, deconstructed, shaped, tested, and experienced' (Weber and Mitchell, 2008, p. 27). But this means digital media, including social networking spaces, offer a tremendous space for critical reflection and analysis.

In particular, such spaces afford opportunities for educators to help young people become conscious of their own *situated-ness* in the world. Multimodal articulations of identity 'are tangible and visible, and so they may be shared, critiqued, and possibly changed through interaction with others' (Drotner, 2008, p. 174). Because they are objectifications of young people's feelings, they also offer a way to talk about key issues in teenager's lives as aesthetic and technical questions, rather than as personal issues. Moreover, because many of the images, sounds, and texts used by young people on Facebook or blogs are drawn from commercial sources, such spaces afford opportunities to examine and deconstruct how ordinary media products are intertwined with young people's self-narratives.

In their work, Jenkins et al. (2006) also address how online spaces can serve as vehicles for youth to take on fictive identities 'and through this process develop a richer understanding of themselves and their social roles' (p. 28). The virtual worlds of video games, for example, provide a space for a re-staging and performance of self that allows for identity play. By creating avatars and participating in virtual environments, youth are able to disinhibit their minds and displace their physical bodies in favor of simulative, performative virtual selves. In creating an avatar for the social network virtual world *Second Life*, for example, a person can try on a different identity, be it by a change as profound as switching gender or race or as simple as altering their manner of dress. The reactions to this new self from other *Second Life* netizens allow the person to experience their identity differently. As well, simulations created by educators and other '*Second Lifers*' allow users to experience different cultures and historical periods, as well as distinct physical environments. (See the sidebar LEARNING IN SECOND LIFE by Jonathan A. Lazare for a more in-depth discussion.) Through such identity performances, young people develop capacities to solve problems from multiple viewpoints, to assimilate information, to exert mastery over core cultural materials, to improvise in relation to a changing environment, and to conceptualize the social conditions that shape their own *situated-ness* in the world (Jenkins et al., 2006, pp. 92–93).

Some evidence (Drotner, 2008; Weber and Mitchell, 2008) suggests that young people may be gaining these new social and cultural perspectives about their identities through their own digital media practices. But we also know that this is more the exception than the rule. We contend in fact that young people's use of online spaces provides a learning opportunity that may not be taken up by children and youth on their own. The role of educators in Media Literacy 2.0 is thus not to ignore or distain teenager's fascination with online games and social networking spaces but to use this engagement as the basis for exploring how identity itself is being articulated, experienced, and remade by youth today.

Communication

In addition to experimenting with their own identities through online spaces, today's tethered teens (Turkle, 2008) are also constantly in contact

Learning in *Second Life*

Jonathan A. Lazare, McGill University

Second Life (*SL*) is an online virtual reality platform that allows users to establish an online identity, explore a virtual world, and collaborate with others to build new environments within it. Introduced by Linden Lab of California in 2003, *SL* has grown to comprise over 15 million accounts, each representing a unique identity within the *SL* world. With opportunities for learning, entertainment, communication, and exploration all feasible within the *SL* reality, the potentials of this evolving platform are literally endless.

Organized as a database of locations – searchable by name, theme, or interest – users select where they would like to visit and what they would like to learn about or experience, and with a click of the mouse they are sent ('teleported') to their desired destinations. *SL* also has a geographic feel, since the different spaces within the platform are spatially located across an *SL* map, each place having specific and unique geographic coordinates. For educators, the platform offers many different prospects for virtual experiential learning for the youngest learners through to university students. For example, strolling through the galleries of the Louvre museum in France, watching a performance in Shakespeare's Globe Theatre in England, and learning about space exploration at a NASA research institute are all possible learning activities in *SL*.

The chance to explore a virtual Morocco and learn about its geography, culture, and lifestyle (while never leaving the classroom) was something unimaginable just a few years ago. Likewise, delving into the psychology of schizophrenia at the University of California, Davis Virtual Hallucinations room is another unique experience. At the UC Davis site, avatars enter the space and begin to hear voices – the voices in one's head that can be symptomatic of psychological disorders. These malicious messages offer a glimpse into the experience of schizophrenia and its delusions, all the while allowing you to keeping a safe distance from any ill patient or the disorder itself. While not a lived experience of the actual medical condition, the simulation, like the others in *SL*, gives a worthy recreation.

If John Dewey's theories (1938) about the value of experience in learning are taken to heart, this kind of technology – and the access that it can offer to learners – is significant. Dewey theorized that education would have a greater impact on students when they were exposed to experiential learning and learning by doing, rather than learning by rote. Instead of only listening to a lecturer and taking down the necessary notes, learners can immerse themselves in a certain setting, interact with the surroundings and other learners, and gather knowledge from the lived or virtual experience. Just as students' learning about ecology and the environment can be enhanced by a visit to a local biology museum, this same subject matter could be further extended and detailed by time spent in *SL* experiencing such sites as the Escapade Zoo and Safari Park or the Abyss Museum of Ocean Science.

In *SL*, avatars can walk along city sidewalks or jog through country fields, all the while seeing the surrounding urban or rural settings flowing by. Fellow pedestrians cross at intersections, and cows and sheep graze in farmers' fields. Sights and sounds are part of the richness of the *SL* environment and experience, as are the different appearances of users, who design and shape their avatars according to their own likes and tastes. Media plays prominently in *SL*, with most areas and islands having their own customized soundtrack. Many rooms also integrate real-life video, and a strange phenomenon occurs when the cartoon-like avatars sit down to watch a real-life video or movie clip – it is as if the real life portrayed in the clips is the simulation for the virtual avatars. Picture a scene where robots watch humans on television or in the movies, as if reality is turned on its head.

Early impressions of *SL* are highly encouraging for those seeking advanced opportunities for experiential teaching and learning. The diversity of the content and subject matter available on the online platform is impressive, and the simulation technology is cutting edge. Advances are even being made within the current program by improving user experiences through increasingly smoother and quicker interactions between the user and the interface, which is an Internet-based system dependent on high bandwidth. This is *SL*'s weakness, however – it is a demanding program that can prompt functional difficulties on slower computers as well as slowdowns resulting from an inadequate Internet connection speed. Nonetheless, this virtual world is a blueprint for the future of the Internet and is of intense interest and potential for educators.

Reference

Dewey, J. (1938). *Experience and Education.* London: Collier-Macmillan.

with their peers, using new media to get connected and stay in touch. The primary means of communication are instant messaging, narrowcasting to peers over social network sites such as Cyworld (Asia), Sonico (Latin America), and Facebook, and texting over cell phones. Of course, socializing with friends is nothing new or extraordinary, but rather an essential part of transitioning into adulthood. In previous decades, street corners, bedrooms, and family phones were the nexus of youth communication, but young people today have an abundance of communicational capacities, both stationary (in home, school, library, and Internet cafes) and mobile (cell phones), as well as greater restrictions in their everyday lives. Internet ethnographer danah boyd (2007) argues that young people are in constant negotiation between public, private, and controlled space, particularly in an era when hanging out on streets is considered more hazardous and when teen lives are increasingly regulated by activities and obligations:

> Adults with authority control the home, the school, and most activity spaces [...] To [teenagers], private space is youth space and it is primarily found at the interstices of controlled space [...] By going virtual, digital technologies allow youth to (re)create private and public youth space while physically in controlled spaces. IM serves as a private space while [social networking sites] provide a public component. Online, youth can build the environments that support youth socialization.

Adults may worry about what youth are doing on the Internet, but, for the most part, young people seem to be hanging out, gossiping, coordinating offline meetings and events, and sharing media, some homemade (particularly photos shot of one another) and some from the vast array of amateur and professional material online (particularly music-related). Concerns about who is watching kids are important, but, in an audit of existing research studies on adolescent online communication, Subrahmanyam and Greenfield (2008) dispute the stereotype of vulnerable adolescents who unwittingly leave themselves vulnerable to strangers. For the most part, it turns out, youth do use the privacy settings available online, and many text communications are followed up by a phone call. Issues of privacy for younger Internet users are still a concern, however, and so it is worth noting that a number of media education organizations have designed helpful lesson plans aimed at teaching students how to protect their privacy in a digital world.

Beyond concerns about privacy, young people's avid online communication raises two further issues educators need to address as part of Media Literacy 2.0. First, in the process of inhabiting and exploring the virtual worlds of the Internet, young people inevitably travel across diverse communities, encountering challenging negotiations between self and others. Culture – including popular commercial culture such as hip hop and children's movies, Japanese manga, and video games – moves easily today, as do cultural consumers. As a result, young people are more and more being provoked by cultural difference and new experiences and communities of all sorts. Communication today thus requires one to learn how to negotiate multiple perspectives while grasping alternative sets of norms (Jenkins et al., 2006). People online encounter conflicting values and assumptions and are forced to come to grips with competing claims about the meaning of shared artifacts and experiences. In response, there seem to be two ways forward for educators.

One way forward is for educators to help young people develop an orientation whereby 'mutual tolerance and dialogue' come to be seen as the way to develop consensus and understanding, based around an idea of individual choice (Drotner, 2008, p. 182). This model of negotiating cultural difference aligns with politically liberal models of citizenship education that are certainly the most common discourses on citizenship taught in North American schools (Westheimer and Kahne, 2004; Knight Abowitz and Harnish, 2006). The second way forward is 'to follow a route of critique, in which mutual respect and dialogue are defined as joint conditions of living together in one world, including with people whose outlook on life may not be shared but without whom no life is feasible' (Drotner, 2008, p. 182). Here the idea is that students learn to negotiate difference in online environments by learning that, to be ourselves, we need the difference of others, because it is through the presence of others who are different from us that the specificity of each one of us is realized (Arendt, 1958). In other words, cultural difference is not approached as a threat or something to compromise over; it is seen as an essential aspect of a public culture in which we are all involved.

The second issue educators need to address as part of Media Literacy 2.0 is as follows: in order to sift through the information flow that is part of rich-media environments, to discern material of value from spurious or irrelevant information, young people's communication competencies must also include a form of network thinking. We define network thinking as thinking or actions that produce meaningful connection with significance for those participating in the network. As such, network thinking is to be contrasted with a more essentialized form of thinking that focuses on discrete artifacts or pieces of information. Another way to say this is that a literate student today is not one who possesses a vast array of discrete bits of information but rather 'one who is able to successfully navigate an already abundant and continually changing world of information' (Jenkins et al., 2006, p. 49).

To do this, students require skills to search out vital information. Many schools and educators have recognized this and have turned to 'webquests' as activities to help students gather images and texts from various sources that can be assessed and compiled in final projects. Another way to help students access information on the web is for them to learn how to use platforms such as Netvibes (www.netvibes.com) or igoogle.com, which are free web services that allow one to direct relevant news, images, photos, and other material related to a specific topic to one's own webpage using RSS feeds. Finally, leveraging information flow in rich-media environments also means young people need to learn how to disseminate their work across multiple communities using Web 2.0 platforms. Historically, where youth media is concerned, the youth film festival, film nights (at schools or in other public forums), and proprietorial websites (operated by art institutes or like organizations) have been the key means for disseminating youth-made media. Today, while these vehicles remain important, students also need to identify alternative strategies to disseminate their work by engaging with various networked communities. For instance, the use of Facebook by social and political activists demonstrates how social networking sites, along with content delivery platforms such as Scribd, legal Torrents, Flickr, YouTube, and TeacherTube can be used to extend the reach of youth communication. Of course, there are hazards online, including interactions with troublesome strangers, but these are perils also found in the offline world and they must be weighed against the benefits of leveraging online communication to reach networked communities.

Consumption and surveillance

Of course, as young people are communicating with each other and larger communities, there are also issues of consumption and surveillance that arise. Not unlike in the history of broadcast media, for the most part, the new media environments inhabited by youth are dominated by private enterprise. Many sites visited by youth advertise products for purchase, and the gadgets and service packages people need to access online and cell communication are commodities and for-profit services. Despite the fact that, once online, much activity is free of charge, there is no free lunch in new media environments. For instance, Sefton-Green, Nixon, and Erstad (2009) describe how in the 1990s personal computers made their initial entrance into the mainstream through the home market as part of a broad marketing strategy targeted at parents to help their kids '"get ahead" and [...] "keep up" with the information and communication requirements of contemporary society' (p. 111). With an average shelf life of three years before hardware and software becomes outdated, computers and their accessories are ideal commodities for producers and merchants. That the new online functionalities require a stable broadband connection, which is also a mercantilized 'service,' adds greater value to home computing from a commercial perspective. The ongoing proliferation of mobile media – also discrete commodities that require pricey service contracts – enables some to get into the new digital markets for the first time, as is the case particularly in the developing world, and offers others a secondary product/service to link to the primary communication hub while on the go. Many middle and upper class households in the global North have a minimum of three, but often more, digital nodes (discrete computers and mobile media). Each of these apparatuses requires some form of updating from time to time, whether in hardware renewal, software upgrades, or service contract renewals. But that is only the tip of the iceberg.

Beyond hardware and software commerce, the pervasive marketing and cross-marketing of products on web domains is now of single importance to the way consumption and surveillance operate online. The rise of immersive advertising and the increasingly pervasive role of all forms of online advertising to children and youth were discussed in Chapter 2. What matters about the development of these increasingly sophisticated strategies is that for young people 'commercial influences [online] [...] are often invisible' (Buckingham, 2007, p. 15; see also Shade, Porter, and Sanchez, 2005). Making the situation all the more complex, on social networking sites and in online game spaces, children are increasingly targeted with demographic-specific advertising. One of the many interesting innovations of Google, the world's number-one website, is intuitive advertising, a Web 3.0 innovation that responds to the user's online profile, the sites they visit, and the clicks they make on individual sites. (Web 3.0 is the semantic web that aggregates user data to learn more about each user for primarily commercial purposes.) Thus, part of the social networking experience, and web trolling in general, is to view ads that have been specifically chosen to knit in with users' online habits and concerns so as to maximize purchasing messages.

To facilitate the behavioral target marketing of children, the emergent surveillance architecture of Web 2.0 and 3.0 environments is key. In a very real sense, the Internet is an archive of our increasingly public lives where prospective partners, teachers, employers, and commercial agents can scroll through images and texts posted by ourselves or others. Beyond seeing what we post, however, the more effective surveillance work today is geared toward collecting aggregate statistics – on children's online movements, interactions, and chat with others – that can be used to peel back young people's online privacy. A simple bit of data exchange called a 'cookie' allows better user interface with websites but it also allows websites to track and collect user data. Aggregated over many users and many sites, data collected can prove very useful to advertisers, among other interested parties. Today, in fact, a detailed file on a million children, with names and addresses, can be bought for as little as five US dollars (Electronic Privacy Information Center, 2003; Steeves, 2007). Using this information, marketers can develop intimate relationships with children. In fact, 'marketers play upon children's developmental needs to experiment with roles, communicate with peers, take risks, and seek advice on issues that are important to them, in order to encourage children to reveal information about themselves' (Steeves, 2007, p. 5). In this way, marketers 'spy' on children, collecting aggregate data in order to build the most effective relationships between children and brands.

The upshot of this is that, while there is considerable concern about young people's online safety, particularly from predators and bullies, the elephant in the room is really increasing corporate governance of everyday life. Qualitative research with children indicates that the problem of 'stranger danger' has been communicated to young people (Livingstone and Bober, 2004; Media Awareness Network, 2005; Steeves, 2007). Ironically, however, alongside attempts to warn children about the dangers of strangers online, children have been encouraged to provide their personal information to marketers and commercial interests. For example, while Viacom's Neopets (www.neopets.com) and Disney's Club Penguin (www.clubpenguin.com) both warn children not to reveal any personal information to other children or to strangers – thus posing as part of the solution to the problem – they are simultaneously two of the most sophisticated sites for collecting children's online information (Chung and Grimes, 2005; Grimes and Shade, 2005). The argument that children need to be protected from strangers, then, is something of a 'moral panic.' Schools are especially important in this light. Rather than taking up the challenge of addressing how young people's privacy and identity are being shaped by commercial intrusions into children's online experience, schools often turn to forms of virtual surveillance or simply shut down adolescents' access to key sites (such as Facebook, YouTube, MySpace, and so on) for fear that they will allow strangers to reach children. But this just defers the problem, because young people are avid users of these sites when out of school. Consequently, youth simply continue to use these resources unaware of how their data is being tracked and captured as they move from one site to the next.

For progressive educators, however, the function of immersive advertising is deeply troubling because it situates marketing as a naturalized, difficult-to-see element of children's leisure time. In her sidebar, IMMERSIVE ADVERTISING AND CHILDREN'S GAME SPACES, Sara M. Grimes notes as much while also pointing out that various transnational agencies, including the Organization for Economic Co-operation and Development; governments in Australia, the UK, and the US (Children's Privacy Online Privacy Protection Act, 1998); and the European Commission have all responded to this situation with policies and advisories on what is appropriate when advertisers target children online. Given the fact that many children do not notice the advertising that is being directed at them on the web, educators may want to use part or all of these documents to explore why policy-makers in some countries have developed positions intended to protect young people and inform them about online advertising. In addition, it would be worthwhile to ask students to think about whether these policies go far enough. Do they in fact seem useful and capable of addressing the evolving marketing practices that are being

Immersive advertising and children's game spaces

Sara M. Grimes, University of Toronto

Digital games and virtual worlds have opened up a number of important new opportunities for children's play and cultural participation while providing a promising new forum for informal and formal learning. However, digital game technologies have also enabled media corporations to introduce increasingly deceptive forms of advertising, as well as highly intrusive forms of marketing, into children's digital culture. These range from using games to conduct covert market research (by tracking users and collecting personal information from them) to in-game advertising (wherein ads appear within the game environment) and 'advergames' (interactive advertisements loosely disguised as games).

An increasingly common form of advertising found within children's game spaces is 'immersive advertising,' a term originally trademarked by Neopets, Inc. (owners of the virtual pet-themed online community for children and teens, www.neopets.com) and used to describe embedded forms of product placement that integrate brands and products into the very fabric of a game's environment and activities. What makes this development unique is the unprecedented level of intimacy it enables marketers to build with their target audiences. Not only do digital game technologies allow ads to be integrated directly into a dynamic game play experience, where promotional messages can be altered and updated as needed, they also enable the systematic tracking and analysis of players' interactions with the ads and the role of advertised brands within emerging communities of practice.

Most of the immersive advertising found within children's game spaces promotes the same products advertised in traditional children's media – including toys, sugary cereals, candy, and fast-food restaurants. Despite the ongoing convergence of traditional and 'new' media, governments have been slow to articulate and enforce comprehensive regulation of advertising to children within game spaces and other digital venues. Given the highly deceptive nature of product placement and the challenge it poses to younger children's ability to identify promotional intent (issues that have justified the regulation of advertisements in children's media since the 1970s), the phenomenon of immersive advertising raises concern among children's advocates, educators, and scholars. Immersive advertising displays many of the characteristics of product placement, including the integration of specific products and brand names into storylines and dialogue. Players are often able to interact with the product in some way and are frequently encouraged to reference brands and products in their own in-game contributions. By creating opportunities for children to play with digital versions of real-life products, toys, and media brands – all within the confines of a corporately controlled branded environment – the children's industries gain ever greater access to children's time, attention, and cultural practices.

The most important and prevalent form of immersive advertising found within children's game spaces involves cross-promotion and branding. For example, many children's television networks use immersive advertising in online games to promote their programs – enabling kids to play with digital versions of their favorite characters and interact with items featured in certain episodes or series. In *Nicktropolis*, a virtual world for children produced by Nickelodeon (at the time of writing, the online world has been closed down and is under development into a new form), several areas featured virtual screens that played webisodes of popular Nickelodeon television programs. In addition, the game environment included a number of branded areas where players could explore program-themed rooms (such as 'SpongeBob's House' from *SpongeBob SquarePants* or the 'Air Temple' from *Avatar: The Last Airbender*) and 'purchase' program-themed items using in-game currency. These strategies enable the expansion of established media brands across children's digital landscape while simultaneously referring players back to the television program and other ancillary texts.

As children's game spaces are increasingly social spaces, allowing for multiplayer collaboration and various opportunities for peer play and social networking, immersive advertising can also foster a controlled form of viral marketing. Many virtual worlds for children limit communication between players to a sort of bricolage, wherein players communicate by selecting from a scroll-down menu of preconstructed sentences (or sentence fragments). While promoted as a 'safe-chat' alternative, the feature also enables the integration of product placement within player-to-player communication. For example, of the 634 preconstructed 'safe-chat' sentences available in *Nicktropolis*, 237 contained explicit references to a Nickelodeon property – including references to television programs and films. By restricting inter-player communication to corporate-friendly speech, players find themselves enlisted as brand ambassadors.

While child advocacy and digital democracy groups in the US have successfully initiated regulatory action on specific issues relating to children's game spaces (namely the collection of personally identifiable data from children, which is now regulated by the Children's Online Privacy Protection Act, and the ongoing public debates about using game spaces to promote fast food and junk food to children), very little attention has thus far been paid in North America to the games' more implicit promotional features. The Organization for Economic Co-operation and Development first identified a number of potential problems and risks to children's rights and wellbeing in this very area as early as 1999. Since then, governments in Australia, the UK, and across the EU have taken a proactive stance against immersive advertising and other forms of product placement within children's game spaces and digital media, often in conjunction with child obesity task force initiatives.

For more on these initiatives, see:

- Ofcom's Final Statement on Television Advertising of Food and Drink Products to Children in the UK, as well as follow-up research they have since conducted on the impact of the new restrictions: www.ofcom.org.uk/consult/condocs/foodads_new/statement.
- The European Commission's regulatory framework for the protection of minors within media development in the EU: ec.europa. eu/avpolicy/reg/minors/index_en.htm.
- Recent reports published by the Australian Government's Preventative Health Taskforce (such as the Obesity Policy Coalition submission, 'Obesity: A need for urgent action': www.fairfieldcity. nsw.gov.au/upload/pfpib32593/nathealth_prevant_obesity.pdf) and the Australian Greens Party ('Dissenting Report': www.aph. gov.au/Senate/committee/clac_ctte/protecting_children_junk_ food_advert/report/d01.pdf) outlining the debates currently unfolding around these issues in within the Australian context.

developed by Madison Avenue to target children and young people? Beyond these ideas, various media education organizations including the Media Awareness Network in Canada and the Center for Media Literacy in the US have developed curriculum and public awareness initiatives to address surveillance issues in new media environments. Also valuable for educators is the DVD and curriculum package *Consuming Kids: The Commercialization of Childhood* (2008), which is produced by the Media Education Foundation and is a great resource that can be used to help young people explore the terms and ethics of marketing in new media environments.

Convergence

At the root of young people's identity and communication practices as well as the new marketing strategies developing today is a convergence of media and communication platforms. There are both centripetal (towards the center) and centrifugal (away from the center) aspects to media convergence. In centripetal terms, the personal computer – whether desktop, laptop, or mobile media – serves as a central node into which all information flows. Increasingly, this singular portal to the world enables wide searches across centrifugal horizons: distinct databases, multimodalities of communication, and multiple perspectives that transcend cultural and ideological bias. These convergences, enabled and enhanced in new media environments, are not just technological. While the personal computer enables users to be present as a single node on the World Wide Web, the data and perspectives of differing people, cultures, and social groups also converge on the Internet in a polyphony of modalities that afford users complex knowledge fields expressed in multiple forms. Ultimately, this rich resource of vast and often unfiltered streams of ideas, knowledge, and information demands requisite skills of judgment and evaluation. As Jenkins et al. (2006) state,

> we must all learn how to read one source of information against another; to understand the contexts within which information is produced and circulated; to identify the mechanisms that ensure the accuracy of information as well as realizing under which circumstances these mechanisms work best. (pp. 98–99)

Alongside this capacity to discern what is truthful and plausible is the need for a visual literacy that enables users to read across platforms and modalities. To a great extent, this requires users to rethink how knowledge and information is produced and received. Simply stated, the new literacies involve, among other things, the revenge of the right brain function. Knowledge is not simply linear and objective in its multimodal form. Rather, there is an emotional and affective component released by the visual and auditory domains that enhances what is known and how it is received. Thus, a visual literacy that adequately responds to the new literacies combines the characteristics of visual reading introduced in Chapter 4 with non-linear, a-rational (intuitive) forms of comprehension.

A competency required in the era of convergence is thus 'transmedia navigation' (Jenkins et al., 2006, pp. 99–100), the capacity to produce and consume information and narratives across media platforms. In a research-based setting, this may involve sorting through a variety of modalities to seek or impart information. In schools and universities, we see this transmedia negotiation most directly in the use of PowerPoint presentations, which unite text and image (and sometimes sound) in the expository and analytical processes of instructors and students. Arguably, this has not been a fully smooth process, with visual sophistry sometimes substituting for scholastic rigor. Nonetheless, when used effectively, multimodal forms of communication can express information and perspectives on a number of registers, tapping into affective domains in a manner that is more difficult to attain in traditional oral presentations.

In the case of entertainment-based narratives, transmedia navigation might involve combining media such as a video game, a movie, a comic book, and a rock video. Stories and themes transcend individual media texts and are enriched by other media texts and experiences. An example of this is the Pokémon franchise, which is consumed through video games, film, books, and playing cards. This highly interactive narrative universe brings video game sensibilities out of the screen and on to the streets. Children routinely collect Pokémon cards and play a complex game that requires knowledge drawn from across platforms. A broader area of convergence and transmedia production in the public domain is 'mashups' (combined applications), for example projects on Google Maps and Google Earth, which link community or geographic knowledge with imagery and other forms of media. (We will return to mashups and remixes in more detail in the section on copy-paste below.)

Another significant implication of convergence in young people's lives is multitasking, the simultaneous connection to telephone, instant messaging, social media, music, and, when pertinent, homework. While there has been

considerable concern expressed that young people are less able to concen-
trate on tasks and texts than previous generations, there is no conclusive
evidence to prove this true. Further, as Jenkins et al. (2006) point out,
multitasking is a key workplace competency and a necessary skill in
contemporary information gathering: 'multi-tasking is often confused
with distraction, but as understood here, multi-tasking involves a method
of monitoring and responding to the sea of information around us'
(pp. 94–95). A hallmark of print literacy is the silence of libraries, the
stillness seen as prerequisite for higher-level thinking and concentration.
Conversely, multitasking environments are marked by the randomness
and cacophony congruent with many workplaces such as newsrooms – an
example we choose because it is a knowledge-producing context of the
print-literate age. While we are not intending to advocate multitasking
environments as the new cultural commons of higher-level knowledge
production, we do argue that these environments have much to offer. In
fact, for some tasks, and some students' learning styles, multitasking
environments offer a marked improvement over the heavy silence of a
traditional library.

Another key element of convergence is the area of human–machine
interaction. Cyborg (part human, part machine) intelligence enables discoveries, enhanced capacities, and new forms of knowledge management.
Human–machine interaction in educational contexts is not new – think, for
example, of the calculator – but this interaction has been much amplified
in the digital era. Jenkins et al. (2006) describe 'distributed cognition' as a
new functionality:

> Challenging the traditional view that intelligence is an attribute of indivi-
> duals, the distributed cognition perspective holds that intelligence is dis-
> tributed across 'brain, body, and world,' looping through an extended
> technological and sociocultural environment [...] [and including] forms
> of reasoning which would not be possible without the presence of artifacts or
> information appliances which expand and augment human's [sic] cognitive
> capacities. (pp. 95–96)

An example of human–machine interaction may indeed be a person using
a calculator to perform quick calculations while working on a larger
mathematical problem. But the more robust sense of distributed cognition
enabled by the new technologies is in the plural when a number of humans
and machines collectively create something. Wikipedia is again a significant

example, but so is TakingITGlobal (www.tigweb.org), a website and social change project coproduced by young people around the world. (We will have more to say about this website below.) Another example is when a large number of people view a homemade video posted on YouTube and some respond with their own videos, as was the case with Modern Oracle's 'Original Music Database – (No Cover Songs).' Here, YouTube users/ participants co-created a set of perspectives greater than the sum of its parts. (By May 2010, this challenge to YouTubers to submit v-logs featuring original music had prompted 6252 video responses.) Similarly, TheOne-MinutesJr. site (www.theoneminutesjr.org), which features brief videos produced by youth from around the world, is a collaborative form of knowledge production. Even when directed by an individual, as is the case with Mark Johnson's 'Playing for Change,' where songs are performed collectively by people from around the world not in physical contact with one another, distributed cognition enables co-creation. And these forms of collaboration are not limited to the arts and social movements, but rather also take place in science and commerce, as documented by Tapscott and Williams in *Wikinomics* (2006).

To draw on the potentials of convergence in contemporary educational contexts is to acknowledge that our students will cull knowledge from a variety of sources, will produce and consume knowledge across a number of platforms and modalities, will engage in a number of distinct tasks simultaneously, and will use the technological resources at hand. These are not revolutionary insights, particularly in relation to developing and ongoing classroom practice in many jurisdictions. What is called for in these new times, however, is a highly collaborative and dispersed model of teaching and learning. Where assessment regimes have traditionally relied on individual portfolios, collaborative project-based assessment with nuanced attention to individual effort and achievement are required. In regard to multitasking and learning styles, recognition should be given to students' complex and sometimes chaotic out-of-school literacy practices in order that schools not be a place where learning is dull and under-stimulating.

Creativity

We identify two aspects of interactive creativity under this heading: the creative media arts as occasioned by the producers of media content and the creative engagement with technology through game playing. The lower cost of the hardware and software needed to produce videos and (audio) podcasts has helped to create an explosion of user-generated multimodal content. (For a discussion of various institutionally mediated forms of youth media production in relation to questions of agency see Chapter 5.) The webcam alone is responsible for a new generation of i-journalism. These factors are augmented too by the distribution capacities afforded by Web 2.0 file-sharing sites today, which have made it easy to circulate material. Web 2.0 has also proved a fertile terrain for the written word, especially the first-person journalism of much blogging. There are of course many forms of creative participation online, however, some sophisticated and complex and some very simple. As such, it would be rash to suggest that Web 2.0 has created a generation of artists, writers, and media producers. There might be a great deal of cultural production today, in other words, but there are distinctions to be made between posting a photo alongside one's social networking home page and creating an elaborate 'text' such as a video, a song, or an 800-word blog. In the next section, we address some of the specific concerns about young people's cultural production that relate to the practices of remixing and mashups. Here, however, we focus on the other aspect of interactive creativity in new media contexts: video gaming.

Video gaming is a hot-button issue in contemporary discussions of children and youth. Video games have been criticized for contributing to young people's violence, alienation, obesity, and short attention spans. For the most part, they are thought to be products of a booming industry that is challenging pop music as the most profitable entertainment industry. Unlike the introduction of other major technological innovations in the delivery of media products such as silent movies, radio, and television, however, video games predated their cultural impact by a couple of decades. Unbeknownst to casual players of Pong back in the 1970s, this new technology would take time to bear its most tantalizing fruit. While the movies, radio, and television had rapid and dramatic effects on cultural practices, video games entered the pond of everyday social and cultural interactions with hardly a ripple and stealthily sneaked into the bedrooms and rec rooms of a generation. Given that gaming was largely a subcultural practice, rather than a universal media technology such as radio or television, the reach and impact of video games in the lives of young people came initially as something of a surprise. In the wake of the Columbine High School massacre in 1999, which some pundits attributed to the video gaming habits and social isolation of its perpetrators, video games and gaming have been widely held in disrepute. While there is some merit, some of the time, to criticisms leveled at video games and gamers, the hyperbole associated with their reception by adult authorities overwhelms the verifiable negative effects so easily attributed to them. It can be argued, in fact, that the diversity of video game types is sufficiently wide that they cannot be painted with the same brush. Moreover, we know that few kids play only one kind of video game and very few kids only play video games on their own. (See Chapter 2 for more details.)

Despite the rhetoric of video games detractors, then, it is encouraging to note that a number of critics have argued their merits, some going so far as to describe video games as learning machines. The creator of *SimCity*, Will Wright, for instance, argues for his game's pedagogical merits, stating that '*SimCity* comes right out of Montessori – if you give people this model for building cities, they will abstract from it principles of urban design' (quoted in Henderson, 2009, p. 57). In *Everything Bad is Good for You* (2005), Steven Johnson describes probing and telescoping, two central conceptual tools used by gamers. Probing is the ability to learn by trial and error, identifying and extracting principles upon which to build one's knowledge of the functions and functionalities of a game. Telescoping is the capacity to anticipate the next tasks while focusing on the current ones. Johnson (2005) does not try to exalt this new digital literacy, but makes a case for video games as learning economies that hone '*different* mental skills that are just as important as the ones exercised by reading books' (p. 23). Video game learning also involves play, another key competency of the new media literacy as articulated by Jenkins et al. (2006):

> Play [...] is a mode of active engagement, one that encourages experimentation and risk-taking, one that views the process of solving a problem as important as finding the answer, one that offers clearly defined goals and roles that encourage strong identifications and emotional investments. (p. 90)

The role of play in new media learning goes far beyond video gaming. In this learn-to-play and play-to-learn era, in fact, the capacity to probe in particular is key to learning new software applications and developing greater mastery in others. Video games are, however, the quintessential play-and-learn platforms. Jim Gee developed a set of 36 learning principles he observed in video game practice (2003). For the sake of brevity, we include here only the eight most salient to our purposes:

- *'Psychosocial moratorium' principle*: Learners can take risks in a space where real-world consequences are lowered (pp. 207–208).
- *Committed learning principle*: Learners participate in an extended engagement (lots of effort and practice) as extensions of their real-world identities in relation to a virtual identity to which they feel some commitment and a virtual world that they find compelling (p. 208).
- *Achievement principle*: For learners of all levels of skill there are intrinsic rewards from the beginning, customized to each learner's level, effort, and growing mastery and signaling the learner's ongoing achievements (p. 208).
- *'Regime of competence' principle*: The learner gets ample opportunity to operate within, but at the outer edge of, his or her resources, so at those points things are felt as challenging but not 'undoable' (p. 209).
- *Explicit information on-demand and just-in-time principle*: The learner is given explicit information both on-demand and just-in-time, when the learner needs it or just at the point where the information can best be understood and used in practice (p. 211).
- *Discovery principle*: Overt telling is kept to a well-thought-out minimum, allowing ample opportunity for the learner to experiment and make discoveries (p. 211).
- *Dispersed principle*: Meaning/knowledge is dispersed in the sense that the learner shares it with others outside the domain/game (p. 212).
- *Insider principle*: The learner is an 'insider,' 'teacher,' and 'producer' (not just a 'consumer') able to customize the learning experience and domain/game from the beginning and throughout the experience (p. 212).

As should be apparent from these few principles, the learning community Gee describes is marked by motivation, flexibility, teamwork, and agency. It makes room for different learning styles (and speeds), it pushes learners without overwhelming them, and it weaves together action and reflection. In short, it is a dynamic and collaborative learning environment, much like a well-functioning workplace. Arguably, the cultural legacies of video games and gaming will not become apparent at these early stages of development. Just as it was unclear at the turn of the twentieth century that film would become one of the century's most powerful cultural repositories of narrative and exposition, the same could hold true in the twenty-first century for the interactive, simulative realm of video games. With this in mind, the tremendous educational potential of video games has not gone unnoticed by researchers and game developers alike. For instance, Jenkins et al. (2006) label simulation as a key competency of new media literacy: 'Contemporary video games allow youth to play with sophisticated simulations [...] These simulations expose players to powerful new ways of seeing the world and encourage them to engage in a process of modeling' (p. 91). (For example, in the sidebar RETHINKING MEDIA LITERACY THROUGH VIDEO GAME PLAY, Michael Dezuanni describes a project where young male game players were encouraged to interrogate their subjectivities.)

Adding to this, games allow students to project an identity different from their own, whether a historical figure or a contemporary person of a different culture, race, or gender. In sophisticated role-playing exercises set 'in situ' alongside historical events, for instance, students gain an insider perspective to phenomena such as warfare and migration. The celebrated game *ICED* (*I Can End Deportation*: www.icedgame.com), for example, puts players in the shoes of five young immigrants to the US who must navigate a complex and often unjust set of rules and restrictions on their presence in the US. Similarly, the University of California, Davis Virtual Hallucinations room in *Second Life* (www.secondlife.com) allows players to experience the effects of schizophrenia, thus helping to break down stereotypes through lived experience (see the sidebar LEARNING IN *SECOND LIFE*). As mentioned, video game simulation can also transport players to a historical period or geographic location. Finally, when used in a pedagogical setting with dialogue and feedback between instructor and peers, even seemingly problematic video game content can be used to teach (see the sidebar RETHINKING MEDIA LITERACY THROUGH VIDEO GAME PLAY). Our point, then, is that video games can enable creative and critical interpretive communities of practice to develop, given the everyday interactions of young gamers who are not dependent on school structures to see through the problematic elements of many games they play (Squire, 2008). A remarkable opportunity is thus present for media educators to plug into this exciting new educational domain as part of the project of Media Literacy 2.0.

Copy-paste

While gaming provides one creative outlet for learning in new media environments, it is also true that young people now have direct access to an unprecedented number of digital information sources and resources. This has changed how and when information is accessed, and it has transformed the nature of research and composition. In particular, it has

Rethinking media literacy through video game play

Michael Dezuanni, Queensland
University of Technology

New media forms such as video games pose challenges for media educators. Many of the classroom strategies, techniques, and approaches that have worked in the past seem inadequate for dealing with a media form that is much more participatory than older iterations. The knowledge that media teachers have about film, television, news media, and advertising cannot be easily transferred to forms such as video games. As gamers, many young people are already 'expert' in areas of games knowledge to an extent that far exceeds their teachers' knowledge. Further, many young people are not just playing games. They are producing digital artifacts for games in the form of mods, reworked levels, and characters. They are also remixing games through the production of games-based animation such as machinima. There is a plethora of cultural material associated with game play produced by young people, for example written commentary in games blogs, in discussion forums, and in 'walkthrough' websites.

Despite the difficulty of responding to these complex forms of engagement, video games should not simply be ignored by media literacy advocates. Of course, most media educators would want their students to be critically reflective on their video game experiences. More broadly, parents, social commentators, and politicians worry about game violence, the perpetuation of gender norms, and the amount of time young people devote to game play. Video games are clearly an important popular cultural form for young people and all the justifications used to include traditional media education in the classroom apply equally to video games. Like other new media forms such as online social networking and mobile media, video games challenge media educators to reconceptualize the aims of media education. These participatory forms of media draw attention to an aspect of the relationship between young people and media that media educators often overlook: media literacy is not an outcome, but a practice; it is produced via our interactions with media in specific social contexts. A new objective for media education may therefore be to provide students with experiences that allow them to use media to experiment with producing representations of themselves in a range of different ways, in different relationships with media and social contexts.

A potential objection to this conception of media literacy is that it suggests that all media responses are equally valid, but this is not the case. When students produce themselves with media, it is important for teachers and other students to raise questions and concerns. Indeed, a fundamental aspect of learning in this approach should be the multiple perspectives that are produced by different classroom participants. The social context of the classroom requires that students and teachers recognize each others' responses as valid but open to further response. In this sense, 'media literacy' is fluid and evolving, but not a 'free-for-all.'

I observed this in practice in a video games project I worked on with a group of teenage boys. The Video Games Immersion Unit consisted of an intensive three-week focus on the study of video games by year-10 boys. Students learned about games, social issues, game design, and production processes for six or more hours per day over 15 days. The focus on social issues such as gaming, gender, and game violence included several 'traditional' media literacy activities and some more 'open' activities. The more open activities included online chat and forum discussions in which there were no 'correct' answers. These open activities seemed to provide the students with more space or potential for variation than the more traditional activities. For example, an online chat about gender and games that included female gamers from a local university provoked the expression of complex and varied masculinities. Via their responses to the chat, many of the students presented themselves as progressive thinkers about gender and games. Moreover, most of the students enjoyed the activity. The same students complained about the boring nature of the more traditional theory-based media literacy activities.

My analysis of the students' responses to both the more structured and open activities suggests that, rather than this work leading to students becoming more 'critical' about video games, it provided them with opportunities to produce themselves as masculine and technological subjects. The students were able to repeat and vary the masculine and technological norms relevant to the communities to which they belonged. Different versions of masculinities were produced as students played, designed, and discussed games, and some activities seemed to provide more opportunities for variation than other activities. This approach to media education focuses on the production of student subjectivities, which I think is appropriate for the participatory media cultures young people are involved in via new media technologies. Older approaches to media education are not sufficient in contemporary cultures, where anyone can be a media producer. This is not to suggest that more established approaches lack value, but that they often fail to account for the complex ways in which young people are using new media.

enabled new forms of cultural production, specifically the remix and mashup, where different types of media are brought together to create new forms of expression. A key feature of digital data is the ease with which it can be copied and merged with other material. Contemporary computers with access to the Internet are like library photocopiers on steroids. As a result, it is not unreasonable to expect that in even 10 minutes one could quickly research a subject and prepare a brief treatise complete with illustrations – none of it original, but all of it on target with the subject at hand. While presenting terrific advantages, this new state of affairs also has great potentially negative consequences in educational contexts, not only for assessment purposes but also for the greater good of teaching and learning.

For instance, the ability to copy and paste material from digital sources has created chaos for educational institutions in the form of concerns that students are plagiarizing information. In response to this threat to teaching and learning as we know them, a software application called TurnItIn (www.turnitin.com) has been developed for commercial sale to educational institutions, which use it to assess originality and authenticity of student writing. There have also been pedagogical responses such as 'information literacy,' which seeks to guide learners in their pursuit of knowledge, training students in search methods and ways to ensure authenticity. Information literacy also crosses into the discourse of cyberethics in imparting an ethical approach aimed at curtailing plagiarism and copyright infringement.

Educational institutions may be adapting to the new and digital literacies with creative solutions to rule-breaking and other transgressions, but these are, to a certain extent, old solutions to new problems. For example, while there is genuine concern about student plagiarism in the new era, there is also a clash of cultural mindsets between print and digital literacy about what constitutes intellectual work. Going back to the preprint literacy era, the Roman scholar Quintilian called for five departments of rhetorical composition: invention, arrangement, style, memory, and delivery. Given that these categories were developed for oral presentation, the roles of memory and delivery were made redundant by print, but the remaining three continued to be relevant. Stripping these down to the most basic elements, invention involved thought and inspiration, arrangement involved logic and forms of argumentation, and style involved grammar and writing persona/tone. While all three of these categories were seen as essential to print literacy, it was only the output of invention that could be plagiarized. Structures of argumentation could be mimicked, and genres, formulas, and forms of writing could be adapted. Style involved mastering the rules of grammar and developing a signature tone, or authorial flair. The emphasis in much school writing on the centrality of invention ignored for the most part that most human knowledge is dialogic and that every great thought and invention is preceded by other intellectual labor, except in as much as students were encouraged to read other authors and make citation or reference to their work. In the digital era, it can be argued, writing is inherently collaborative, and arrangement is the competency increasingly required by writers and authors. This is not to say that invention is dead and that all new authorship will be based on rearrangement, but rather to bring arrangement out of invention's shadow and recognize it as a key competency of contemporary composition.

In the domains of multimodal cultural production, there is a wildfire of creative reworkings of existing cultural material taking place alongside a raging debate about the legitimacy of the resulting material. One of the most prevalent forms of youth online cultural production is the homemade video with a favorite song as the soundtrack. Whether kids dance to the music or create a collage of images to go with the song, they are technically breaking copyright if the music is commercially available. Lawrence Lessig, a copyright lawyer and scholar, is one of the foremost proponents of free and fair use of cultural material. He takes this position because, he argues, we are a read/write culture today, no longer a read only one. This is to say, we have shifted away from a model of cultural production where a few experts – curators, authors, composers, and so on – create the culture that others consume. Lessig (2008) argues in fact that we should value the aesthetic and intellectual acumen required to remix material into new forms, arguing that 'it takes extraordinary knowledge about a culture to remix it well' (p. 93).

Similarly, Jenkins et al. (2006) state that appropriation is a complex new competency: 'Sampling intelligently from the existing cultural reservoir requires a close analysis of the existing structures and uses of this material; remixing requires an appreciation of emerging structures and latent potential meanings' (pp. 93–94).

Of course, as schools and kids adapt to the reality of free and simple access to words, sights, and sounds of cultural producers and intellectuals, a question of cyberethics arises. One strand of thought in the discourse of cyberethics sees all copyright infringement as theft, but a tremendous debate exists over the broader question of the ownership of the icons, key texts, sounds, and images of our culture. When young people create new productions from the artifacts of the mass media, for example, are they stealing or creating totally new texts? Lessig argues that, if the former position becomes dominant, we will begin (as some jurisdictions already have) to criminalize kids because they lack the political voice to make a case for remix culture (2008). But alternative communities have already sprung up that seek to make software and media available for the public good, the most famous cases being the collaboratively produced Linux software and the Creative Commons archive. Moreover, to put this whole discussion into perspective, imagine a future where you are not allowed to sing the Mickey Mouse Club theme song or show someone a picture of Donald Duck. Like members of an oral culture, young people take elements of their cultural landscape – key themes, resonant images, powerful tropes – and remake them into new cultural forms today. This is the reality of online youth productions, which for the most part are not intended for commercial sale.

The products of this work are remixes and mashups, and we note that there is some overlap in the use of the terms (see Giuliana Cucinelli's sidebar, UNDERSTANDING REMIX AND DIGITAL MASHUP, for a close examination of these terms and the types of hybrid cultural production these approaches enable). For the sake of distinction, however, we prefer to reserve the term 'mashup' for those productions that involve the use of distinct computer applications, or APIs (application programming interfaces). Some of the most circulated mashups are those using Google Earth or Google Maps, for example those that can be viewed at the Google Maps Mania website (googlemapsmania.blogspot.com; this site is independent of Google). Mapping projects allow for a new, highly effective presentation of knowledge. Whether seeking independent book stores in the US or region-by-region breakdowns of an election somewhere in the world, much data has been mapped. To a great extent, the Web 2.0 revolution has involved

Understanding remix and digital mashup

Giuliana Cucinelli, McGill University

In a world where discovery is more important than delivery, it's the people who find, remix and direct attention to old stuff that should be rewarded, not the people who deliver it or sit on it waiting for someone to show up. (Joichi Ito, n.d.)

In recent years, remixing has become a form of Internet currency, a way for netizens to share, exchange, alter, and play with media texts made available by the Internet. Further, user-generated and open-source material accessible through social networking and Web 2.0 sites, such as Remix.vg and YouTube, have encouraged people to contribute to the remix and mashup culture. This online fan culture goes as far as to provide wikis and tutorials on 'how to remix.' As a result, new material and remixed texts appear daily and easily become a form of viral media.

What exactly are remixes and digital mashups? The histories and paths of remix and digital mashup are rich and complex, and it is important to note that they are two distinct practices. Often, the term 'remix culture' is used to include both remix and digital mashups, and it is described by Lawrence Lessig as a 'society which allows and encourages derivative works' (Lessig, 2008, p. 56). This society is comprised of amateur creators 'who are no longer willing to be merely passive receptors of content' (O'Brien and Fitzgerald, 2006, p. 1). Eduardo Navas (2009) believes remix culture can be defined as 'the global activity consisting of the creative and efficient exchange of information made possible by digital technologies that is supported by the practice of cut/copy and paste' (para. 5). Both remix and digital mashup exist in a remix culture, and often crossover, but their methods and materials differ.

By definition, remixing involves producing an alternative version of an existing musical piece, whereas a digital mashup is 'a visual remix, commonly a video or website which remixes and combines content from a number of different sources to produce something new and creative' (O'Brien and Fitzgerald, 2006, p. 1). Swedish DJ and producer Eric Prydz's version of Pink Floyd's 'Another Brick in the Wall, Part II' is an example of a remix. Prydz's take of Pink Floyd's classic 'Proper

Education' (2006) hit number one on the US Billboard Hot Dance Airplay chart, making it the first remixed recording of an original song to reach the top spot. Conversely, a good example of a digital mashup is 'Teletubbies Lean Wit It' on YouTube, created by senseigmg, which as of October 2010 had over six million views. This mashup includes video segments from the BBC's children's television series *Teletubbies* synched to the Dem Franchize Boyz's 2005 hit 'Lean wit It, Rock wit It.'

The purpose of a digital mashup is to bring together as many sources as possible to create a unique mix of media texts. Occasionally, digital mashups offer poignant and valuable social commentary. One example is ParkRidge47's YouTube mashup 'Vote Different,' the political message of which is to vote for change – and hence Barack Obama. The mashup includes Apple's '1984' commercial with images and sounds of Big Brother replaced with Hilary Clinton, who at the time was a candidate in the 2008 US presidential election. With over six million views as of October 2010, this video exemplifies the power of mashups as a form of social commentary.

It would be naïve to ignore the questions of copyright infringement and ethical problems that plague remix culture. Many consider remix and mashup to be tantamount to theft. In 2001, Joi Ito and Lawrence Lessig established Creative Commons, a non-profit organization devoted to promoting 'copyleft' licensing and building a community where people share and build upon the work of others (Creative Commons, 2009, para. 1). In an effort to promote remix culture, American musician Gregg Michael Gillis, also known as Girl Talk, in collaboration with the National Film Board of Canada and Director Brett Gaylor, produced a feature-length open-source documentary named *rip!: A Remix Manifesto* (2008), which explores remix, the Internet, intellectual property, and copyright culture. The documentary encourages people to mashup existing segments of the documentary online through the Open Source Cinema Project. There are several other documentaries and infographic videos available online that explore remix culture and copyright wars, for example *Steal this Film* (2006) and *Good Copy Bad Copy* (2007).

Remix culture continues to grow despite an ongoing copyright battle, and will do so for a very long time. According to Mark Getty (2006), 'intellectual property is the oil of the twenty-first century' (*Steal this Film*) and very few of us are willing to consider the ethical weight of our choices when media texts can be so easily accessed via the Internet for creative and artistic purposes. Cultural producers continue to make and upload new and exciting remixes and mashups despite the fear of someday losing that freedom. Until then, the only limit is creativity.

References

Creative Commons. (2009). 'About.' Retrieved October 8, 2010 from http://creativecommons.org/about.

Ito, J. (2005). Does 'the long tail' mean we need longer copyrights? Retrieved April 4, 2010 from http://joi.ito.com/weblog/2005/03/07/does-the-long-t.html.

King, J. (director). (2007). *Steal this Film*. The League of Noble Peers (producer). UK and Germany: Independent and BitTorrent.

Lessig, L. (2008). *Remix: Making Art and Commerce Thrive in the Hybrid Economy*. New York: Penguin.

O'Brien, D. and Fitzgerald, B. (2006). Mashups, remixes and copyright law. *Internet Law Bulletin*, 9(2), pp. 17–19.

Navas, E. (2009). Remix: The bond of repetition and representation. Retrieved October 8, 2010 from http://remixtheory.net/?p=361.

individual programmers in the creation of content, and, increasingly, this involves many amateurs. The fluidity and ease with which web applications can be incorporated onto blogs and websites has made it possible for newcomers to digitally design highly sophisticated websites using print, video, audio, and applications such as maps. In response to this development, and further encouraging it, Google launched Web Elements (www.google.com/webelements), where users can help themselves to a variety of applications. The key competencies required for creative mashers and remixers are design, curating, and editing, alongside composition and creation. Ultimately, the creative reworking of material and applications is a key competency of Media Literacy 2.0 and one that will be recognized more fully in educational contexts before long.

Community

Finally, we note that social networking involves developing networks and community-building (usually by collecting friends and joining groups) and so community represents a last conceptual problem central to Media

Literacy 2.0. The process of developing virtual communities has been much advanced by the advent of online social networking. Each user in social networking spaces builds their own network and no two networks are identical, each always representing the character and idiosyncrasies of its producer. These peer-centered virtual communities lie at the heart of Internet activity, functioning as communicational and identity hubs for young people. In relation to the latter, 'who you know' is increasingly public and status can be attained by securing certain 'friends' to your network. While we would argue that these peer-centered communities are the most prevalent form of networking online, there is a vast set of more specialized networks to which youth belong.

Other important forms of online community include affinity groups, for instance, which are usually organized around shared interests. These may involve advocacy (e.g., yahanet.org), creativity (MySpace was originally created as a site for musicians), fantasy (fanfiction sites such as harrypotterfanfiction.com), game playing (multiplayer online video games such as Sony's *Everquest*), conventional politics (e.g., Obama's Facebook page), or self-help and group therapy (e.g., www.healthdiscovery.net). (For a discussion of social networking and activist research, see the sidebar YAHANET: YOUTH, THE ARTS, HIV AND AIDS NETWORK by Katie MacEntee and John Murray.) Community can be built in a slow and stable manner or in the manner of the 'flash mob,' which develops and recedes quickly. Belonging to an online affinity group can take the form of a hobby or correspond to a social or personal need, yet the line between the two can blur. If someone wishes to lose weight and uses the Health Discovery site to reach out to others, for instance, it seems apparent that this fulfills a social and personal need. Yet, if that same person plays *Everquest* and writes fiction at harrypotterfanfiction. com, this apparent hobby might also be a remedy for social isolation. It is possible that the very same person visits yahanet.org to feel socially involved, maintains a page at MySpace to stay plugged in to the music community, and visited the Obama Facebook page regularly during the presidential election of 2008 to express political views.

The diversity of possible communities available to young people online has been a cause for much celebration and anticipation over the past decade, in part because the Internet seems to offer significant new opportunities for community-building and youth civic engagement. These two objectives often work hand in hand, but, if we focus on community-building for the moment, it seems clear that blogging, social network sites, and other web domains now provide vital new spaces for identification and belonging,

YAHAnet: Youth, the Arts, HIV and AIDS network

Katie MacEntee and John Murray, McGill University

YAHAnet.org is an arts-based networking and resource tool launched in early 2009 that provides youth from around the world with the opportunity to actively and creatively participate in HIV and AIDS awareness and education. Dedicated to a participatory action framework, YAHAnet focuses on how the arts and arts-based methods can give youth a voice on topics that affect them. To support youth expression and engagement, the webtool offers how-to guides on a wide range of art forms, including collage art, drawing, photovoice, murals, painting, comic strips, magazines, newsletters, narrative writing, fiction and non-fiction writing, poetry, forum theatre, street theatre, puppetry, dance, hip hop, music, radio drama and documentary, television, video-making, storytelling, and websites. An integral part of YAHAnet is the online gallery space, which houses photos, videos, audio files, and written art created and uploaded by members. The webtool also features a user-controlled resource database and fact guides on such topics as gender, stigma, sexual behavior, and myths surrounding HIV and AIDS. The 'workgroup' function on the webtool gives youth the opportunity to network and initiate projects with other like-minded peer activists and artists on both a local and global level. In addition to workgroups, members can share stories and discuss any problems arising from arts-based approaches to advocacy in the site-wide forum, which also provides a space to discuss topics such as recent medical research, global news and facts, health-related questions, and gender and stigma. To encourage regular participation, YAHAnet hosts online artistic competitions for individuals and groups and posts regularly updated polls and quizzes. In addition, an events calendar provides a way to get involved and take action beyond the webtool. YAHAnet is a unique and comprehensive resource designed by a youth team who feel the peer-to-peer spread of accurate information and innovative creative messages is of global importance.

YAHAnet views youth leadership as vitally important in halting and reversing the current trends affecting the wellbeing of youth. Globally, young people (aged 15–24) account for an estimated 50 percent of newly HIV-infected people (Public Health Agency of Canada, 2007). Women, compared to men, are disproportionately affected by HIV, and this is even more pronounced in young women (UNAIDS, 2008). Biological difference, gender violence, increased poverty, and a growing culture of violence among youth all contribute to the vulnerability of girls and young women (Mitchell et al., 2005). The number of children orphaned as a result of HIV and AIDS is also a serious concern. The loss of one or both parents to AIDS-related deaths leads not only to emotional suffering among young people, families, and communities but also to spiritual and economic trauma. Increasingly, grandparents or siblings – some struggling to care for themselves – are left with the responsibility of caring for younger family members. 'AIDS orphans' are often forced to leave school in order to find work and/or look after younger siblings (AVERT, n.d.). The global AIDS situation has real and devastating effects. Youth live in the age of AIDS.

Young people have been subject to numerous AIDS awareness campaigns, which have had varying degrees of success and have often made young people feel like passive targets. In Sub-Saharan Africa, for example, the barrage of AIDS messages has resulted in a certain amount of AIDS fatigue:

> As one group of disadvantaged black youth just outside of Johannesburg expressed a few years ago, 'AIDS, AIDS, AIDS, that's all we ever hear – we are sick of AIDS.' Testament of how distinctly situated people's relationships are to the disease, another group from a more privileged private school about 20 km away lamented, 'AIDS, it has nothing to do with us. We are sick of AIDS.' (Mitchell and Smith, 2001, p. 513)

However, young people today are growing up in the wake of the Convention on the Rights of the Child (adopted on November 20, 1989) (UNICEF, 2009). As a result of this convention, a declaration was born that recognizes the special circumstances and risks of the child. It also ensures that young people's voices are heard and considered on decisions concerning them and their wellbeing. Although youth are overwhelmingly affected, both directly and indirectly, by HIV and AIDS and also by apathy towards the pandemic, many young people still say, 'we want to do something.' YAHAnet uniquely strives to give youth around the world a place where they can make their voices heard and seize the opportunity to make a difference in their own lives through active participation in a creative online meeting space. When engaged and in charge of their own HIV and AIDS initiatives, youth can play a strong role in tackling the obstacles of the pandemic. But *are* the voices of young people actually going to be heard? And will youth voices affect the global pandemic?

The voices of young people are already beginning to be heard. There are groups, centers, and organizations around the world dedicated to this goal. For example, the Gendering Adolescent AIDS Prevention project (GAAP, www.wgsi.utoronto.ca/GAAP/news/index.html), organized through the University of Toronto and officially partnered with YAHAnet, works with different community groups to use arts-based methods to educate and raise awareness around youth, gender, and HIV and AIDS. In GAAP's project 'Performed Ethnography on HIV/AIDS Prevention,' researchers, playwrights, and Aboriginal youth work together to produce short scenes discussing the socio-political and postcolonial context that contributes to the high rates of HIV and AIDS within Aboriginal communities in Canada. These scenes effectively disseminate data based on a series of focus groups with Aboriginal youth in the greater Toronto area that help discuss the youths' contextual understanding of race, colonial legacies, gender, sex, and drugs in connection with HIV and AIDS.

Similarly, another official partner of YAHAnet, the Centre for Visual Methodologies and Social Change (CVMSC, cvm.za.org), at the University of KwaZulu-Natal in South Africa, works with youth, teachers, and community health workers to support and build comprehensive and effective arts-based research dedicated to social change. In the CVMSC project 'Seeing for Ourselves,' youth created videos on gender-based violence, rape, and sexual abuse. These videos are now being shown to young people and teachers as a way to initiate discussion about the issues. In this case, youth are the experts and their knowledge and understanding are contributing to the development and sustainability of the education system. These projects highlight the opportunities for and potential of the arts to bridge gaps between academia, research, education, and youths' lives.

YAHAnet.org exists to support such initiatives and to promote self-started, grassroots youth involvement. The youth team that designed and that currently maintains, promotes, and expands YAHAnet believes that every user of the site has the potential to become a leader in his or her community. Creative collaborative discussion among individual youth and youth groups/organizations combined with knowledge of facts and understanding of stigma, gender, and cultural difference will produce youth-developed arts-based strategies to educate about HIV and AIDS in communities around the world. These strategies will empower their creators and promote the global voice of youth to make a positive difference in the age of AIDS. The webtool can be explored at www.yahanet.org.

References

AVERT. (n.d.). Worldwide HIV & AIDS statistics commentary. Retrieved May 22, 2011, from http://www.avert.org/worlstatinfo.htm.

Mitchell, C., de Lange, N., Moletsane, R., Stuart, J., and Buthelezi, T. (2005). Giving a face to HIV and AIDS: On the uses of photo-voice by teachers and community health care workers working with youth in rural South Africa. *Qualitative Research in Psychology*, 2(3), pp. 257–270.

Mitchell, C. and Smith, A. (2001). 'Sick of AIDS': Life, literacy and South African youth. *Culture, Health & Sexuality*, 5(6), pp. 513–522.

Public Health Agency of Canada. (2007). *HIV/AIDS epi updates, November 2007*. Retrieved May 22, 2011, from http://www.phac-aspc.gc.ca/aids-sida/publication/index.html.

UNAIDS. (2008). *2008 Report on the Global AIDS Epidemic*. Retrieved May 22, 2011, from http://www.unaids.org/en/KnowledgeCentre/HIVData/GlobalReport/2008/2008_Global_report.asp.

UNICEF. (2009). Voices of youth: Fact sheet. Retrieved May 22, 2011, from http://www.unicef.org/voy/explore/rights/explore_148.html.

especially for young people, who have historically been 'isolated and individualized within their everyday lifeworlds' (Driver, 2006, p. 230). Much attention has focused in particular on the way gay, lesbian, bisexual, transgender, queer, and questioning young people are developing cyber-communities. The appeal of such communities is that they allow participation to be spatially and temporally flexible. Teenagers do not need to live in the same physical community to interact, and yet they can still come together based on various shifting interests, ideas, sentiments, and values. This includes personal lifestyle issues but also 'vulnerable experiences that take on broader social significance' (Driver, 2006, p. 231). The complexity of such conversations and the online spaces needed to facilitate them has led some to wonder whether queer cybercommunities risk homogenizing marginalized kids, even when such spaces provide 'a welcome relief from the [everyday] violences that accrue to members of marginalized sexual and/or gendered subcultures' (Bryson et al., 2006, p. 794). While an important concern, it is of note that new cybercommunities are also changing the way public and private lives intersect.

Social networking spaces offer informal realms for social engagement and thus it is in such spaces where the boundaries between private life and public political life are changing. Where queer youth are concerned, this means seemingly private discussions and postings have a bearing on teens' shifting political sentiments. Conversely, any number of organizations, industries, and foundations are using digital media today to engage young people in civic and political life. The hope is that the popularity and familiarity of new technologies can be leveraged in such a way as to help reverse declines in civic and political participation by youth (Montgomery, 2008). Drawing on the work of Peter Levine, Bennett (2008) argues that this is essential if young people's apparent interest in community volunteer work, consumer activism, environmental issues, and economic injustice are to be leveraged into real change in the political life of nations and communities. Since the late 1990s, various websites have been set up to initiate these very possibilities, including WireTap (www.wiretapmag.org), an online magazine delivering youth writing on various cultural issues; Teaching Tolerance (www.tolerance.org), a web project of the Southern Poverty Law Center that promotes activist approaches to fighting 'self-segregation' and hate in all forms in schools; TakingITGlobal (mentioned earlier), a tremendous resource for promoting youth media production and international dialogue on various issues; and YouthNoise (www.youthnoise.com), a project initiative of Save the Children that provides information from more than 300 non-profit partners to spark youth action and voice.

It is also worth noting that the dialogic interactions enabled by the new media often make possible outcomes where the sum is greater than the individual contributions, something that Jenkins et al. (2006) refer to as 'collective intelligence.' At root, collective intelligence refers to the fact that online spaces enable participants to pool knowledge and compare notes with others towards a common goal. As such, 'collective intelligence [is] an alternative source of power, one that allows grassroots communities to respond effectively to government institutions [...] or to corporate interests' (Jenkins et al., 2006, p. 40). The idea of collective intelligence is that a community is a vast repository of knowledge and that individuals who know how to tap the community to acquire knowledge on a just-in-time basis are in a better position to shape their own and others' social futures. Unfortunately, collective intelligence is a capacity that has not been adequately harnessed in traditional school settings. Over time, pedagogical models that rely on team work have been developed, but they have created problems for evaluation and assessment models predicated on individual performance. In their out-of-school lives, however, young people are increasingly engaged in collaborative contexts, which approximate workplace cultures, not school cultures. Indeed, the notion that knowledge production is enhanced by collaboration is gaining currency, as witnessed by the impact of James Surowiecki's *The Wisdom of Crowds* (2004) and Don Tapscott and Anthony Williams' *Wikinomics* (2006).

While the spectacularly successful contributor-driven knowledge-sharing site Wikipedia has set the new standard for mass collaboration (it was the seventh most visited website in the world in August 2009), it is met with suspicion in school cultures still beholden to lay literacy assumptions from the print era about authoritative sources of knowledge (university presses, mainstream media, and so on). But, in fact, Wikipedia offers a tremendous resource for educators to demonstrate to students how knowledge is produced today. First, it defies the myths of expertise inherited from print-based culture. When *Nature* magazine (2005) compared the accuracy of scientific information on Wikipedia and in the *Encyclopedia Britannica*, for instance, they found that on average they were the same. With the exception of a few closed entries, most items on Wikipedia can be edited by anyone. Contributors can write a new entry or passage, or simply correct a word or a phrase. A small cadre of volunteer editors review the site daily for changes and additions, as do the random hordes who visit the site daily. An interesting exercise involves adding a passage to an existing section and seeing it change over time as others change or transform it. The reliability of information on Wikipedia often depends on the number of contributors; the more authors there are of a particular entry, the greater is the likelihood of accuracy and veracity. The point of this for our purposes, then, is that this exercise in 'crowdsourcing' demonstrates the power of collective intelligence and the fallibility of yesteryear's autonomous expert. The caveat here, of course, is that yesteryear's expert has not faded quietly away, but rather is collaboratively producing knowledge on Wikipedia, now as a contributor to the global pluriverse.

Conclusion

This chapter has covered vast ground in articulating the conceptual problematics central to Media Literacy 2.0. Going forward, a Media Literacy 2.0 agenda must be attendant to the conceptual framework provided by the seven Cs of contemporary youth media practices. Too often in the early years of new media education, the emphasis has been on prevention, on protecting young people from the potential dangers of the Internet, on discouraging them from harassing one another online, and on stopping them from violating copyright. Arguably, there is a growing awareness on the part of media educators of the importance of media production and of the central roles of creativity and collaboration in this process. Nonetheless, much of the response to the challenges posed by the new media is contingent on the relatively rare local conditions of an enlightened program or an inspired teacher. Collaboration, for example, is usually taught as teamwork, not as collective intelligence and distributed cognition. Virtual worlds are for the most part ignored or disdained. And the cultural centrality for young people of consciousness, communication, and community is left to out-of-school contexts.

If Media Literacy 1.0 puts the focus on media – evaluating its structures, institutions, and audiences – Media Literacy 2.0 should be seen as an opportunity to focus on a new kind of literacy that is central to education, working futures, and leisure spaces. This hybrid approach to literacy, which includes youth leisure spheres, runs counter to traditional assumptions of the division between school learning and everyday life. Today, however, many youth come to classrooms with capacities and competencies that emerge from communication and play that scaffold with school learning in interesting but not direct ways. One of the major tasks at hand for Media Literacy 2.0 proponents is to encourage the playful engagements youth have with new technologies in order then to problematize them and to scaffold from them into learning activities congruent with the classroom. The other major task is to develop hybrid new literacies that reach back to traditional textual practices and forward to multimodal literacies. This is a period of tremendous opportunity to retask education to meaningfully engage with situated literacy practices that run the gamut of learning, working, and playing. That is to say, if today's youth are encouraged to 'prosume' their education, schooling will emerge as a meaningful site of learning and development for young people.

8

Critical Citizenship and Media Literacy Futures

The time is right for media literacy to assume a more central role in school curricula worldwide. The important work of media educators in the critical interpretation of media texts and institutions is as imperative today as ever, and the new potentials for production-oriented media education to shape the use of technology across learning environments gives urgency to expanding the role of media education in schools and community settings. Despite these terrific potentials, however, there continues to be a prevailing sentiment of doubt on the part of some key educational stakeholders. In response, we quote from a 2009 commentary in *The Guardian* by media literacy scholar David Buckingham:

> The suspicion of media studies is very similar to that which greeted sociology in the 1960s, or English literature in the 1920s. Then, the suggestion that young people might study books in their native language rather than just in ancient Greek and Latin was little short of scandalous. Now, the idea that young people might study the media of modern communication seems equally scandalous. Newspapers have been around for more than 250 years, the cinema for more than 100 and television for more than 60. Perish the thought that schools should recognise, and interrogate, their existence.

Irony aside, underlying Buckingham's remarks is a clear sense that the transmission of touchstone cultural narratives operates through multiple media forms today. Films such as *Slumdog Millionaire* (2009) and *Jackass 3D* (2010), television shows such as *The Simpsons* and *American Idol,* and video games such as *Grand Theft Auto* and *Spore* shape cultural experience and are used by adolescents and adults to make sense of their own lives and their

Media Literacies: A Critical Introduction, First Edition. Michael Hoechsmann and Stuart R. Poyntz.
© 2012 Blackwell Publishing Ltd. Published 2012 by Blackwell Publishing Ltd.

connections with others. The need to take these media seriously is thus obvious, not only as objects of study, but as pedagogical texts and artifacts that form our identities, our relationships, and our visions of the future.

The suspicion that media literacy is somehow a trivial and unimportant subject, a reflection of the popular culture it seeks to critically interpret, is a misgiving that also threatens the field's development. To this fear, Buckingham (2009) offers another response:

> Much of the discussion of media studies reflects a fundamental confusion about its aims. On the one hand, it is chided for being not vocational enough: after all, media studies isn't going to get you a job in the BBC. Yet on the other, it is condemned for not being academic enough: [...] a Mickey Mouse subject [...] The charge of being insufficiently academic is one that media studies students – who routinely struggle with the complexities of social and cultural theory – would find [...] ridiculous.

That Buckingham needs to make such arguments in a public forum demonstrates how far media literacy proponents still have to go in legitimizing our work. But, of course, the agenda for media literacy is for the most part not being set by the pundits and malcontents who deride its educational value, but by teachers, researchers, and policy-makers. Nonetheless, Buckingham's spirited defense of Media Literacy 1.0 demonstrates the precarious foothold media literacy continues to have in educational and policy circles. This precariousness often has less to do with the strides being made in educational and policy circles, however, and more to do with public discourses that are hostile to educational change that is seen to pander to the worst excesses of youth anomie and transgression.

Broadly speaking, discussions of youth engagement with new and old media appear in the public domain whenever youth are harming themselves and others or falling short of perceived standards of what it means to be an educated subject. At worst, new technologies appear to enable cheating, theft, harassment, bullying, victimization, violence, and even mass murder, and encourage young people to become lazy, distracted, and poor learners. That these claims have been leveled at previous new communication technologies is largely forgotten. That such claims ignore the material circumstances of poverty, decreased funding for public schooling, and the criminalization of various youth sectors (Giroux, 2009) is also largely overlooked. Perhaps this is because communication technologies make good scapegoats; they don't speak back and they are popular enough that their very ubiquity makes for an easy target. Those who live on the 'right side' of the fence can thus find easy solutions to society's woes without turning the mirror back on themselves. Critical traditions in media literacy have always sought to undermine simplistic arguments about social and cultural issues. If this is a strength in media education, it is also a kind of weakness. What critics of the media so often seem to want is straightforward answers, when what is really needed is the rich and challenging work of critically analyzing and transforming how media orchestrates dominant narratives of the day, while also affording new resources and experiences for understanding and reimagining these narratives and our own relationship to them.

Ironically, Buckingham makes no reference to the new communication technologies, perhaps the strongest new tools in the toolkit of media literacy's advocates, in his piece. We make a plea for a reinvigorated version of Media Literacy 1.0 in this book, set within a framework of Media Literacy 2.0. Together, this work exists at the crossroads between a critically generative past and a yet-to-be-determined future. It also acknowledges media interpretation, production, and participation as central to the core of media education. The future of education, technology, work, and culture – four intersecting forces of uncertainty and change – will ensure that the field continues to transform and evolve. In many educational jurisdictions, transformative curricular reform is in place, in process, or under consideration. How this plays out in educational policy and classroom practice is yet to be seen. At a minimum, and under normal circumstances, educational change takes at least 12 years – the life cycle of one student – to make itself known. In the realm of technology, change is blindingly fast, but practice always lags behind. The future of work is also uncertain, not only in the unstable circumstances of globalized economies but in the micro-practices of workplaces and workers grappling with technological change. The discourse of 'creative economies' (Hesmondhalgh, 2007; see also Miranda Campbell's sidebar, YOUTH CULTURAL PRODUCTION AND CREATIVE ECONOMIES, in Chapter 5) attempts to address new work practices arising at the wellspring of economic and technological change, but it does not translate easily into educational discourse and practice. Ultimately, the impulse to react to new economic imperatives and creative futures can lead to a strict vocationalism in media and technology education, a prospect we despair at. In contrast, we argue in favor of a media literacy project that includes the development of operational literacies across a range of modalities (print, visual, and audio) in such a way that enables young people to become active citizens and vital contributors to the public life of our shared worlds. It is important to recognize that the growing significance of networked and multimodal forms of communication will take at least another decade to be fully felt. Some of this operationalization of emerging literacies will take place in workplaces and educational institutions, but much will be worked out in the cultural practices of everyday life, where the new and older media are consumed, experienced, and increasingly produced.

As much as sites of everyday culture are where many emerging literacies are operationalized, these too are the sites where new forms of practice are contested, transformed, and consolidated. Here we note briefly two bellwether topics that are of concern to contemporary media educators: consumerism and media violence. Despite the expansion of non-commercial media that circulate through the conduits of Web 2.0 and the development of copyright-free cultural sandboxes such as the Creative Commons, the ethical, environmental, and political dimensions of consumerism remain a central preoccupation within media education. Media audiences and participants continue to be counted, traded, and sold by media corporations, and the advertising and sale of products and services is central to the media strategies of these same corporations. As the number of platforms through which we consume (and participate with) the media have proliferated, the webs of commodification and commercialization have continued to grow in both reach and complexity. Given that young people are hard pressed to learn and come to terms with these evolving webs of commodification, media education retains an absolutely vital calling as one of the primary counter-strategies through which consumption and the 'nighttime of the commodity' – that is, the environmental, ethical, and political dangers posed by consumerism – can be interrogated, contested, and moved to change.

It is also the case that media violence debates will continue to be an important vector through which media education is discussed in the popular press and taken up in schools. In particular, video gaming and cyberbullying will continue to resonate as part of media violence debates in the future. In response, what matters is that such debates – and the actions that follow from them – steer clear of the moral panics that have so often tainted thinking about children and the media. We know that media violence rarely if ever is the direct cause of children's and youths' actions in the world. Moreover, where video games are concerned, the work of a growing number of educators and researchers is showing how video games can be designed for educational and pro-social aims (de Castell and Jenson, 2007a; Delwiche, 2010). Other research (Gee, 2003; de Castell and Jenson, 2007b; Squire, 2008) demonstrates that young people often interpret and use games in wildly creative and educationally significant ways that hint at emergent forms of critical understanding that can be explored and developed in media education classrooms.

Where cyberbullying is concerned, the stakes are enormous. Just as we are completing this text, a new wave of concern over cyberbullying – here focused on a young, queer college student at Rutgers who committed suicide after being harassed online – has drawn the attention of mainstream media, families, and educators. This is one incident but it is telling of how new technologies can be manipulated by young people to cause harm. In response, the discussion of harm reduction in media education needs to include new definitions of harassment and hate crime so that the energies spent on discussing how technology provokes cyberbullying can include a debate on how and why young people continue to harass one another. Ultimately, technology exacerbates a problem – bullying – that has been consonant with youth culture for decades. But this means it is the task of media educators and young learners to carefully negotiate the multiple uses and potentials of digital media to develop ethical uses and to quickly recognize abuses. While it is true that there is a generalized misunderstanding of the role of Web 2.0 media in the lives of young people, there is enough evidence of harm, or the potential thereof, that media educators must play a central role in both shaping public debates about harm reduction and making harm reduction central to learning contexts.

Alongside consumption and media violence (harm reduction), the issues of intellectual property and copyright (see Chapter 7 for a more extensive discussion) will also be immensely important for media educators in the near future. In short, as well as criminalizing youth for reworking cultural artifacts that circulate in culture at large, the concern in media literacy circles has to do with access to primary materials for media production, much of which is held in copyright and not available legally to children and youth. How this problem is resolved depends on the courts on the one hand, but also on the advocacy and political participation of educators, students, and everyday citizens. With this in mind, it is to the question of critical citizenship that we wish to turn in closing this book.

Thinking, Judging, and Critical Citizenship

Equipping young people to be critical participants in public spheres has long been a key objective within media education. It is consonant with the moral agenda that circumscribes the field (see Chapter 1 on this point) and is crucial in societies and cultures that are increasingly semiotic and digital, where to be a citizen means to participate critically online and in everyday life through images, sounds, and written texts. If this is the case, we argue that critical citizenship has less to do with the way young people learn to become certain kinds of activists or to take part in the formal mechanisms of politics (i.e., voting, membership in political parties, and so on) via media education and more to do with the way media education fosters students' modes of thinking, judging, and acting.

We do not only argue thus because it is clear that young people themselves are increasingly engaging in multiple forms of civic participation, including consumer activism, social movements, issue-based politics, and new forms of volunteerism that circumvent or ignore more traditional liberal democratic institutions (Bennett, 2008). More important is the fact that it is not the job of media educators to determine the political project young people will inherit, and public life itself is not sustained by mere acts of voting once every three or four years. Public life is sustained through a culture of speech and action that counteracts thoughtlessness. By this we mean that democracy is fostered through a rich social, cultural, and political field, an everyday lifeworld in which conformity is contested, and thoughtful and vigilant resistance to the power of ideology, bureaucracy, and artificiality are enabled. Such a field is not a singular space, however; it is 'a space of conflicting and competing discourses, of stories, and images, and performances' that do not reveal truth as much as 'the worldliness of the world' (Silverstone, 2007, p. 49). But this means a vital social, cultural, and political lifeworld is sustained as much by the complexity and richness of the stories and perspectives we find there as by the way truth itself is articulated in public life.

If media education offers the potential to examine the lifeworlds of our students, we wish to amplify the discussion to open up a debate over what really matters. Does media education open doors for our students to re-envision the world around them? Arguably, it has the potential to do so, as many contributors to the discourse and practice of media education have demonstrated and as we have argued in this book. But we are, nonetheless, struck with a simple but fundamental question: 'so what?' So what if our students learn to critically interpret the media, to produce probing media of their own, and to question the social, cultural, political, and economic circumstances in which they live? So what?

We invoke here the critical interventions of a number of theorists, specifically Paulo Freire, Antonio Gramsci, Mikhail Bakhtin and Hannah Arendt, all of whom advocate a vision of dialogue and getting outside of one's own skin to experience the world of others. Freire gives us a vision of education based on dialogue. Both the teacher and the student are learners – not only of the subject matter, but also of the specific conditions of one another. Gramsci tells us that democracy involves a struggle over ideas, that there may be unusual alliances, but that, ultimately, there is a war of position around the question of which ideas win the day in democratic societies. Bakhtin gives us the concept of dialogism, that one person's ideas are influenced by what comes before. This dialogism is informed by a heteroglossia of voices – 'hetero' meaning different and distinct, and 'glossia' referring to voices (or tongues). To sum up the work of Freire, Gramsci, and Bakhtin, to be is to be in relation to, and conversation with, others.

It is the presence of others – the plurality of other people, other stories, other images, other performances – that sustains that 'the worldliness of the world,' in other words. It is in this sense that plurality acts as a bulwark against thoughtlessness because the presence of other people, new ideas, and images – what Hannah Arendt (1958) calls the 'web of human relationships' – ensures our mediated lives are open to change. Plurality thereby counters a kind of oblivion that can blind us to the possibility that things might be different from how they are. Plurality nurtures thoughtfulness and thus constitutes the ground on which democratic dreams might be born. As such, it is essential for developing a common world, a public culture in which we are all involved.

Our question, then, is how does media education foster plurality (and thereby thoughtfulness) among children and youth? We argue it does so by 'preserving newness' (Arendt, 1968, p. 189), which is to say, by working with young people in such a way that our students learn that new beginnings, new directions in their own and other people's lives are possible. This happens, first, when media education enables thinking itself, the habit of examining 'whatever happens to come to pass or attract attention' in our lives (Arendt, 1978, p. 5). It is through our faculty of thought, our ability to reflect on the world, that we move beyond routine circumstances and routine behaviors and begin to consider these circumstances and behaviors in relation to other problems, other people, other possible answers. A more complex (or plural) field of social, cultural, and political life is thereby opened up.

Where media education enables thinking and contributes to the critical citizenship vital to public life, it does so by helping young people to denaturalize the images and mediated experiences that are so much a part of our lives. By helping young people to become historians of the present, to read into the fabric of everyday consumer life, media education demystifies the given world. Distance is thereby introduced into the way young people experience their identities, their relationships with others, and their sense of the world itself. The constructedness of our social and cultural lives is thus brought into view. Certainly, the fact that our lives are constructed in and of itself is not the problem; but, unless we learn to think about how this constructedness operates, change is not possible. Media education also fosters thinking by helping young people to question bias in media, to see how figures of authority are constituted as such, to examine the production of media texts and practices in relation to an ecology of structures and forces, and by helping children and youth to use media texts – including personalities like lonelygirl15 – as looking glasses into the cultural patterns and pressures shaping their lives.

If thinking of this sort is consonant with Media Literacy 1.0, the intertwined project of Media Literacy 2.0 also fosters thinking by helping students to learn how to leverage the networking form and capabilities of the Internet. This includes learning to think via forms of collective intelligence, but, more broadly, network thinking refers to thinking enabled *through* the production of meaningful connections in a world rich with information and digital media. This is a central ambition of Media Literacy 2.0, as are efforts to foster thinking by developing young people's abilities to sift through and assess the information and narratives produced across media platforms.

Thinking works to open up routine behaviors and practices; nevertheless, on its own it is still not enough to foster young people's democratic habits of mind, because thinking is typically something we do on our own, or, at the very least, in our own minds. To preserve newness and nurture democratic cultures, however, also requires that we engage with that culture, by *being in the world*. To do so requires that we learn to judge (Arendt, 1978). Judging brings us into the world because judging is something we can only do by forming opinions *with* and *through* our encounters with others. Judging is not something we can do on our own. To judge is to form points of view or positions regarding others, and to do this requires that we involve ourselves in 'a talking through, a bringing forth, a constant engagement with one's own thought and that of others' (Silverstone, 2007, p. 44). This requires us to act in the world, to go out and engage with others in order to understand others. Through this, judging involves risk-taking and, often, a challenge to the status quo, because to judge is to see things from many sides and thus to understand perspectives not yet taken.

Media education nurtures young people's ability to judge by affording opportunities for children and youth to talk back to various publics, to leverage the production possibilities made available by new (social networking spaces, blogs, podcasts, and increasingly accessible video production tools) and older media (including written text) to contest, engage, visit, and act with others. These resources make it possible – as perhaps never before – for students to be active agents in their lives and the lives of others. That said, young people do not take on such roles automatically or easily. Rather, a willingness to judge with others develops at least in part as students are provoked and challenged (by teachers and those working in less formal learning environments) to examine how media cultures operate in and through their lives, including how these cultures might be changed to make way for more equitable futures. To do this work, a production-oriented media education curriculum is not only an interesting add-on to the critical analytic work media education has long been committed to; in our view, it is also crucial for ensuring that media literacy programs nurture a kind of engagement that challenges and invites students to share their views with others, to learn to judge in such a way that thoughtfulness is the result. Where media production opens up these possibilities, so too do a range of web spaces – see Chapter 7 for a more detailed list and discussion of such spaces – that address issues of culture, race, sexuality, and youth action on global issues. Such spaces enable dialogue and the sharing of media resources among youth and educators. It is also of note that these sites often emphasize a 'learning to play, playing to learn' orientation that appears to be a powerful motivating force for young learners. What media educators must do is develop ways to translate these learning practices toward engagement with the issues and concerns that are shaping young people's daily experiences. By doing so, critical citizenship can be fostered in relation to the media young people increasingly see as their own.

This process involves opening the door to some forms of narrative and story that the young people in our classrooms value and consider 'edgy,' both in the sense of being on the cutting edge of contemporary youth culture and being on the edge of what is permissible in terms of topics and issues normally discussed with adults. While youth are often portrayed as a threat to the fabric of social life, this is a way of controlling, disciplining, and managing youths' sense of agency and belonging. 'For psychological and social reasons,' however, youth quite typically

> engage in [...] 'boundary performance' – risk-taking [that] is often publicly performed as part of the process of identity construction in a peer group context [...] [The result is that] whatever we as adults worry about, whatever social norms we seek to defend, children will be motivated to transgress precisely those norms that society has constructed as vital to the preservation of childhood innocence. (Livingstone, 2009, p. 155)

If this is so, media education should open a space for dialogue with young people that can help sustain a democratic world by ensuring that 'the digital and analogue spectrum' is available for all those who are marginalized in contemporary culture (Silverstone, 2007, p. 143). This involves going past pithy commentaries on pop culture trends – which are valuable but not enough on their own – by also drawing attention to those voices and bodies (including people who are homeless, refugees, migrant labor, sex trade workers, and others) that are regularly disappeared from view in the mainstream press; by helping young people to experiment with new forms of association, including 'crowdsourcing' and online community forums that are changing the political spaces of our cities and neighborhoods; and so on. Most importantly, media education fosters democracy when it enables young people to confront 'fundamental and structuring wrong[s], a miscount, a radical and unjust exclusion' of people, of ideas, of media practices 'that cannot be tolerated' (Barney, 2010). When we do this, media education helps to nurture a form of thinking and doing, a critical citizenry conscious of the ways all meaning (including that revealed through media texts and experiences) has a social and historical context, a form of contingency that is susceptible to change.

Last Words

Reflecting on the contemporary circumstances of change in the world, Divina Frau-Meigs and Jordi Torrent (2009) recently proposed that 'media education is an agent for soft change' in the sense that 'it produces inclusion and helps fight poverty, marginalization and segregation' (p. 17). If soft change sounds excessively modest, we contend that a critically informed and participatory global citizenry is better positioned to steward through more fundamental changes, and that a critical education agenda is central to this vision. Today, technological change is turning media into 'intrusive and extensive prostheses' (p. 18) that impact upon economic development, subjective identities, and our social and political futures. This is an era in which information rivals knowledge, and humanistic *logos* competes with corporate logos. This is also an era of connectivity and surveillance. 'Communicational transparency,' the French philosopher Jean-François Lyotard (1984) reminds us, ensures that every person is jacked into the informational circuitry, 'located at "nodal points" of specific communication circuits' (p. 6). While Lyotard was speaking about a much earlier information era, his words still capture a dimension of our lives today. Says Lyotard (1984), for instance:

> one is always located at a post through which various kinds of messages pass. No one, not even the least privileged amongst us, is ever entirely powerless over the messages that traverse and position him at the post of sender, addressee, or referent. (p. 15)

From Lyotard (1984), we learn that the guiding conception of a cybernetic public sphere was, and is, to 'be operational (that is, commensurable) or disappear' (p. xxiv). The question of inclusion and exclusion still begs the question of the digital divide between cybernetic haves and have-nots. While investment is being made globally to bring more people online and into the new international cybersphere, the patterns of participation continue to follow the path of economic divides that separate the privileged and underprivileged. Still, what is clear is that, when people are exposed to the new technologies for the first time, media education and media literacy are the front-line responses to ensuring meaningful participation. Media education is essential for ensuring young people a form of critical engagement with mediated cultures that allows them to make sense of their lives and identities and to engage with the technologies, literacies, and everyday cultural practices that can foster economic participation and social inclusion. As policy-makers worldwide are recognizing, media literacy facilitates hands-on, grassroots lessons in civic engagement that enable participation and meaningful engagement in our increasingly semiotic and digitally mediated world.

To continue this work in the decades to come, what is required is a concerted and sustained effort by policy-makers, working alongside educators, teacher associations, community groups, and, most of all, young people themselves. The goal is to create the policy frameworks and curricular initiatives that will help to sustain the promise of a robust media literacy project into the future. At the root of this agenda should always be a democratic vision of education that is emancipatory and inclusive and that seeks to engender knowledge and inquisitiveness by building minds and communities and preparing current and future generations for the challenges ahead in the realm of media and technology, but also in the realm of participation in cultural, social, political, and economic life.

References

Adorno, T. and Horkheimer, M. (1972). *The Dialectic of Enlightenment.* New York: Herder and Herder.

Anderson, C. A., Bushman, A. C., Schmitt, K. L., Linebarger, D. L., and Wright, J. C. (2001). Early childhood television viewing and adolescent behavior: The recontact study. *Monographs of the Society for Research in Child Development,* 66(1, serial no. 264), pp. 1–147.

Anderson, D. R., Huston, A. C., Wright, J. C., and Collins, P. A. (1998). Initial findings on the long term impact of *Sesame Street* and educational television for children: The recontact study. In R. Noll and M. Price (Eds.), *A Communications Cornucopia: Markle Foundation Essays on Information Policy* (pp. 279–296). Washington, DC: Brookings Institute.

Arendt, H. (1958). *The Human Condition* (2nd edn.). Chicago, IL: University of Chicago Press.

Arendt, H. (1968). *Between Past and Future: Eight Exercises in Political Thought* (enl. edn.). New York: Viking Press.

Arendt, H. (1978). *The Life of the Mind.* New York: Harcourt Brace Jovanovich.

Arnold, M. (1993 [1869]). *Culture and Anarchy and Other Writings.* Cambridge, UK: Cambridge University Press.

Bakardjieva, M. (2010). The internet and subactivism: Cultivating young citizenship in everyday life. In T. Olsson and P. Dahlgren (Eds.), *Young People, ICTs and Democracy: Theories, Policies, Identities, and Websites* (pp. 129–146). Göteborg, Sweden: Nordicom, University of Gothenburg.

Bakhtin, M. (1981). Discourse in the novel (C. Emerson and M. Holquist, trans.) In M. Holquist (Ed.), *The Dialogic Imagination: Four Essays by M. M. Bakhtin* (pp. 259–422). Austin, TX: University of Texas Press.

Bakhtin, M. (1984). *Rabelais and His World* (H. Iswolsky, trans.). Bloomington, IN: Indiana University Press.

Media Literacies: A Critical Introduction, First Edition. Michael Hoechsmann and Stuart R. Poyntz.
© 2012 Blackwell Publishing Ltd. Published 2012 by Blackwell Publishing Ltd.

Barbaro, A. and Earp, J. (writers and directors) (2008). *The Commercialization of Childhood.* S. Jhally (producer). Amherst, MA: The Media Education Foundation.

Barney, D. (2004). *The Network Society.* Cambridge, UK: Polity Press.

Barney, D. (2010). 'Excuse us if we don't give a fuck': The (anti-) political career of participation. *Jeunesse,* 2(2), pp. 138–146.

Barthes, R. (1957). *Mythologies.* Paris: Editions du Seuil.

Barthes, R. (1977). The death of the author (S. Heath, trans.). In *Image-Music-Text* (pp. 142–148). New York: Hill and Wang.

Benjamin, W. (1986). The author as producer. In P. Demetz (Ed.), *Reflections: Essays, Aphorisms, Autobiographical Writings* (pp. 220–238). New York: Schocken Books.

Benkler, Y. (2006). *The Wealth of Networks: How Social Production Transforms Markets and Freedom.* New Haven, CT: Yale University Press.

Bennett, W. L. (2008). Changing citizenship in the digital age. In W. L. Bennett (Ed.), *Civic Life Online: Learning How Digital Media Can Engage Youth* (pp. 1–24). Cambridge, MA: MIT Press.

Berko, L. (1989). Video in search of a discourse. *Quarterly Review of Film Studies,* 10(4), pp. 289–307.

Bloom, A. (1987). *The Closing of the American Mind.* New York: Simon and Schuster.

boyd, d. (2007). Why youth (heart) social network sites: The role of networked publics in teenage social life. In D. Buckingham (Ed.), *McArthur Foundation Series on Digital Learning – Youth, Identity, and Digital Media Volume* (pp. 119–142). Cambridge, MA: MIT Press.

Boyd-Barrett, J. O. (1982). Cultural dependency and the mass media. In M. Gurevitch, T. Bennett, J. Curran, and J. Woollacott (Eds.), *Culture, Society and the Media* (pp. 174–195). London: Methuen and Co. Ltd.

Bragg, S. (2000). Media violence and education: A study of youth audiences and the horror genre. Unpublished Doctoral Thesis. London: University of London, Institute of Education.

Bragg, S. (2007). 'Student voice' and governmentality: The production of enterprising subjects? *Discourse: Studies in the Cultural Politics of Education,* 28(3), pp. 343–358.

Bryson, M., MacIntosh, L., Jordan, S., and Lin, H.-L. (2006). Virtually queer? Homing devices, mobility, and un/belongings. *Canadian Journal of Communication,* 31(4), pp. 791–814.

Buckingham, D. (1996). *Moving Images: Understanding Children's Emotional Responses to Television.* Manchester, UK: Manchester University Press.

Buckingham, D. (1999). The place of production: Media education and youth media production in the UK. In C. von Feilitzen and U. Carlsson (Eds.), *Children and Media: Image, Education, Participation* (Vol. Yearbook 1999, pp. 219–228). Göteborg, Sweden: UNESCO International Clearinghouse on Children and Violence on the Screen.

Buckingham, D. (2000). *After the Death of Childhood: Growing Up in the Age of Electronic Media.* Malden, MA: Polity Press.

Buckingham, D. (2003a). *Media Education: Literacy, Learning and Contemporary Culture.* Cambridge, UK: Polity Press.

Buckingham, D. (2003b). Media education and the end of the critical consumer. *Harvard Educational Review,* 73(3), pp. 309–327.

Buckingham, D. (2006a). *The Media Literacy of Children and Young People: A Review of the Research Literature.* London: Centre for the Study of Children, Youth, and Media, Institute of Education.

Buckingham, D. (2006b). Is there a digital generation? In D. Buckingham and R. Willett (Eds.), *Digital Generations: Children, Young People, and New Media* (pp. 1–13). London: Lawrence Erlbaum Associates.

Buckingham, D. (2006c). Children and new media. In L. A. Lievrouw and S. M. Livingstone (Eds.), *Handbook of New Media: Social Shaping and Social Consequences of ICTs* (2nd edn., pp. 75–91). London, UK: Sage Publications.

Buckingham, D. (2007). Selling childhood? Children and consumer culture. *Journal of Children and Media,* 1(1), pp. 15–24.

Buckingham, D. (2009). In defence of media studies. Retrieved October 1, 2009, from http://www.guardian.co.uk/commentisfree/2009/aug/22/media-studies

Buckingham, D., Niesyto, H., and Fisherkeller, J. (2003). Videoculture: Crossing borders with young people's video productions. *Television and New Media,* 4(4), pp. 461–482.

Buckingham, D. and Sefton-Green, J. (1994). *Cultural Studies Goes to School: Reading and Teaching Popular Media.* London: Taylor and Francis.

Buckingham, D. and Sefton-Green, J. (2003). Gotta catch 'em all: Structure, agency and pedagogy in children's media culture. *Media, Culture & Society,* 25(3), pp. 379–399.

Burke, K. (1966). *Language as Symbolic Action.* Berkeley, CA: University of California Press.

Burn, A. and Durran, J. (2006). Digital anatomies: Analysis as production in media education. In D. Buckingham and R. Willett (Eds.), *Digital Generations: Children, Young People, and New Media* (pp. 273–293). Mahwah, NJ: Lawrence Erlbaum.

Burnett, R. (1996). Video: The politics of culture and community. In M. Renov and E. Suderburg (Eds.), *Resolutions: Contemporary Video Practices* (pp. 283–301). Minneapolis, MN: University of Minnesota Press.

Byers, M. (2008). Education and entertainment: The many reals of Degrassi. In Z. Druick and A. Kotsopoulos (Eds.), *Programming Reality: Perspectives on English-Canadian Television* (pp. 187–204). Waterloo, ON: Wilfred Laurier University Press.

Casey, B., Casey, N., Calvert, B., French, L., and Lewis, J. (2008). *Television Studies: Key Concepts* (2nd edn.). New York: Routledge.

Castells, M. (2001). *The Internet Galaxy*. Oxford, UK: Oxford University Press.

Cazden, C., Cope, B., Fairclough, N., Gee, J. P., Kalantzis, M., Kress, G., Luke, A., Luke, C., Michaels, S., and Nakata, M. (2000 [1996]). A pedagogy of multi-literacies: Designing social futures. In B. Cope and M. Kalantzis (Eds.), *Multiliteracies: Literacy, Learning and the Design of Social Futures* (pp. 9–37). London: Routledge.

Ceruzzi, P. (1986). An unforeseen revolution: Computers and expectations, 1935–1985. In J. J. Corn (Ed.), *Imagining Tomorrow: History, Technology and the American Future* (pp. 188–201). Cambridge MA: MIT Press.

Charmaraman, L. (2006). Cognitive and social development through digital media construction in an urban after-school community. Unpublished Doctoral Dissertation. Berkley, CA: University of California, Berkley.

Children's Television Workshop. (1988). *International Adaptations of Sesame Street: Description and Evaluation*. New York: Children's Television Workshop.

Chung, G. and Grimes, S. M. (2005). Data mining the kids: Surveillance and market research strategies in children's online games. *Canadian Journal of Communication*, 30(4), pp. 527–548.

Connell, I. and Hurd, G. (1989). Cultural education: A revised program. *Media Information Australia*, 53, pp. 23–30.

Cook, D. T. (2004). *The Commodification of Childhood*. Durham, NC: Duke University Press.

Danesi, M. (2006). *Brands*. New York: Routledge.

de Block, L. and Rydin, I. (2006). Digital rapping in media productions: Intercultural communication through youth culture. In D. Buckingham and R. Willett (Eds.), *Digital Generations: Children, Young People, and New Media* (pp. 295–312). Mahwah, NJ: Lawrence Erlbaum Associates.

Debord, G. (1994). *The Society of the Spectacle* (D. Nicholson-Smith, trans.). New York: Zone Books.

de Castell, S. and Jenson, J. (2007a). Digital games for education: When meanings play. *Intermedialities*, 9, pp. 113–132.

de Castell, S. and Jenson, J. (Eds.) (2007b). *Worlds in Play: International Perspectives on Digital Games Research*. New York: Peter Lang.

del Vecchio, G. (1997). *Creating Ever-Cool: A Marketer's Guide to a Kid's Heart*. Grenta, LA: Pelican.

Delwiche, A. (2010). Media literacy 2.0: Unique characteristics of video games. In K. Tyner (Ed.), *Media Literacy: New Agendas in Communication* (pp. 175–191). New York: Routledge.

Demetz, P. (Ed.) (1986). *Reflections: Essays, Aphorisms, Autobiographical Writings* (E. Jephcott, trans.). New York: Schocken Books.

Dery, M. (1993). *Culture Jamming: Hacking, Slashing and Sniping in the Empire of Signs* (Vol. 25). Westfield, NJ: Open Magazine Pamphlet Series.

de Saussure, F. (1974). *Course in General Linguistics.* London: Fontana.

Driver, S. (2006). Virtually queer youth communities of girls and birls: Dialogical spaces of identity work and desiring exchanges. In D. Buckingham and R. Willett (Eds.), *Digital Generations: Children, Young People and New Media* (pp. 229–249). Mahwah, NJ: Lawrence Erlbaum Associates.

Drotner, K. (1999). Dangerous media? Panic discourses and dilemma of modernity. *Paedogogica Historica,* 35(3), pp. 593–619.

Drotner, K. (2008). Leisure is hard work: Digital practices and future competencies. In D. Buckingham (Ed.), *Youth, Identity and Digital Media* (pp. 167–184). Cambridge, MA: MIT Press.

Dyson, A. H. (1997). *Writing Superheroes: Contemporary Childhood, Popular Culture, and Classroom Literacy.* New York: Teachers College Press.

Electronic Privacy Information Centre. (2003). The children's online privacy protection act (COPPA). Retrieved May 15, 2009, from http://epic.org/privacy/kids

Farrelly, M., Davis, K., Haviland, L., Messeri, P., and Healton, C. (2005). Evidence of a dose-response relationship between 'truth' antismoking ads and youth smoking prevalence. *American Journal of Public Health,* 95(3), pp. 425–431.

Fleetwood, N. (2005). Authenticating practices: Producing realness, performing youth. In S. Maira and E. Soep (Eds.), *Youthscapes: The Popular, the National, the Global* (pp. 155–172). Philadelphia, PA: University of Pennsylvania Press.

Frau-Meigs, D. and Torrent, J. (2009). Media education policy: Towards a global rationale. In D. Frau-Meigs and J. Torrent (Eds.), *Mapping Media Education Policies in the World: Visions, Programmes and Challenges* (pp. 15–21). New York: UN-Alliance of Civilizations and Grupo Comunicar.

Gandy, O. H. (2002). The real digital divide. In L. A. Lievrouw and S. M. Livingstone (Eds.), *Handbook of New Media: Social Shaping and Consequences of ICTs* (pp. 448–460). Thousand Oaks, CA: Sage Publications.

Gee, J. P. (2003). *What Video Games Have to Teach Us about Learning and Literacy.* New York: Palgrave MacMillan.

Gee, J. P., Hull, G., and Lankshear, C. (1996). *The New Work Order: Behind the Language of New Capitalism.* Sydney, Australia: Allen and Unwin.

Giddens, A. (1976). *New Rules of Sociological Method.* London: Hutchinson.

Giddens, A. (1984). *The Constitution of Society.* Cambridge, UK: Polity Press.

Giddens, A. (1990). Structuration theory and sociological analysis. In J. Clark, C. Modgil, and S. Modgil (Eds.), *Anthony Giddens: Consensus and Controversy.* Basingstoke, UK: Falmer.

Giroux, H. A. (1994). *Disturbing Pleasures: Learning Popular Culture.* New York: Routledge.

Giroux, H. A. (2009). *Youth in a Suspect Society: Democracy or Disposability?* New York: Palgrave Macmillan.

Goldfarb, B. (2002). *Visual Pedagogy: Media Cultures in and Beyond the Classroom.* Durham, NC: Duke University Press.

Goodman, S. (2003). *Teaching Youth Media: A Critical Guide to Literacy, Video Production, and Social Change.* New York: Teachers College Press.

Goodman, S. (2005). The practice and principles of teaching critical literacy at the educational video center. In G. Schwarz (Ed.), *Media Literacy: Transforming Curriculum and Teaching* (Vol. 104, pp. 206–228). London: Blackwell Synergy.

Goody, J. (1977). *The Domestication of the Savage Mind.* Cambridge, UK: Cambridge University Press.

Gore, J. (1993). *The Struggle for Pedagogies.* New York: Routledge.

Grace, D. J. and Tobin, J. (2002). Pleasure, creativity, and the carnivalesque in children's video production. In L. Bresler and C. M. Thompson (Eds.), *The Arts in Children's Lives* (pp. 195–214). Dordrecht, The Netherlands: Kluwer Academic Publishers.

Graff, H. J. (1987). *The Legacies of Literacy: Continuities and Contradictions in Western Culture and Society.* Bloomington, IN: Indiana University Press.

Green, B. and Bigum, C. (1993). Aliens in the classroom. *Australian Journal of Education,* 37(2), pp. 119–41.

Grimes, S. M. and Shade, L. R. (2005). Neopian economics of play: Children's cyberpets and online communities as immersive advertising in neopets.com. *International Journal of Media and Cultural Politics,* 1(2), pp. 181–198.

Hall, S. (1980). Encoding/decoding. In S. Hall, D. Hobson, A. Lowe, and P. Willis (Eds), *Culture, Media, Language* (pp. 128–139). London: Unwin Hyman.

Hall, S. (1994). Cultural identity and diapora. In P. Williams and L. Chrisman (Eds.), *Colonial Discourse and Post-Colonial Theory: A Reader* (pp. 392–403). New York: Columbia University Press.

Hall, S. (1996a). Cultural studies and its theoretical legacies. In D. Morley and K.-H. Chen (Eds.), *Stuart Hall: Critical Dialogues in Cultural Studies* (pp. 262–275). London: Routledge.

Hall, S. (1996b). Introduction: Who needs identity? In S. Hall and P. du Gay (Eds.), *Questions of Cultural Identity* (pp. 1–17). London: Sage Publications.

Healton, C. (2003). *Progress Report, 2002–2003.* Washington, DC: American Legacy Foundation.

Henderson, L. (2009). Let's all be neighbours on Will Wright Street. *Walrus Magazine,* March, pp. 56–58.

Hesmondhalgh, D. (2007). *The Cultural Industries* (2nd edn.). London: Sage Publications.

Hodge, R. and Tripp, D. (1986). *Children and Television: A Semiotic Approach.* Cambridge, UK: Polity Press.

Hoechsmann, M. (2001). Just do it: What Michael Jordan has to teach us. In D. Andrews (Ed.), *Michael Jordan Inc* (pp. 269–276). Albany, NY: State University of New York Press.

Hoechsmann, M. and Low, B. E. (2008). *Reading Youth Writing: 'New' Literacies, Cultural Studies and Education.* New York: Peter Lang.

Hoggart, R. (1957). *Uses of Literacy: Changing Patterns in English Mass Culture.* Fair Lawn, NJ: Essential Books.

Illich, I. (1987). A plea for research on lay literacy. *Interchange,* 18(1/2), pp. 9–22.

Ito, M. (2008). Education vs. entertainment: A cultural history of children's software. In K. Salen (Ed.), *The Ecology of Games: Connecting Youth, Games, and Learning* (pp. 89–116). Cambridge, MA: MIT Press.

Jankowski, N. W. (2002). Creating community with media: History, theories and scientific investigations. In L. A. Lievrouw and S. M. Livingstone (Eds.), *Handbook of New Media: Social Shaping and Consequences of ICTs* (pp. 34–49). Thousand Oaks, CA: Sage Publications.

Jenkins, H. (2006a). *Convergence Culture.* New York: New York University Press.

Jenkins, H. (2006b). *Fans, Bloggers, and Gamers: Exploring Participatory Culture.* New York: New York University Press.

Jenkins, H., Clinton, K., Purushotma, R., Robinson, A. J., and Weigel, M. (2006). *Confronting the Challenges of Participatory Culture: Media Education for the 21st Century.* Chicago, IL: The MacArthur Foundation. Retrieved October 7, 2009, from http://www.newmedialiteracies.org/files/working/NMLWhitePaper.pdf

Johnson, R. (1986–1987). What is cultural studies anyway? *Social Text,* 16, pp. 38–80.

Johnson, S. (2005). *Everything Bad is Good for You: How Today's Popular Culture is Actually Making Us Smarter.* New York: Riverhead Books.

Kelly, D. M. (2006). Framework: Helping youth counter their misrepresentations in media. *Canadian Journal of Education,* 29(1), pp. 27–48.

Kenway, J. and Bullen, E. (2008). The global corporate curriculum and the young cyberflaneur as global citizen. In N. Dolby and F. Rizvi (Eds.), *Youth Moves: Identities and Education in Global Perspective* (pp. 17–32). New York: Routledge.

Kidd, B. (1987). Sports and masculinity. In M. Kaufman (Ed.), *Beyond Patriarchy* (pp. 250–265). Toronto, ON: Oxford University Press.

Kline, S. (1993). *Out of the Garden: Toys, TV and Children's Culture in the Age of Marketing.* Toronto, ON: Garamond Press.

Kline, S. (2005). Countering children's sedentary lifestyles: An evaluative study of a media-risk education approach. *Childhood,* 12(2), pp. 239–258.

Kline, S. and Woo, B. (2008). Toxic gaming? On the problems of regulating play. In J. Greenberg and C. Elliott (Eds.), *Communication in Question: Competing Perspectives on Controversial Issues in Communication Studies* (pp. 97–104). Toronto, ON: Nelson Canada.

Kline, S., Stewart, K., and Murphy, D. (2006). Media literacy in the risk society: Toward a risk reduction strategy. *Canadian Journal of Education,* 29(1), pp. 131–153.

Knight Abowitz, K. and Harnish, J. (2006). Contemporary discourses of citizenship. *Review of Educational Research*, 76(4), pp. 653–690.

Kubey, R. W. (2003). Why U.S. media education lags behind the rest of the English-speaking world. *Television and New Media*, 4(4), pp. 351–370.

Lanham, R. (2006). *The Economics of Attention*. Chicago, IL: University of Chicago Press.

Lankshear, C. and Knobel, M. (2006). *New Literacies: Everyday Practices and Classroom Learning* (2nd edn.). Maidenhead, UK: Open University Press.

Lankshear, C. and Knobel, M. (2007). Introduction: Digital literacies – concepts, policies and practices. In C. Lankshear and M. Knobel (Eds.), *Digital Literacies: Concepts, Policies and Practices* (pp. 1–16). New York: Peter Lang.

Leander, K. and Frank, A. (2006). The aesthetic production and distribution of image/subjects among online youth. *E-Learning*, 3(2), pp. 185–206.

Leavis, F. R. and Thompson, D. (1933). *Culture and Environment: The Training of Critical Awareness*. London: Chatto and Windus.

Lenhart, A., Kahne, J., Middaugh, E., Rankin Macgill, A., Evans, C., and Vitak, J. (2008). *Teens, Video Games, and Civics*. Washington, DC: Pew Internet and American Life Project.

Lessig, L. (2008). *Remix: Making Art and Commerce Thrive in the Hybrid Economy*. New York: Penguin.

Levine, L. (1988). *High Brow/Low Brow*. Cambridge, MA: Harvard University Press.

Lévi-Strauss, C. (1966). *The Savage Mind*. Chicago, IL: University of Chicago Press.

Lewis, J., Cushion, S., and Thomas, J. (2005). Immediacy, convenience or engagement? An analysis of 24-hour news channels in the UK. *Journalism Studies*, 6(4), pp. 461–478.

Livingstone, S. (2002). *Young People and New Media: Childhood and the Changing Media Environment*. London: Sage Publications.

Livingstone, S. (2009). *Children and the Internet: Great Expectations, Challenging Realities*. Cambridge, UK: Polity Press.

Livingstone, S. and Bober, M. (2004). *UK Children Go Online: Surveying the Experiences of Young People and their Parents*. London: Economic and Social Research Council.

Livingstone, S. and Haddon, L. (2009). *Young People in the European Digital Media Landscape: A Statistical Overview*. Göteborg, Sweden: International Clearinghouse on Children, Youth and Media.

Lowndes, D. (1968). *Film Making in Schools*. London: Batsford.

Luke, A. (2003). Literacy and the other: A sociological approach to literacy research and policy in multilingual societies. *Reading Research Quarterly*, 38(1), pp. 132–141.

Luke, C. (2000). Cyber-schooling and technological change: Multiple literacies for new times. In B. Cope and M. Kalantzis (Eds.), *Multiliteracies: Literacy Learning and the Design of Social Futures* (pp. 69–91). London: Routledge.

Luke, C. (2002). Re-crafting media and ICT literacies. In D. Alverman (Ed.), *Adolescents and Literacies in a Digital World*. New York: Peter Lang.

Lury, C. (1996). *Consumer Culture*. Oxford, UK: Polity Press.

Lyotard, J.-F. (1984). *The Postmodern Condition: A Report on Knowledge* (G. Bennington and B. Massumi, trans.). Minneapolis, MN: University of Minnesota Press.

Madge, N. and Barker, J. (2007). *Risk and Childhood*. London: Royal Society for the Encouragement of Arts, Manufacturers and Commerce.

Martin-Barbero, J. (1987). *De los Medios a las Mediaciones: Comunicacion, Cultura y Hegemonia*. Barcelona, Spain: Editorial Gustavo Gili, S.A.

Masterman, L. (1985). *Teaching the Media*. London: Comedia Publishing Group.

McChesney, R. (2008). *The Political Economy of Media: Enduring Issues, Emerging Dilemmas*. New York: Monthly Review Press.

McKenzie, J. (2007). Digital nativism, digital delusions and digital deprivation. *From Now On*, 17(2). Retrieved October 7, 2009, from http://fno.org/nov07/nativism.html

McLuhan, M. (1994 [1964]). *Understanding Media: The Extensions of Man*. Cambridge, MA: MIT Press.

McMahon, B. and Quin, R. (1999). Australian children and the media. In C. von Feilitzen and U. Carlsson (Eds.), *Children and Media: Image, Education, Participation* (pp. 189–203). Göteborg, Sweden: UNESCO International Clearinghouse on Children and Violence on the Screen.

McRobbie, A. (1994). *Postmodernism and Popular Culture*. New York: Routledge.

McRobbie, A. (2000). *Feminism and Youth Culture*. London: Routledge.

McRobbie, A. (2005). *The Uses of Cultural Studies*. London: Sage Publications.

Media Awareness Network. (2005). *Young Canadians in a Wired World*. Ottawa, ON: Media Awareness Network.

Meikle, G. (2007). Stop signs: An introduction to culture jamming. In K. Coyer, T. Dowmunt, and A. Fountain (Eds.), *The Alternative Media Handbook* (pp. 166–179). London: Routledge.

Mercer, K. (1994). *Welcome to the Jungle: New Positions in Black Cultural Studies*. New York: Routledge.

Messaris, P. (1994). *Visual 'Literacy': Image, Mind, and Reality*. Boulder, CO: Westview Press.

Ministry of Education, Ontario. (1989). *Media Literacy: A Resource Guide*. Toronto, ON: Queen's Printer of Ontario.

Minow, N. N. and LaMay, C. L. (1995). *Abandoned in the Wasteland: Children, Television, and the First Amendment*. New York: Hill and Wang.

Montgomery, K. C. (2008). Youth and digital democracy: Intersections of practice, policy, and the marketplace. In W. L. Bennett (Ed.), *Civic Life Online: Learning How Digital Media Can Engage Youth* (pp. 25–49). Cambridge, MA: MIT Press.

Montgomery, K. C. (2009). *Generation Digital: Politics, Commerce, and Childhood in the Age of the Internet*. Cambridge, MA: MIT Press.

Montgomery, K. C. and Chester, J. (2008). Food advertising to children in the new digital marketing ecosystem. In K. M. Ekstrom and B. Tufte (Eds.), *Children, Media and Consumption: On the Front Edge* (pp. 179–193). Göteborg, Sweden: International Clearinghouse on Children, Youth and Media.

O'Brien, S. and Szeman, I. (2004). *Popular Culture: A User's Guide*. Scarborough, ON: Nelson.

O'Neill, B. (2009). Communication rights, digital literacy and ethical individualism in the new media environment. Paper presented at the International Association of Media and Communication Researchers, Mexico City, MX.

Orner, M. (1992). Interrupting the calls for student voice in liberatory education: A feminist poststructuralist perspective. In C. Luke and J. Gore (Eds.), *Feminisms and Critical Pedagogy* (pp. 15–25). New York: Routledge.

Osgerby, B. (2004). *Youth Media*. New York: Routledge.

O'Sullivan, T., Hartley, J., Saunders, D., Montgomery, M., and Fiske, J. (1994). *Key Concepts in Communication and Cultural Studies*. London: Routledge.

Oswell, D. (2002). *Television, Childhood and the Home: A History of the Making of the Child Television Audience in Britain*. Oxford, UK: Oxford University Press.

Oswell, D. (2008). Media and communications regulation and child protection: An overview of the field. In K. Drotner and S. Livingstone (Eds.), *The International Handbook of Children, Media and Culture* (pp. 475–492). London: Sage Publications.

Parker, J. (2000). *Structuration*. Buckingham, UK: Open University Press.

Pettitt, T. (2007). Before the Guttenberg Parenthesis: Elizabethan-American Compatibilities. Media in Transition 5 Conference. Cambridge, MA: MIT. April 27.

Postman, N. (1985). *Amusing Ourselves to Death: Public Discourse in the Age of Show Buisness*. New York: Penguin.

Poyntz, S. R. (2008). Producing publics: An ethnographic study of democratic practice and youth media production and mentorship. Unpublished Dissertation. Vancouver, BC: University of British Columbia.

Poyntz, S. R. (2009). 'On behalf of a shared world': Arendtian politics in a culture of youth media production. *Review of Education, Pedagogy and Cultural Studies*, 31(4), pp. 365–386.

Prensky, M. (2001). Digital natives, digital immigrants. Retrieved October 7, 2009, from http://www.marcprensky.com/writing/Prensky%20-%20Digital%20Natives,%20Digital%20Immigrants%20-%20Part1.pdf.

Prout, A. (2008). Culture-nature and the construction of childhood. In K. Drotner and S. Livingstone (Eds.), *The International Handbook of Children, Media and Culture* (pp. 21–35). London: Sage Publications.

Public Broadcasting System. (2001). *Merchants of Cool*. Retrieved October 7, 2009, from http://www.pbs.org/wgbh/pages/frontline/shows/cool.

Quin, R. (2003). Questions of knowledge in Australian media education. *Television and New Media*, 4(4), pp. 439–460.

Rampton, B. (2006). *Language in Late Modernity: Integration in an Urban School*. Cambridge, UK: Cambridge University Press.

Rheingold, H. (2008). Using participatory media and public voice to encourage civic engagement. In W. L. Bennett (Ed.), *Civic Life Online: Learning How Digital Media Can Engage Youth* (pp. 97–118). Cambridge, MA: MIT Press.

Rideout, V. J., Foehr, U. G., and Roberts, D. F. (2010). *Generation M2: Media in the Lives of 8- to 18-Year-Olds*. Menlo Park, CA: Henry J. Kaiser Family Foundation.

Robins, K. and Webster, F. (1999). *Times of the Technoculture: From the Information Society to the Virtual Life*. London: Routledge.

Robinson, T. N., Wilde, M. L., Navacruz, L. C., Haydel, K. F., and Varady, A. (2001). Effects of reducing children's television and video game use on aggressive behavior: A randomized controlled trial. *Archives of Pediatrics and Adolescent Medicine*, 155(1), pp. 17–23.

Rosenblatt, L. (1938). *Literature as Exploration*. New York: Appleton-Century.

Rousseau, J.-J. (1963). *Émile* (B. Foxley, trans.). London: Dent.

Royal Ontario Museum. (1995). *Watching TV* (L. Jeffrey and S. Shaul, Eds.). Toronto, ON: Royal Ontario Museum.

Schlesinger, P., Dobash, R. E., Dobash, R. P., and Weaver, C. K. (1992). *Women Viewing Violence*. London: British Film Institute.

Sefton-Green, J. (1995). Neither reading nor writing: The history of practical work in media education. *Changing English*, 2(2), 77–96.

Sefton-Green, J. (2006). Youth, technology and media cultures. *Review of Research in Education*, 30, pp. 279–306.

Sefton-Green, J., Nixon, H., and Ertstad, O. (2009). Reviewing approaches and perspectives on 'digital literacy'. *Pedagogies*, 4(2), pp. 105–127.

Seiter, E. (1993). *Sold Separately: Children and Parents in Consumer Culture*. New Brunswick, NJ: Rutgers University Press.

Seiter, E. (2008). Practicing at home: Computers, pianos, and cultural capital. In T. McPherson (Ed.), *Digital Youth, Innovation, and the Unexpected* (pp. 27–52). Cambridge, MA: MIT Press.

Shade, L. R., Porter, N., and Sanchez, W. (2005). 'You can see anything on the internet, you can do anything on the internet!': Young Canadians talk about the internet. *Canadian Journal of Communication*, 30(4), pp. 503–526.

Silverstone, R. (1999). *Why Study the Media?* London: Sage Publications.

Silverstone, R. (2004). Regulation, media literacy and media civics. *Media, Culture & Society*, 26(3), pp. 440–449.

Silverstone, R. (2007). *Media and Morality: On the Rise of the Mediapolis*. Cambridge, UK: Polity Press.

Singhal, A. and Rogers, E. M. (1999). *Entertainment-Education: A Communication Strategy for Social Change*. Mahwah, NJ: Lawrence Erlbaum Associates.

Smythe, D. W. (1981). *Dependency Road: Communications, Capitalism, Conscious-ness and Canada.* Norwood, NJ: Ablex Publishing.

Soep, E. (2006). Beyond literacy and voice in youth media education. *McGill Journal of Education,* 41(3), pp. 197–213.

Sourbati, M. (2009). Media literacy and universal access in Europe. *The Information Society,* 25, pp. 248–254.

Spring, J. (2009). *Globalization of Education: An Introduction.* New York, NY: Routledge.

Squire, K. (2008). Open-ended video games: A model for developing learning for the interactive age. In K. Salen (Ed.), *The Ecology of Games: Connecting Youth, Games and Learning* (pp. 167–198). Cambridge, MA: MIT Press.

Stack, M. (2008). Spectacle and symbolic subversion: Canadian youth-adult video collaborations on war and commodification. *Journal of Children and Media,* 2(2), pp. 114–128.

Starker, S. (1989). *Evil Influences: Crusades against the Mass Media.* New Brunswick, NJ: Transaction Publishers.

Steeves, V. (2007). Children's online privacy policy concerns. Paper presented at the Terra Incognita: Privacy Horizons, 29th International Conference of Data Protection and Privacy Commisioners, Montreal, QC.

Street, B. (1984). *Literacy in Theory and Practice.* Cambridge, UK: Cambridge University Press.

Subrahmanyam, K. and Greenfield, P. (2008). Online communication and ado-lescent relationships. *The Future of the Children,* 18(1), pp. 119–146.

Surowiecki, J. (2004). *The Wisdom of Crowds.* New York: Little, Brown.

Tapscott, D. (1998). *Growing Up Digital: The Rise of the Net Generation.* New York: McGraw-Hill.

Tapscott, D. and Williams, A. (2006). *Wikinomics: How Mass Collaboration Changes Everything.* New York: Portfolio.

Toffler, A. (1980). *The Third Wave.* New York: Bantam Books.

Tornero, J. M. P. (2009). *Study on Assessment Criteria for Media Literacy Levels: A Comprehensive View of the Concept of Media Literacy and an Understanding of How Media Literacy Level in Europe Should be Assessed (Final Report).* Brussels, Belgium: European Commission Directorate General Information Society and Media, Media Literacy Unit.

Trend, D. (1997). *Cultural Democracy: Politics, Media, New Technology.* Albany, NY: State University of New York Press.

Tufte, B. (2000). Media education in Europe, with special focus on the nordic countries. In C. von Feilitzen and U. Carlsson (Eds.), *Children and Media: Image, Education, Participation* (Vol. Yearbook 1999, pp. 205–217). Göteborg, Sweden: The UNESCO International Clearinghouse on Children and Violence on the Screen.

Tufte, T. (2004). Entertainment-education in HIV/AIDS communication: Beyond marketing, towards empowerment. In C. von Feilitzen and U. Carlsson (Eds.), *Promote or Protect? Perspectives on Media Literacy and Media Regulations* (Vol. Yearbook 2003, pp. 85–97). Göteborg, Sweden: International Clearinghouse on Children, Youth and Media.

Tufte, T. and Enghel, F. (2009). Youth engaging with media and communication: Different, unequal and disconnected? In T. Tufte and F. Enghel (Eds.), *Youth Engaging with the World – Media, Communication and Social Change* (Vol. Yearbook 2009, pp. 11–18). Göteborg, Sweden: International Clearinghouse on Children, Youth and Media.

Turkle, S. (2008). Always on/always on you: The tethered self. In J. Katz (Ed.), *Handbook of Mobile Communications and Social Change* (pp. 121–137). Cambridge, MA: MIT Press.

UNESCO. (1982). *Grunwald Declaration on Media Education.* Retrieved October 7, 2009, from http://www.unesco.org/education/pdf/MEDIA_E.PDF.

van Dijk, T. A. (1991). The interdisciplinary study of news as discourse. In K. B. Jensen and N. Jankowski (Eds.), *A Handbook of Qualitative Methodologies for Mass Communication Research* (pp. 108–120). New York: Routledge.

Virilio, P. (1986). *Speed and Politics: An Essay on Dromology.* New York: Semiotext(e).

von Feilitzen, C. (2009). *Influences of Mediated Violence: A Brief Research Summary.* Göteborg, Sweden: International Clearinghouse on Children, Youth and Media.

Vygotsky, L. S. and Cole, M. (1978). *Mind in Society: The Development of Higher Psychological Processes.* Cambridge, MA: Harvard University Press.

Wakefield, M., Flay, B., Nichter, M., and Giovino, G. (2003). Role of the media in influencing trajectories of youth smoking. *Addiction,* 98(Suppl 1), pp. 79–103.

Wasko, J. (2008). The commodification of youth culture. In K. Drotner and S. Livingstone (Eds.), *The International Handbook of Children, Media and Culture* (pp. 460–474). London: Sage Publications.

Weber, S. and Mitchell, C. (2008). Imaging, keyboarding, and posting identities: Young people and new media technologies. In D. Buckingham (Ed.), *Youth, Identity, and Digital Media* (pp. 25–48). Cambridge, MA: MIT Press.

West, C. (1993). *Keeping Faith: Philosophy and Race in America.* New York: Routledge.

Westheimer, J. and Kahne, J. (2004). What kind of citizen? The politics of educating for democracy. *American Educational Research Journal,* 41(2), pp. 237–269.

Willett, R. (2005). Constructing the digital tween: Market forces, adult concerns and girls interests. In C. Mitchell and J. R. Walsh (Eds.), *Seven Going on Seventeen: Tween Culture in Girlhood Studies* (pp. 278–293). Oxford, UK: Peter Lang.

Willett, R. (2008). Consumer citizens online: Structure, agency, and gender in online participation. In D. Buckingham (Ed.), *Youth, Identity, and Digital Media* (pp. 49–69). Cambridge, MA: MIT Press.

Williams, R. (1958). *Culture and Society, 1780–1950.* London: Chatto and Windus.

Willis, P. (1990). *Common Culture.* Buckingham, UK: Open University Press.

Wimsatt, W. K. and Beardsley, M. C. (1946). The intentional fallacy. *Sewanee Review,* 54(3), pp. 468–488.

Winsten, J. A. (1990). *The Designated Driver Campaign.* Cambridge, MA: Harvard School of Public Health, Harvard University.

World Internet Project. (2009). Retrieved March 12, 2010, from http://www. worldinternetproject.net.

Index

Lightning Source UK Ltd.
Milton Keynes UK
UKHW05f2358240818
327723UK00007B/224/P